THE

21ST

CENTURY

PASTOR

THE 21ST CENTURY PASTOR

*A Vision
Based on the
Ministry of Paul*

DAVID FISHER

ZondervanPublishingHouse

Grand Rapids, Michigan

A Division of HarperCollins*Publishers*

The 21st-Century Pastor
Copyright © 1996 by David Fisher

Requests for information should be addressed to:

ZondervanPublishingHouse
Grand Rapids, Michigan 49530

Library of Congress Cataloging-in-Publication Data

Fisher, David, 1943–
The 21st-century pastor : a vision based on the ministry of Paul / David Fisher.
    p.   cm.
Includes bibliographical references.
ISBN 0-310-20154-3 (pbk.)
1. Pastoral theology. 2. Christianity—United States—Forecasting. 3. Pastoral
theology—Biblical teaching. 4. Bible. N.T. Epistles of Paul—Theology. I. Title.
BV4011.F55 1996
253—dc20   95-52768
                                                                                CIP

The quotation from *How Shall They Preach?* by Gardner Taylor on pages
246–47 is used with the kind permission of the author.

Edited by Jack Kuhatschek and Laura Weller
Interior design by Sue Vandenberg Koppenol

Printed in the United States of America

---

97 98 99 00 01 02 / ❖ DH/ 10 9 8 7 6 5 4 3

CONTENTS

Introduction:
Welcome to the Ministry

THE PASTORAL CRISIS

Being a pastor today is more difficult than anytime in memory. This century witnessed the collapse of the Christian consensus that held American culture together for centuries. The secularization of our culture pushed the churches to the margins of our nation's consciousness. The moral relativism that accompanies a secular view of reality deeply affects the work of the church and its ministry. According to a 1992 *Christianity Today* survey,[1] 66 percent of Americans believe there is no absolute truth. Significantly, among Americans ages eighteen to twenty-five, the number is 72 percent. The Christian faith adheres to a multitude of absolutes. No wonder ministry in and to this culture is more complex than ever. No wonder pastors and churches are increasingly viewed as curiosities or even threats to the public.

The world is experiencing rapid and perpetual change. Cultural quakes and shifts are documented in books like Russell Chandler's *Racing Toward 2001,* Leith Anderson's *Church for the 21st Century,* and Leonard Sweet's *Faith-Quakes.*[2] Suffice it to say, each of these quakes and shifts deeply affects the church and pastors.

The result of culture quakes and shakes is an increasingly unchristian America. George Hunter claims that 120 million Americans are virtually secular. They have no Christian influence, no Christian memory or vocabulary, and no Christian assumptions or worldview. Hunter thinks that America is the largest mission field in the Western world, noting that the percentage of practicing evangelical Christians in Uganda, once a Western mission field, is higher than in America.[3] The challenge for Christian ministry is unprecedented, and the opportunity for the church to be the church is staggering—but only if we change the way we think about the church and the ministry.

Hunter and others are calling for change in the way we do ministry. We must come to terms with the fact that we labor in a mission field and then change the ministry and the church to meet the new order. Loren Mead suggests that because we are at a shift in the ages, we are going to experience a reformation in church and ministry.[4]

I hope so. However, a huge reality stands in the way of reformation: Widespread evidence shows that pastoral ministry is in trouble. Greg Asimakoupoulos began a review of two books on the pastoral crisis in *Leadership* magazine with these words, "Warning: the list of endangered species is growing. To bald eagles, koalas, and spotted owls, add another: ordained pastors energized by what they do."[5] He goes on to claim that the majority of American ministers are suffering from burnout.

The two books Asimakoupoulos reviewed have ominous titles: *Pastors at Risk* by H. B. London and Neil Wiseman and *Pastors Off the Record* by Stefan Ulstein. London and Wiseman quote a Focus on the Family study that claims that 70 percent of the pastors they surveyed wonder if they should remain in ministry. The conclusion, "Pastors are discouraged and often outraged."[6]

A friend told me he is leaving pastoral ministry. Though he loves the ministry, he is tired of dealing with the pettiness that characterizes so much of church life. Another surrendered his credentials because, in his words, "I can't take the pounding any more." Why is it that so many of us begin with such high hopes and dreams and end up tired and discouraged?

Psychiatrist Louis McBurney reports that low self-esteem is the number-one problem pastors face. Why? We are in a high-demand, low-stroke profession in a culture that does not value our product or our work. We labor among people with unrealistic expectations, and deep inside we expect far more from ourselves and the church. It's no wonder McBurney's study identified depression as the second most identified pastoral problem.[7]

The problem is not new. For fifty years church leaders have spoken about a "crisis in the ministry" and "ferment in the ministry." Back in 1954, H. R. Niebuhr wrote about the church and ministry and called pastorate the "perplexed profession."[8] Niebuhr correctly suggested that the crisis in ministry is primarily a crisis of identity. The communities in which we work no longer value our product or our role the way society once honored the church and its ministry. We are providing a service to a world that no longer wants it. Professional religious leaders are an anachronism in a secular culture. Even our congregations wonder about us. Contemporary Christians are affected by the secular nature of our world more than they may realize. By calling, by training, and quite often by personality type and interests, we pastors are different. We work and speak for God in a world that recognizes no God, a world in which it is not politically correct to speak openly of God. Increasingly, we are pushed to the margins. What is a Christian pastor in our society? Who are we in churches of the last part of the twentieth century?

THE HEART OF THE CRISIS

Since Niebuhr's book, more books have rolled off the presses in response to the crisis. In 1960, James Smart correctly noted that the crisis goes beneath the obvious identity crisis.[9] The personal and professional identity crisis is the symptom of a systemic ecclesiastical disease. There is no accepted theology of the ministry in our time. Instead, the practice of ministry has become the theology. The task itself is the model.

Seward Hiltner put it another way. He wrote that pastoral ministry has no unifying theory by which it organizes itself. The ministry is no longer based on a theology. Hiltner's

Preface to Pastoral Theology (1956)[10] was his early attempt to create a new theology of the ministry.

Somewhere along the way the old theological discipline called "pastoral theology" was lost. For centuries each theological tradition had a classic pastoral theology text, and pastoral theology was a central part of the theological curriculum. Around the turn of the century, pastoral theology disappeared, and in conservative quarters it was replaced by "practical theology"—"how-to" pastoral training. In the mainline churches "pastoral care," in which the pastor became primarily a counselor, was the new discipline. In most of American Protestantism, biblical and theological reflection on pastoral ministry ceased. The practice of ministry became the theology of ministry.

Hiltner's *Preface to Pastoral Theology* changed the face of pastoral ministry in America. Protesting the lack of a pastoral theology, Hiltner proposed a psychological/sociological base as a unifying theory for ministry. "Pastoral care" became increasingly therapeutic. "Shepherding," the ancient practice of the cure of souls, became more and more counseling. Clinical pastoral education moved to the center of pastoral training.

Because the base was social science, not theology, the pastoral art was reduced to human skill. The transcendent dimension of ministry, its grounding in God himself, was removed from pastoral theology. In fact, theology itself disappeared as the practical work of ministry was removed from seminary theology departments to a practical division that tended to describe pastoral ministry in human terms. Biblical and theological reflection on pastoral ministry soon faded away. Reflection on the church and its ministry was separated from the body of theology and is now conducted on a largely human level.

What is most curious to me is that evangelicals unquestioningly embrace nontheological ministry models. Some move the model to therapeutic and others to management models of ministry. In either case, evangelicals tend to think of both the church and ministry in human terms, an unreflective immanence. It is ironic that the liberal theological agenda that centered in anthropology and featured immanence is now implicitly championed by conservatives. The result is, more often than not, a failure of theological-biblical integration and, at the heart of it, a base for ministry that is not properly biblical or theological.

Yet a pastoral ministry equipped and empowered for this generation must have a proper biblical and theological base. Methodology without a proper base is dangerous and ultimately powerless. In other words, we had better figure out our identity before we start dealing with the work of the church and the ministry in today's world. We dare not form pastoral roles based on human models, or we will accomplish little for God. Note how Paul's certain identity as an apostle in Galatians 1:11–24 forms the foundation for his pastoral exhortation that follows.

Part 1 of this book asks four critical questions that lie at the heart of pastoral life and flow out of real pastoral life in the modern world. In each case the answer given is grounded in Christology and the Incarnation. These theological answers form a foundation for both a biblical and contemporary pastoral ministry.

Part 2 paints a portrait of the pastor from a biblical or apostolic source. While the theological *foundation* for pastoral ministry is the person and work of Christ, the biblical *framework* for pastoral ministry is found in the ministry of the apostles, especially Paul. Paul described his pastoral and apostolic ministry with a variety of metaphors, ten of which I develop in part 2 to paint a biblical portrait of a pastor. Each metaphor is centered in Christ and describes a different area of pastoral work.

A biblical and apostolic understanding of the ministry is the proper framework for pastoral work in times like these and is the core of a contemporary theology of pastoral ministry.

PART 1

Four Crucial Questions for Pastors

1

Who Am I?
The Question of
Pastoral Identity

A thunderbolt of truth struck me my last semester of seminary: Within months I would be a Christian pastor. Frightened into good sense, I began to study and pray quite differently. And deep inside me a gnawing question began to grow: *What would I do every day?* At first it was very practical. Soon it became more basic and very real.

WELCOME, REVEREND!

One hot July day I drove a U-Haul truck packed with all my family's earthly belongings over a mountain pass and into a little town in the Pacific Northwest. Since I was alone in the truck—my wife and children would join me in a few days—I had lots of time to think and more than enough time to worry. The closer I got to town the more anxious I became. An indefinable and awesome "something" awaited me in that town. I slowed the truck down to delay the inevitable.

Yet I was thrilled too. Seminary had been hard. I had worked full-time to support a family while also maintaining a strict study schedule. I wanted to learn everything necessary to go out in the power of the Spirit to conquer principalities and powers in the name of the Lord. A little group of us had gathered for prayer each week that last semester. How we prayed for the fruit and power of the Holy Spirit to fill us. We longed to do something significant for Christ and his church.

But it was scary to think that we would soon stand in pulpits, speaking for God, and sit in offices counseling the people for whom Christ died. I was acutely mindful that I was twenty-six years old and had no experience in the work that would soon be my life. I had a growing awareness that I wasn't ready.

Yet here I was driving down the mountain into town. I couldn't stop the truck or the inevitable. Too soon, it seemed, I entered the city limits and drove to the parsonage, which sat next to a century-old white frame church. I had driven right into a scene from a Norman Rockwell painting.

WHAT DO THEY EXPECT?

Back on the mountain pass I had been a fresh seminary graduate, a young man with promise. Now, in a single and mysterious moment, I had become a Christian pastor. Three months before, when I had come to interview and to preach for the church, I had been a student. In an act of amazing trust, the members had voted to call me to be their pastor. Then I had been a "pastor-in-training," not the real thing. Now I was something very specific, a pastor—*their pastor*. School was over; reality was at hand.

As I crossed the city limit, I entered a world of images and expectations, none of which I chose and few of which I then understood. I was expected to fill a role established by predecessors whom I had never met. But I knew they were important. People talked about them and quoted them. Some had near-mythic reputations. One, they had tried to forget. I lived in the shadow of them all and was expected to live up to the best of them, avoiding the ways of the one that nobody wanted to remember.

I listened hard and long, to understand and apply what this meant. Some was very good. My immediate predecessor had died a month before I arrived. He had come there to finish his ministry and retire. Sadly, he became very sick, and his last several years were difficult for him and the church. But the congregation loved him and learned to care for a dying pastor. One day as I listened to a man talk about it, it dawned on me that if they loved him they would probably love me too. And they did.

Some of the expectations weren't so good. A woman told me she expected me never to take a day off. After all, Reverend Ketcham never did!

The townspeople had expectations too. Local citizens defined me by a common tradition a century long. They expected certain behavior of their ministers. These expectations were seldom verbalized, and when they were, I was usually surprised. Once a man from another church told me that my predecessor was a great pastor because he spent so much time with people outside his congregation. I'm pretty sure he was criticizing his pastor. At any rate, what he meant was that I should spend less time with my people and more with him! Another man dropped by one day to ask me to pray at an American Legion memorial service at the cemetery. I'd never met him before. In his view, pastors prayed for dead soldiers—once a year!

But I, too, had expectations of my church and community. My background and training created a whole set of expectations. I expected Christians to act like Christians, leaders to lead, and the congregation to love God and his Word. On top of all that, they should take good care of me! After all, I was giving them my life. Since I was working for God in what many of them thought was the highest calling on earth, I expected them to respect me. And I also thought the town should give me the respect I had been taught that educated and dedicated clergy deserve.

I had some vague expectations of myself too. I knew I was a teacher and preacher of the Bible. In my tradition, that was and is primary. But I knew pastoral ministry was much more than Sunday sermons. It had dawned on me during my last year in seminary that I would spend the rest of my life leading worship. In fact, I would spend as much public time leading worship as preaching. Yet worship was not addressed in any seminary course I had taken. So I quickly signed up for an elective course in worship taught by a working pastor. It was one of best choices I made in seminary.

I knew I needed to be a leader. That was an unspoken but very real part of my tradition. I had grown up watching pastors lead, yet I didn't know the first thing about leadership except what I had seen and a few instincts yet unnamed. My seminary teachers hadn't talked about leading churches. How could they? They were academicians, most of whom were neither pastors nor leaders. I suppose they figured an excellent and accurate preacher and teacher was a leader. Nonetheless, I quickly discovered that I would spend the rest of my life leading God's people. A wise man told me, "Everything rises and falls on leadership." He was right—as I soon discovered.

Above all, I wanted and expected by God's grace to be a success. My dad and his friends all lived to do something great for God. They didn't pastor large or well-known churches, but they did know what God considers success. They lived in the firm confidence that the gospel is the power of God and that pastoral ministry under that gospel changes lives. Then as now, I cannot imagine a God who doesn't want his servants to accomplish great things for him. I desperately wanted God to bless my ministry with changed lives and transformed churches.

All of this seemed a crushing burden as I drove into town and parked the truck in front of the parsonage. I turned the motor off and sat in the quiet. I was both anxious and excited. My new life had begun.

WHERE DO I START?

I spent that first day unloading the truck with the help of one of the church's trustees and a teenage girl who showed up and asked to help. We carried the last boxes off the truck to my office next door at the church. Those boxes held my precious few books. I stood there in my new office, thrilled at the sight of my desk and bookshelves. But the thrill was soon overcome by anxiety. Tomorrow I would begin my pastoral life. *What would I do?* I didn't know, but I couldn't wait to get started.

Early the next morning I went to the office. I sat down at my desk and tried to figure out what to do first. I thought I must have missed the day in seminary when they covered "getting started." So, for lack of a better idea, I put my books on the shelves, sat down, and stared at them. *Where do I start?* I wondered. I knew Sunday was coming and two sermons were expected. But what else? What about running, managing, or leading this church? What about the people whom I had come to serve?

I thought I should find a list of the church members, but I didn't know where to find one. As I was looking, the volunteer secretary came in to show me how to work the mimeograph machine. She was going on vacation for a month, and the bulletins were now my responsibility. I guess I had missed the day they covered "mimeographs and stencils" too. This wasn't starting the way I had imagined. The secretary told me that no list of members existed, but she thought she could create one. She left. I was alone in an office in a strange town. I was responsible for several hundred people, the truth of God, and a mimeograph machine.

I learned the tasks of pastoral ministry quickly. I preached sermons, taught lessons, visited members in homes and in the hospital, gave pastoral advice, and got to know the town and its people. Whatever I forgot to do or didn't know I should do, some kind soul quickly filled in. But my nagging question, "What do I do?" took on another and much more troubling form.

THE REAL QUESTION

As I went about my duties—meeting people, tending to the church, preparing for sermons and lessons, and conducting a wider variety of meetings than I had ever imagined—I suddenly was aware that I really didn't know *who* I was supposed to be.

This much I knew: I was seen as different from the ordinary young man about town. At the hospital I was a semi-official member of the healing team. At the post office I wasn't just David Fisher; I was one of the town's pastors. At high school football games my presence was noted, and I received good marks for being there. Walking down Main Street one day, it dawned on me that I would never be seen as an "ordinary" man again—at least not in that town. I had been David Fisher for twenty-six years. Suddenly I was "Reverend Fisher." A new identity was laid on me, and I couldn't be just me anymore. I didn't think I liked that. I knew I didn't like some of the stereotypes that accompanied the title *Reverend*.

I was invited to civic events simply because I was a pastor in town. I was asked to pray at a governor's prayer breakfast. I even got to sit with the governor. That was a nice benefit to ministry, I thought.

The funeral director went out of his way to provide business for me. I was the new and young pastor in town. I guess he thought I needed the work. "Shoes for the kids," he winked. He needed me too. He firmly believed no one could be buried without a proper "Christian" service. Twice, only three of us were at the graveside: he, the grave digger, and I. I didn't know whether to cry or laugh.

I became increasingly uneasy being "something." I didn't like being defined by expectations, roles, and titles. Some people called me "Reverend," others "Pastor," and one man always referred to me as "Preacher." Some people asked me what they should call me. But I still felt like the old me despite the titles and role expectations.

Things went very well. The church grew, and I was thought to be a success. People even told me they admired me. The role of "The Reverend" was growing, but I knew deep inside it was still me. The distance between what people thought I was and who I knew I was seemed to be expanding.

Sometimes being a clergyman hurt. One day I was playing with my children in the yard between the church and parsonage. A big logging truck roared by. The driver honked his horn and gave me an obscene gesture. It bothered me— deeply. Who was I that I should get that kind of abuse? The guy didn't know me. He just saw a pastor and gave me his load of anger and resentment. Then one day when I was jogging, I stopped to talk to a farmer on his tractor. He was part of the church, and we had an interesting conversation. As I jogged off, he yelled, "If you had a real job, you wouldn't need to run around like that!" I knew he was teasing, but beneath all humor lies some truth. *Who am I to him?* I wondered. My daily walk to the post office took on added meaning.

Having the title *reverend* certainly wasn't all bad. In fact, most of my pastoral life was wonderful. Most of the congregation loved me and my family simply because I was their pastor. People wanted to be our friends. But even an evening with a young couple who might become our friends seemed to be colored by the fact that I was their pastor, something "special" to them. I thought I was me. They agreed but added "Pastor." I was concerned about their not being able to separate the role from the man. Besides, I had the nagging suspicion that most of them wouldn't love me as much if I were a lousy pastor.

There was more. A man called and said his wife had locked herself in the bathroom with a gun and was about to shoot herself. By the time I arrived, he had talked her out of the bathroom and into bed. I sat on the edge of the bed, and she held on to me so tightly it hurt. She told me I was her only link to life. Now who was I? This identity question got murkier and a bit frightening. I really didn't want that kind of responsibility. I began to intensely dislike the identity question.

The funeral director called and said that a former member of the church had died—a suicide. It was my first funeral. I didn't know anyone in the room, yet I stood to offer them a word from the Lord. Now who was I? This much I knew for sure: I was more to them than David Fisher, the recent seminary graduate. To these people I was "something," and they expected something. Yet I wasn't sure of what that "something" was, and they probably weren't either.

A woman with a dark past came to faith in Christ and then decided that she needed to talk to me about her history. She was trying to exorcise some horrid memories and destructive habits. She thought that, because I was a man of God, I could help her straighten out her twisted life. Her story of sexual perversion and violence was unbelievable and enormously distressing, yet she believed my hearing and counsel would put her broken life together. Now who was I?

Even routine pastoral duties were filled with the identity question. I visited people in the hospital regularly. Who was I now? Nice young man? Neighbor and friend? The preacher?

And of course there was the inevitable question: Who was I when I went home to my wife and kids? They knew the real me, not "the Reverend." They didn't want a pastor at home; they wanted me. This was getting complicated. I was becoming lots of things to many people. How was I to juggle all these roles? Could I take on so many roles with integrity?

And who were we, my wife and I, when we were together? People had as many or more expectations of her, the "first lady" of the church. She wasn't just another woman, and we were not an ordinary family. Like it or not, we were models for the community. The question for us was, models of what?

I talked to my local colleagues in ministry and found that they were as uncertain as I. Each seemed to have a distinct and different role, and each resisted the roles and expectations of his congregation and the town. One saw himself as an evangelist. Another thought he was a social reformer. Still another visited in homes and the hospital from morning to night. Their spouses' self-understanding was just as diverse. Some were partners in ministry; others weren't. Their participation in the life of the church varied widely.

At my denomination's clergy retreat I sought direction from my experienced peers but could find no clear sense of pastoral identity among my colleagues. Most seemed burdened with discouragement. My closest clergy friend desperately wanted out of the ministry. He wondered how to lose his "call." I found that quite troubling.

I too became increasingly dissatisfied with my pastoral duties and role. I learned that there is little satisfaction in performance of tasks without a clear and foundational identity. Nothing in seminary prepared me for this identity crisis. I knew who I was at 11:00 Sunday morning. My evangelical roots and training were certain. In the act of preaching, I was God's herald proclaiming God's Word in power. But who was I the other 167 hours of the week? I certainly didn't walk around town preaching continually.

I was troubled also because the role and expectations in the church and in the community seemed to have no biblical or theological basis. Pastors were expected to do certain things simply because that's what pastors did. Not many people were interested in discussing the biblical role of a pastor, and fewer were willing to deal with the underlying and more fundamental question: What is a Christian pastor?

I reviewed my seminary notes and found nothing to help. I must have skipped that day too! I realized that I had never been in a conversation about pastoral identity that went beyond "preacher." Desperately I searched for contemporary literature on pastoral ministry. It was not an easy search. I had to start from scratch since, curiously, my training ignored the literature in the field. I read about "change-agents," "poimenics," "pastor-teachers," "relational theology," "the pastoral director," "the sacramental person," "the Reformed pastor," "player-coaches," and "the pastor as manager"—all recent models for the ministry. These were a few of the twenty-or-so contemporary models of ministry available at the time. I identified with none of them. They were remote from small-town church life and my emerging pastoral experience. My colleagues in churches large and small, rural and urban seemed as confused as I was. The question grew larger, "What is a Christian pastor at the end of the twentieth century?"

The literature on contemporary pastoral ministry is remarkably diverse but tends to agree that we are at a crisis point and that at least part of the problem is pastoral identity in our modern society. My personal struggle was a small part of the larger reality of ministry in our time. The profound irony is that although it is a fundamental question at the heart of the ministry, in three years of seminary the question was never raised.

Now here I was, 2000 miles from seminary and 120 miles from the nearest theological library, sitting in a little office with my one hundred-or-so books. The few books I did have on pastoral ministry only sharpened my questions. My colleagues were as confused as I was. And my wonderful congregation, as helpful as they were, couldn't walk down this road with me.

A SURPRISING ANSWER

Help came in an unexpected way. One morning I was reading 1 Thessalonians. Suddenly a vivid metaphor jumped up and waved at me, and my life has never been the same. Paul said he was gentle, like a mother caring for her children, to the Thessalonian church (2:7). I was dumbfounded. I had never thought of myself as a mother, and I certainly had not thought of my ministry as motherhood. The idea simply exploded in my head.

I read on. Paul added a second half to the metaphor: he was also a father to the Thessalonians (1 Thess. 2:11). Paul thought of himself as a pastoral parent. I had never thought of Paul as a working pastor before. This two-sided metaphor indicated to me that Paul had a deep pastoral self-consciousness. I began to look for other metaphors in Paul's writings that reveal his pastoral sense of identity. I found them everywhere: farmer, architect, engraver, general, steward, ambassador, clay pot, slave, master builder, herald, and more.

I began to wonder if Paul was providing the pastoral identity I had been looking for. Was his experience the place to begin my search for identity and the framework for a pastoral theology? As I studied, I discovered that Paul's metaphors taken together provide a compelling and powerful portrait of a pastor. Here was the pastoral identity I longed for.

Paul and other first-century apostles and pastors lived in circumstances similar to our own. They represented a faith on the very margin of life in their world. More often than not their message was despised by the larger culture, whether Jewish or Gentile. Paul could declare that he and his fellow apostles were the "scum of the earth, the refuse of the world" (1 Cor. 4:13) and that the gospel was "a stumbling block to Jews and foolishness to Gentiles" (1 Cor. 1:23).

Imagine Paul's first visit to proud Greek Corinth. If the second-century description of Paul is correct, he was a small man, bent and bald. He entered a city that featured statues of perfect physiques and that gloried in economic power and philosophical prowess. Besides that, the city was a cesspool of moral perversion in religious dress. Paul had come to tell them that their spirituality was defective and that the answer to their need was a Near Eastern savior, a Jew at that. This Savior was an exclusive Lord who was crucified to pay for their sins, rose from the dead, and demanded moral purity from his followers. Talk about an alienating message! No wonder Paul confessed that he entered Corinth in fear, weakness, and much trembling (1 Cor. 2:3).

Paul knew all about unrealistic expectations. The church in Corinth was a classic case in point. The church didn't like Paul's looks, his personality, or his style. They said, "His letters are weighty and forceful, but in person he is unimpressive and his speaking amounts to nothing" (2 Cor. 10:10). They let Paul know that they expected something quite different in their leader than him. It hurt Paul just as it hurts us. Second Corinthians is the most autobiographical of Paul's letters, and its pages tremble with the agony and tears of personal and pastoral rejection.

I don't think it is by accident that most of Paul's pastoral metaphors are in his letters to Corinth. He was struggling with his pastoral identity against all sorts of cultural and ecclesiastical pressures. Paul doesn't try to hide his humanity but includes us in his struggle while telling us about his sense of himself as a pastor.

Paul was also under attack in Thessalonica. Some accused him of using flattery and dishonesty to make money from the Christians. The first part of the letter, to which I referred above, is Paul's reminder that when he was in Thessalonica he was honest and above board, that his speech was marked by authenticity and accompanied by the power of God. In fact, Paul reminds the church that he was gentle like a mother caring for her little children and encouraging like a father urging his children on. Those are powerful portraits of a pastor. But beneath the metaphors lies an even more potent truth. Paul went to great pains to let the Thessalonian Christians know that, though his love for them was deep and sacrificial, he took his cues from God, not them. His motive was to please God, and his end was to win praise from God (1 Thess. 2:4).

In other words, Paul's strong pastoral identity was rooted in God. God made him a pastoral apostle, God equipped him with the tools of an apostle, and God sent him to Thessalonica. God made Paul the Thessalonians' mother and father in the faith. All the accusations in the world could not shake that firm conviction. Even the praise and admiration of the churches did not alter the fact that he took his identity cues from God and not from the world or the church.

The last part of 1 Thessalonians 2:6 clarifies Paul's unshaken sense of identity. It was "as an apostle of Christ" that Paul was a mother and father to the church. He took his orders from the Lord of the church, and the content of his pastoral work came from his Lord. He was motherly in the way that the Christ who sent him was gentle. He was fatherly in the way that his Lord taught and trained his disciples. Paul's pastoral person and pastoral work were rooted in the Son of God. Paul's model for pastoral parent did not come from his human experience but from God as revealed in Jesus Christ (for more on this see chapter 8 below).

For a Christian, the question of identity is far more than a psychological issue. If our struggle is merely our psychological loss of significance, the answer will be strictly human and will come in the form of therapy or some sense of higher self-esteem. That is no answer to people who are created by God and made new by Christ. Our identity must be filled with Christian content—that is, rooted in God, formed by Christ, and empowered by the Holy Spirit.

For Christian pastors, the question of our identity is far deeper than professional models or cultural adaptation. It is certainly more than regaining some of our lost respect from the culture or the church. Our identity, our sense of calling, our mission in life must be grounded in Scripture and filled with theological integrity.

We must learn to take our cues from God as he revealed himself in Christ. While the changing culture does form a most significant part of our formation and function as pastors, our primary cues must not come from the culture. And though the churches we serve are subcultures with their own forms, styles, traditions, and expectations, the churches do not give us our orders. And although the professional world has much to offer the church and pastors in a rapidly changing world, management techniques dare not define the work of God's servants.

My crisis of identity was, in part, my deep longing for significance in a world that wasn't about to give a professional religious person many strokes. I instinctively adapted to my culture and the subculture of my church in order to find that significance. I suspect my hunger for seminars, books, and advanced degrees is fueled by the same desire. Over a lifetime I have learned to take my cues from my environment. But that's a dead-end street. Our earthly environment can give us significance, but it is severely limited. This world can provide no more than this world can create! If our affirmation comes from earthly sources alone, we have only a meager human resource. As our culture increasingly despises the Christian faith, do we dare think we will get satisfaction by looking to it for affirmation? The church can give its ministers wonderful satisfaction, but if our work in the church is how we get our strokes, that is a very slender hope indeed. Christians love well, but because we are all human, we love conditionally. The best pastors must understand that if we were suddenly maimed or lost our ability to do our work, much of the affirmation would cease.

God wants us to know that our primary cues come from him. Our identity is found in his Son, who calls us to his service. We must learn to live under God's smile, knowing that human smiles are mere frosting on that divine cake. Our sense of purpose and success must come from our identity as Christ's servants.

The difficulty is maintaining the delicate balance between finding our identity and marching orders in Christ and loving people and Christ's church with proper sensitivity. Human nature tends to move us in either direction. We can be so full of our identity as Christ's servant that we become obnoxious and insensitive. Or, we easily respond so deeply to our people and their needs (after all, we're pastors!), we take our identity and measure our worth by them. Most of us are insecure and are people pleasers and are too easily manipulated for good or evil. Yet we live under the orders of Christ. It is a difficult tension.

Paul combines both sides of the pastoral equation in the same paragraph in 1 Thessalonians 2. He doesn't look for praise from the Thessalonian church or from anyone else

(v. 6). But he was gentle among them "like a mother caring for her little children."

At the very foundation of Paul's being he was Christ's possession. Christ, the Lord of the church, called him to a ministry where he stood in Christ's church as pastor and apostle. All he did flowed from his deep sense of being under orders from Christ the Lord. This is the foundation of Christian pastoral identity.

At the same time, Paul could say he was all things to all people (1 Cor. 9:22). He was sensitive to his environment and adjusted his ministry to church and community. But this cultural and ecclesiastical formation, while crucial, was built upon the solid foundation of his identity in Christ.

A friend of mine is a very successful pastor. Thousands flock to hear him preach. His church is a model for evangelism and discipleship. One day he made an astonishing statement. He said, "I don't get any of my significance from my work at this church." He went on to say his significance came from his relationship to Christ, his marriage, and his children. I'm not there yet. I suspect my friend's theology is stronger than his experience. But that is the heart of it. It is true that God calls his pastors to wonderful and divine work. It is also true that we work in a very human environment. I still live with stereotypes, roles, and expectations. I am still filled with doubts and fears too. Often I don't feel good about being a pastor. I want human affirmation and the respect of the community. Sometimes I don't like being a pastor, especially when the abuse comes.

But I know Paul is right. I am a man in Christ. That is the foundation of my life. Back in the study of that little country church, I discovered that Christ called me to this work, and made me for the purpose of pastoring that congregation of his people. Everything else in my ministry flows from that foundational conviction. To the degree I remember who I am in Christ and submit to his call, I am a free man—and, I suspect, a better pastor.

2

What's My Address? The Significance of Geography

In the late 1970s the Alban Institute conducted a study of pastors in their first churches. To no one's surprise they discovered a troubled group of people. The title of the study sums it up well: *Crossing the Boundary Between the Seminary and the Parish.*[1] The study revealed that the boundary between seminary and church is vast and that the journey across that great divide creates anger, grief, loss, doubt, and disillusionment. It strains marriages, questions personal identity, and even increases vulnerability to sickness.

The gap between seminary and ministry in the church is only one of the boundaries that pastors must cross. Geography is another. It is an immense boundary made up of a variety of smaller boundaries. It can be painful to cross, but crossing it is crucial for effective pastoral ministry. Pastors must know their address.

410 WEST BROADWAY
GOLDENDALE, WASHINGTON 98620

During the first chapter of my pastoral ministry my address was 410 West Broadway, Goldendale, Washington 98620. Each part of that address bore tremendous significance for ministry in that place. I soon discovered that Washington, like all the Pacific Northwest, reveres the great outdoors. The spirit of the pioneers still lives. The mood is often, "We made this country without God, and we don't need God now." Washington has one of the lowest per capita church membership rates in the nation. The churches in eastern Washington where I lived tended to be small and struggling, common characteristics of church life in those days. Survival was a real issue.

Small-Town America

I lived and ministered in a small town of three thousand people. Like so many small towns, it seemed to be in decline—at least people thought so. Shops and stores had difficulty making it because the larger town thirty miles south sold products cheaper. The largest employer in town, a lumber mill, teetered on the brink of profit, and the future was anything but certain. Fluctuating grain prices and the high price of business kept farmers guessing about the future. People tended to be discouraged about their town though they loved it dearly. Many fondly remembered the good old days. Before long, a large aluminum plant moved nearby and brought an influx of people, many of whom seemed very different from us and threatening to our community values. Rumors flew through town about drug dealing and deviant behavior. These events changed the character of the town in ways many thought unhealthy, making the good old days look even brighter.

Change is always difficult in a church but is particularly hard when the cultural air is filled with discouragement and nostalgia. I found that the community and church leaders tended to be very cautious, even suspicious. The future didn't seem bright to them, and this feeling was revealed in their actions. This wasn't like the suburban church in which I grew up. I was learning the power of a church's address.

Small-Church Ministry

My address on West Broadway served also as the church's address. Broadway was one of the main streets in town, and a Broadway address indicated that we were one of the established churches in town with a century of history and tradition. Some of the sons and daughters of the pioneers who founded the town and the church were members. Our church, along with the Methodist and Lutheran churches, still had some influence in town. The newer churches lacked tradition and influence.

My congregation was a delightful group of God's children who were a representative cross-section of the community. We had members in the school system, city hall, Main Street, the lumber mill, and later, the factory. We had the potential to reach into every part of the community and to influence the life of the town. The major impediment to mobilizing the church for impact in the community was me. From adolescence I grew up in a large industrial city in the Midwest. I was educated in the liberal arts and graduated from a seminary in a prosperous suburb of Chicago. I didn't realize it at the time, but I carried a world of ideas, assumptions, attitudes, values, and expectations from my old address to my new one in rural America.

More paralyzing was my awareness that seminary did not prepare me for any form of outreach or evangelism. We were taught that expository preaching and biblical teaching were sufficient tools for all pastoral work. Occasionally pastoral care was mentioned, but it seemed an afterthought. Evangelism was neither part of the curriculum nor classroom discussion. I was starting from scratch at an unfamiliar address.

Pastoral Ministry in Small-Town America

I quickly learned that my new address was a different world. I was two thousand miles from my seminary but even farther from the culture of my congregation. I was a stranger in a new land.

I saw the world through tinted glasses shared by very few people at my new address. Small-town America was a foreign land to me. One of the boundaries I had to cross was rural sociology. About the only college graduates in the town were school teachers who, like the local pastors, came from the outside world. Things were done certain accepted ways, and new ways were not tolerated—especially if outsiders suggested them. For example, when the public school teachers went on strike, the school board held several open forums, probably to show the teachers, most of whom were outsiders, how unpopular the strike was. At one of the forums a school board member suggested that these ungrateful teachers should pay the school to come to our community and breathe our clean mountain air. I was astonished. I was also confused. Did I belong at this strange address?

I recall standing in line to vote on a proposal for a new high school. I was talking to some people vehemently opposed to the new school. One of them, a member of my congregation, went on about how he had been educated in a one-room school house, and that was good enough for these kids. But the superintendent of schools and many of the teachers were also members of my congregation. I was discovering that in small-towns little things affect people in big ways. Like the teacher's strike, the new building divided the community and the church.

I wondered how to get things done in a place like this. *How could one live at this unique address and make it work for the kingdom of God?* I desperately longed for a course in rural sociology.

I also discovered that though this congregation deeply loved the Bible and wanted me to teach them, I had to recover my preseminary vocabulary and somehow remember how I thought before my theological training. I had to learn how to communicate in language and thought forms congenial to a small-town congregation. I had to understand how the sawyer and the millwright at a lumber mill viewed the world and understood Christian faith. How did a high school girl or her teacher hear? How did a housewife learn or a farmer think? I was learning that all pastoral work is a cross-cultural experience.

I wanted to influence people for Christ's sake, but they were so different from me. Their interests, backgrounds, and ambitions were not familiar. They heard and understood in ways shaped by their own lives, the history of their church, the ethos of their community, and the values of their culture. And when the aluminum factory added its strange array of new cultures to the old, the town faced a cultural challenge beyond its imagination and the church was confronted with a ministry opportunity it never expected.

I did the only thing possible: I asked questions and listened very carefully. My mentor was an older deacon in the church. He had been in the church for a long time and was the kind of man people listened to and trusted. His passion in life was hunting and fishing. I discovered that if I hunted and fished with him, I'd not only learn a lot, but I'd indirectly influence an entire church. I spent lots of time on rivers and in fields with him. Much of the church business was conducted while we fished.

I learned that big-city notions and complex theological ideas needed to be translated into the language and thought forms of my new community. I listened to people in and out of the church to hear what made them tick and how things worked in the community. It was a priceless educational course as well as a fascinating cross-cultural adventure. In seminary I had learned how to exegete texts; now I was learning how to interpret people and communities.

I discovered that preaching and teaching in small-town America and in this small town in particular was quite different from what I had grown up hearing in the suburbs. The content was the same, since God's Word is timeless, but the presentation had to fit my new address. The application of preaching and teaching had to aim precisely and pastorally at the lives of these people. I needed new ears and eyes.

My pastoral work was intensely particular, and that affected how I viewed my work and my congregation's Christian growth. Every day I dealt with life, death, and everything in-between in the astonishing variety typical of small-town churches. I helped people die, and I welcomed children into the world. I performed weddings and spoke at high school baccalaureates. I spent time on farms and in a lumber mill. I visited the rich and comforted the poor. Teenagers came to talk to me, and so did their grandparents. I prayed with them all. And when I stood to lead worship and preach on Sunday, I began to see those people and our town in new ways.

The Heart of Pastoral Ministry

I discovered the most important cross-cultural pastoral principle by accident. After three years of seminary in the crowded rush of suburban Chicago, I loved this new rural mountain setting. It was quiet, simple, and enjoyable. Almost unconsciously, my wife and I began to adapt to our new culture.

Our friends and neighbors spent a lot of time in the mountains, camping. Soon they invited us to join them. We loved it so much we bought a camp trailer and took trips with people in the church. We were having more fun than we imagined possible.

On Thanksgiving we had a special service during which people told the congregation what they were thankful for that year. Midway through the service I said something I hadn't planned to say, but it seemed right. I confessed that I had nearly gone to graduate school instead of accepting their call. But, I added, I was so very thankful that I had come to their town and our church. I told the people how much I loved them.

That spontaneous declaration of love created a reservoir of trust and affection that stunned me. It was so simple—they loved their town and their church, and they wanted me to love what they loved. Because I loved them and their way of life and told them so, they listened and followed.

Pastors must not only know their address, they must also love their neighbors. Cultural adaptation and respect has far more to do with effective pastoral ministry than many people want to admit. We need to become experts at reading and understanding cultural maps.

READING CULTURAL MAPS

Being the son of a wise pastor gave me a wonderful head start as a cultural map reader. When I was an adolescent, Dad became pastor of a large church in the center of a midwestern industrial city. The city and our church had a large number of Appalachian immigrants who had come to the big city to work. They had a very distinct culture that was different from anything we had known. The issue of culture affected every aspect of that church and all the relationships in it, and my family often felt like outsiders. I recall many conversations between my mom and dad about their new culture. They were determined to understand it and fit into it. Most important was the fact that although they didn't like parts of the culture, they always respected it. Their respect and affection was responded to with love and loyalty.

I came home from seminary once and complained about the "country" style of worship at my father's church. Dad smiled and agreed that he, too, preferred the great hymns and confessions. He went on to explain that traditional worship just wouldn't work in this congregation. He could live that way because he loved his congregation and respected their culture even though much of it was alien to him.

Over the years, I have come to recognize the power and importance of cultures in the life of the church. I now realize that every church is made of overlapping cultures, and each culture must be understood and interpreted for effective ministry. Failure to appreciate and respect culture is the bane of many churches and pastors.

1 Park Street
Boston, Massachusetts 02108

Until recently I pastored a downtown church in a major East Coast city. My address was 1 Park Street, Boston, Massachusetts 02108. I was three thousand miles away from 410 West Broadway in Goldendale, Washington. My pastoral world could scarcely have been more different.

But the task was precisely the same. I was God's man sent to this location with the gospel of Jesus Christ. Equipped with gifts from the Spirit, I was commissioned to proclaim the Word of God, grow Christ's church, and expand the borders of his kingdom.

Nevertheless, the context in which that work took place shaped the task in every way. When I arrived in Boston, it quickly dawned on me that I had to decode a variety of cultures in order to minister effectively. In other words, I had to learn to read several overlapping cultural maps. The city is part of a region and is itself made up of many cultures, and the church is a unique subculture with more subcultures in it. My maps looked like this:

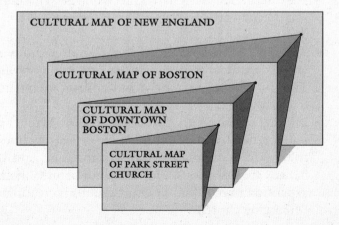

CULTURAL MAP OF NEW ENGLAND

CULTURAL MAP OF BOSTON

CULTURAL MAP OF DOWNTOWN BOSTON

CULTURAL MAP OF PARK STREET CHURCH

A CULTURAL MAP OF NEW ENGLAND

- Tradition: preservationist mentality—resistant to change.
- European Roots: reserved Yankees—resistant to self-revelation or personal sharing.
- Academic Elitism—leaders highly process-oriented, sometimes cynical.
- Adversarial Democracy: rugged independence—boards and committees tend toward discussion/debate rather than action.
- Provincialism—suspicious of experiences and ideas from the outside. See Academic Elitism.
- Liberal and Libertarian Political Tradition—polarization and extremes work against consensus.
- Severe Economic Cycles Plus Puritan Roots—pessimism.

There is more, of course, but this is the spiritual and intellectual air that people in New England breathe. It affects the way people hear, understand, and act. The region is the background to more specific cultures that affect the work of the church.

A CULTURAL MAP OF BOSTON

- Provincial: Self-designated nickname is "The Hub" (of the universe)—if you haven't done it here, it doesn't count.
- Academic Economy: Nearly three hundred thousand university students give the city a very young profile. The city also has a "spirit" that leans toward intellectual arrogance.
- Ethnic Diversity with Adversarial Reality: Magnet for immigration last century and in the present. Politics is tribal, life is adversarial, race is significant, and the natives are suspicious. However, powerful Christian expansion in recent immigrant groups is creating an "emerging church."

- Catholic Majority with Declining Influence: Irish Catholics are the dominant political and religious force. Protestants are a minority and evangelicals a fraction of that minority.
- Advanced Secularism: The universities along with the opinion makers create a profound antireligious bias. Eastern Massachusetts and Boston, in particular, have a centuries-long secular tradition.
- Young Adult Population in Downtown: Large numbers of ambitious, hard-driven, and transient young adults live within walking distance of the financial district.
- Urban Decay: The city reality is darkened by violence, drugs, and poverty in the inner city.
- High-Tech Economy: Many brilliant people with profound needs live in the city.

A CULTURAL MAP OF DOWNTOWN BOSTON: OUR NEIGHBORHOOD.

- Financial District: Three hundred thousand people in high-rise buildings; four seats of government; and a university.
- Historic Residential District: One hundred thousand neighbors who tend to be young and secular.
- Highly Secular: Surveys indicate that our neighbors have little or no interest in organized religion. However, half of them would come to church if asked!
- White Middle-Class: But with a touch of Asia.
- Highly Transient Population: Here today and gone tomorrow.

A CULTURAL MAP OF PARK STREET CHURCH

- Historic and Traditional: Enormous pride and preservationist mentality in long-time members.
- Stability: Four pastors in this century.
- Transient Laity: There is a 50 percent turnover of the congregation every two years.

- Young Adult majority: 67 percent of the congregation is under age forty and single.
- Generational Tension: Aging leadership with emerging young majority who want ownership.
- Academic Orientation: Preoccupation with processes makes it difficult to create movement.
- International Congregation: Thirty nationalities represented with 15 percent from Asian backgrounds.

These maps are unlike any in which I have worked before. Perhaps no other church reads like this one. That's the point: Every church is unique and in its own particular setting. I have had to adjust how I preach, teach, and lead. My pastoral and leadership instincts point in a new direction. God put this church in this place to make an impact here.

I'm still learning, asking, and listening. Recently I saw a headline in one of the Boston newspapers: "Locals Skeptical." I clipped it and put it on my desk to remind me where I am. Reading the multiple cultural maps is a never ending-discipline. I must not forget my address. Most important, every day I ask myself the fundamental question: Do I love this place? I have learned by hard experience in another pastorate that I cannot serve those whom I do not love.

Learning to adapt is not easy, but it is what we expect our missionaries to do. We send them to new cultures, where they learn the language and adjust to the culture for the sake of Christ. The degree to which missionaries can make that transition into another culture—that is, learn their new address—in large measure determines their success there.

An American church leader told me that while he was visiting Haiti, he asked a veteran Haitian Christian what makes a good missionary. The old man answered, "Someone who loves God and loves Haitians." He went on to lament that most of the missionaries he had known seemed to love God but didn't love Haitians. I suspect those missionaries learned their cultural superiority in American churches. We talk a lot about loving God and winning the world, but we often seem angry at the American culture we are called to win. Christian talk sometimes borders on hatred of the culture or even of those whom God calls us to serve. The church cannot win those whom it does not serve in love.

THE FOUNDATION OF PASTORAL THEOLOGY

Whatever our address, we march under orders from a Lord who loves his enemies. Remember Jesus' triumphal entry into Jerusalem on a donkey? He was riding into the last week of his life and what he knew would be his death. The city was full of his enemies, who were committed to getting rid of him. The larger population simply ignored him. He was a strange teacher from Galilee, and no one who amounted to much ever came from there.

Luke tells us that as Jesus rode down the hill into the city he looked at it and began to weep and sob. "If you, even you, had only known on this day what would bring you peace ..." (Luke 19:42). He could have ridden down that hill, filled with resentment and anger for a culture that suppressed the Word of God, opposed and killed God's prophets, and would murder him within a week. Instead he entered the city with a broken heart. Christ's church and its pastoral leaders need to follow Jesus down that hill toward our address. A culture-bashing Christianity does not serve well the Christ who went to a cross to die for his enemies, even the enemies of our church.

We adapt to our culture as a matter of theological integrity, not merely because it works. The foundation of that kind of pastoral thinking is sociological and can produce nothing more than human power can generate. The results of any method cannot be greater than the method itself. We need something more.

Incarnational Base

Christian pastoral reasoning is rooted in the Incarnation. The way we view all reality, especially our work as pastors, flows from the pattern established when God became flesh for

41

us. The Incarnation is the most spectacular example of the missionary decision ever made. God delivered his final revelation to the human race by clothing himself in flesh and entering a particular culture at a particular point in time. Jesus knew his address—"Jesus of Nazareth," they called him. Jesus spoke the language of his people with a Galilean accent. He understood the worlds of Nazareth and Galilee and all Judea, and he entered into life in those worlds.

Jesus learned how to read and write at the village school in the synagogue in Nazareth. He learned carpentry at Joseph's side and built and remodeled homes for his neighbors. He knew their hopes and fears because he listened to them. In fact, he felt what they felt and thought like they thought. He was a Jewish man from Galilee, and he looked like one, talked like one, and acted like one. Thus he could preach and teach in a way his contemporaries could understand, using examples from their world.

Jesus' point in crossing his cultural boundaries was far more than identification. He came to transform people and cultures. And while identifying with his culture, he also stood in judgment against it. Pastors must learn the difficult and often controversial art of full identification with their culture without losing their foundational identity in Christ.

The Incarnation means that God takes human cultures seriously. Christ's church, if it follows the pattern of the Incarnation, will take its culture seriously too. Pastors, as leaders of God's people, must lead the way by living themselves into the lives of their people. Then the church must live itself deeply into its culture. We must learn how to identity with the people God has sent us to win.

Incarnational Pattern of Truth

The Incarnation is the pattern for God's revelation. God has always delivered his truth in ways accessible to particular cultures as exemplified in the way the Hebrew Scriptures bear the marks of ancient Jewish culture. The prophets and apostles who wrote the Bible communicated God's truth in language common to their culture, and they addressed issues present in their culture in appropriate ways.

Paul, for example, knew his address and the addresses of his hearers. His speech at Mars Hill in Athens is a classic example of cultural adaptation. He knew exactly to whom he was speaking, and he shaped his speech to their understanding. He started his speech in their world and moved them to the world of the gospel. The next week, speaking to Jews in a synagogue in Corinth, he used different thought patterns and language to make the same point.

Paul made tents to support himself in Corinth lest he offend the new believers. Later, in Ephesus, he rented a hall where he taught the Christian faith for three years. His constant cultural adaptation is summed up in his powerful statement in 1 Corinthians 9:22–23: "I have become all things to all men so that by all possible means I might save some. I do all this for the sake of the gospel."

Incarnational Church

The Incarnation is the center of the New Testament teaching about the church. Paul calls the church "the body of Christ." As Jesus was the truth of God in flesh and blood, the church expresses the gospel of Jesus in living flesh and blood reality. The church exists to demonstrate the gospel and by that demonstration to spread it. By its very nature, the church is called to live itself into its world in order to transform it.

Sadly, the church doesn't do a very good job of demonstration. Most non-Christians I talk to don't object to Jesus and his teaching, but they have a major problem with the church. And so do many of us.

The hostility of many Christians toward contemporary culture is profoundly anti-Incarnational. While there are always some who want the church to be a safe fortress against the marauding hordes of evil around us, an attitude far from Jesus' Incarnational mind, a more dangerous trend is upon us: parishioners who want us to make the church a crusading army bent on destroying our neighbors for whom Christ died. Nothing could be further from the mind of Christ.

A church leader let me know in no uncertain terms that he expected me to lead a church crusade against homosexuals. The issue was legislation pending in the state house that would ensure legal and civil rights for homosexuals. As we talked he became more and more insistent that I was negligent in my pastoral duties if I didn't lead the charge to the state house to stop this legislation. Finally, when my patience ran out, I answered. "You know," I said, "I have loved ones who are homosexual. More than anything, they need God. I try to keep them away from Christians like you, or they'll never hear the good news of Christ."

Whatever one may think about politics and the church, one thing is clear: The church is called to Incarnational thinking, which at the very least identifies with and understands all the subcultures of the world in which we live. Moral standards and deep convictions do not require alienation from those whom we are called to serve in Christ's name. We cannot speak good news to people we hold in contempt.

Francis Schaeffer used to say that the church must speak a word of judgment to itself and the watching world. But, he added, that word must be accompanied with tears. Like our Lord, our hearts must be broken for those we are called to serve. Then the necessary hard words will bear the grace inherent in the gospel, which is specially designed for people alienated from God.

I love motorcycles. Every year several friends and I take a motorcycle vacation. This year we rode to the fifty-fifth annual Black Hills Rally in Sturgis, South Dakota. Several hundred thousand motorcyclists joined us in the largest assembly of Harley-Davidsons in the world. Leather-clad bikers on loud bikes came to see, to be seen, and to party. The crowd was rough, tough, often profane, and sometimes obnoxious.

I thought a lot about the gospel and the Incarnation in this world so far removed from my life as a pastor among God's people. Sometimes I had to remind myself that God loves each one of these people and that Jesus died for them. I wondered how to tell them about God's love found in Jesus Christ.

I remembered a church in Akron, Ohio, that has a large and effective ministry to bikers. The ministry is led by some converted bikers who live to tell other bikers about the gospel. These ministers don't look like conventional church people. They look like the bikers they are. They hang out in biker bars and attend biker rallies, where they bear witness to the transforming power of God. They were there in Sturgis, telling the good news in a way that that crowd could understand. It was the Incarnation principle at work. The church cannot serve whom it will not embrace in the love of Christ. Whatever the address of the church, it is called to live itself into its neighborhood and world for the sake of the gospel.

A turning point in my life was the day several of us seminary students were complaining bitterly to our seminary dean about the failures and foibles of the church. He listened patiently. When we were finished with our tirade he said, "If Christ loved the church enough to die for it, can't you guys love it enough to serve it?" There it was. My problem wasn't the church. Nor was it the culture. The problem was and continues to be me. Am I willing to make the missionary decision to serve the world God loves and the church for which Christ died?

Every month or so I stop and ask myself the missionary questions: Do I love this place? Do I love this church despite its many shortcomings? Do I love this city? With Jesus can I weep for my Jerusalem?

Incarnational Pastoral Ministry

Pastoral ministry is rooted in the incarnation of Christ. We are the servants of the One who willingly entered into our world and took on the burden of humanity in order to rescue us. The central motivation of an incarnational ministry is the love of Christ, which Paul confessed compelled him to pastoral ministry even with the rogue Christians in Corinth (2 Cor. 5:14).

We are called to specific addresses where Christ's church lives and worships. At its most basic point, our calling demands that we incarnate ourselves into our churches and their communities. That means that we must understand our people and their culture so well that we can think their thoughts and feel their heart cries. We must join Jesus on his brokenhearted ride into the city of Jerusalem.

But incarnational living is even deeper than accurate identification with people or profound understanding of their world. At its very center, incarnation is sacrificial. It cost Jesus everything to be our Savior. Finally, it cost him his life. Pastoral ministry costs us our lives too. While few, if any, of us will be martyrs, all of us are called to give our lives to Christ and his church. I think that is why ministry is inherently painful. The gift of a life is a matter of the heart. We give our lives and our hearts to people, and that gift is more often than not, unappreciated or even rejected. It hurts. It also hurts to live oneself into people's lives. There we stand between God and people bearing the Word of God on one hand and the burdens, pain, and sorrow of people on the other. This no-man's-land cannot be comfortable. Yet it is our calling.

One of the most astonishing texts in the New Testament is Romans 9:3, in which Paul says that he is willing to be cursed if it means the salvation of Israel. Think about it: Paul was willing to be damned if it meant salvation for those he loved. Paul was making the boldest missionary decision humanly possible, and it is the heart of a Christological and apostolic pastoral ministry.

The Incarnation is the heart and soul of pastoral ministry, and it is also the foundation stone of pastoral theology. Our pastoral work finds its center in Christology that is not a mere abstract theological idea but a living reality. Such incarnational ministry always has a specific address. That's what makes it ministry, and that's what makes it challenging.

Now I find myself in a prosperous suburb of Minneapolis in a congregation with its own history and culture. I am listening carefully and learning how to blend into this wonderful and complex congregation and community. It is a never-ending and delightful journey among God's people.

3

What Time Is It?
The Question of Date

King Saul left a mess for David to clean up. King David began his reign surrounded by enemies because, although Saul often fought the Philistines, Israel's traditional enemy and oppressor, he never decisively defeated them. And Moab and Ammon were always on Israel's horizon, threatening peace and prosperity.

Internally, the nation was not sound. Saul had led the nation in a civil war that sapped its military and spiritual strength. The country was divided and dismayed. Jerusalem, the fortress city in the middle of the country, defied Israel's rule. David was king, but parts of the land were not under his rule. So David began by consolidating his power. He ruled from the town of Hebron supported by those 1 Chronicles calls his "mighty men" (11:11). David's task was immense: He had to consolidate a decaying kingdom and defeat Israel's enemies. Such a task would take time. In fact, the king wouldn't capture Jerusalem until seven years later. Only then would he begin attacking Philistia, Moab, and Ammon.

Fighting men from every tribe in Israel joined David in Hebron. Their job, says the chronicler in 1 Chronicles 12, where the fighting men are listed by tribe, was "to turn Saul's kingdom over to [David], as the LORD had said" (v. 23). Thousands came to aid their new king in establishing his rule and sovereignty over the land. Benjamin, King Saul's tribe, who had been resistant to David, sent 3000 warriors. The little tribe of Ephraim sent nearly 20,800 armed warriors ready for battle. Even the priestly tribe of Levi sent 4,600 men. All these warriors, several hundred thousand of them, came "fully determined to make David king over all Israel" (v. 38).

Saul had never known this kind of support. But David was a much better general than Saul, and the warriors of Israel knew it because many of them had served with David in his campaigns. They loved their king and gladly joined in supporting him and his army. The chronicler goes on to tell how various tribes, even the most distant, sent food, wine, clothing, animals, and other supplies to the Hebron (1 Chron. 12:40).

But military power and popular support were not enough. In the middle of the list of tribal armies that came to David's aid lies a profound comment. The tribe of Issachar sent two hundred chiefs to David, *"men ... who understood the times and knew what Israel should do"* (1 Chron. 12:32, emphasis added). The skills of a brilliant military king and the sheer power of hundreds of thousands of trained warriors needed to be informed and directed by two hundred men who "understood the times and knew what Israel should do."

That is the need among God's people in every generation. Our task is the same as Israel's: to expand the reign of God on earth. He is the king, but we are surrounded by a culture that will not recognize his sovereignty. Vast numbers of Christians and powerful churches are necessary but not enough. To defeat the enemies of God and establish his reign in the lives of people, we must be led by people who "understand the times and know what [the church] should do." This is especially necessary in our culture, which is rapidly losing whatever God-consciousness it once had and in which the church often seems powerless against the assault on Christian values and beliefs. While there are plenty of Christians and hundreds of thousands of churches, we must find and deploy people who understand the times and know what to do.

The pattern of the Incarnation demands that we understand the lives, minds, and heart hungers of our neighbors if we are going to win them. Leaders must know national trends and local folk ways. Effective ministry depends on pastors knowing what time it is and knowing what to do about it.

OUR TIME

Everyone seems to agree that we are living at a turning point in history. So many and massive are the changes in our day that *paradigm shift* is the term used to describe this turning of the ages. Management expert Tom Peters notes that escalating change is producing chaos in society and in the marketplace. In his recent book, *Thriving on Chaos*, Peters says that he is promoting a necessary management revolution. The old way of management, he says, was based on "a relatively predictable environment now vanished."[1] His point is that things are changing so rapidly that the only organizations that will survive are those that can manage the chaos the escalating change creates.

Time will tell if Peters' analysis of the business world is correct. The larger question for men and women of God is the state of the church in a world of escalating change. One thing is certain: The world in which the church lives and works is not only changing with escalating speed, it is fundamentally different from the world a generation ago.

The New Reality: The Marginalized Church

Not for centuries has the gulf between the church and culture been wider. The ancient Christian consensus that informed our culture and in some sense guided it has fallen. For centuries the church held an honored and influential place in Western society. In America the moral sense of the nation was formed by Christian moral assumptions. Government and society paid respect to the church and its leaders. Local churches wielded enormous community influence.

Earlier in this century, for example, the pastor of Boston's Park Street Church was A. Z. Conrad. One of the lingering memories of Dr. Conrad is his walking rapidly up the street toward the statehouse, his formal coattail flapping in the breeze. He was constantly going to see local political leaders about matters that impacted the church and the community. He expected to be heard by the legislators and, I suppose, they expected to hear from him. He represented the old Protestant establishment as the cardinal of the archdiocese of Boston represented the new Catholic establishment.

I attended a meeting of the Downtown Boston Clergy when I first arrived in town. The devotional was given by two Hari Krishnas chanting in Sanskrit. I met members of several non-Christian religions who are often part of the program. The purpose of the clergy meetings is to help one another understand the faiths that dot the religious landscape. The larger community, especially the political establishment, doesn't know that the downtown clergy meet, nor does it seem to care. The governor's door is shut to all Christian influence except an occasional nod to the Catholic cardinal. In a city founded and dominated by Puritans for centuries and more recently heavily influenced by a Catholic political establishment, Christianity has very little influence. Boston, like most American cities, is a very secular place; religion is on the margins at best. Christianity is just one of several religious groups striving to stay alive in an increasingly hostile environment.

Most of us are discovering that we live on a mission field. The many and escalating changes of our time have produced a society with less and less Christian presence. Loren Mead puts our present challenge forthrightly in his brief and provocative book, *The Once and Future Church*.[2] The subtitle, *Reinventing the Congregation for a New Mission Frontier,* suggests the enormity of the changes he and most thoughtful observers believe lie before us.

Mead rightly maintains that the church is defined by its mission. Since that is the case, there have been two ecclesiological paradigms in church history. He calls the first the "Apostolic Paradigm." In the Apostolic era, the church clearly understood the distance between itself and its hostile environment. It also understood that its calling was to reach out *to* the environment. Its mission was to cross that missionary boundary, and that mission defined the church and its life.

Mead calls the second paradigm the "Christendom Paradigm." Emperor Constantine erased the boundary between the church and its environment. Since the world was now officially Christian and the Christian environment served the church, the mission of the church naturally became a far-off enterprise, something done in distant lands. That mentality dominated the church through the Reformation and into the present. In most churches we expect our neighbors to come to us, learn our ways and habits, and enter our subculture.

The Need of the Hour

Mead's point is that, like it or not, the Christendom Paradigm is dead. He suggests that we live in an interim period as the third paradigm takes shape. The boundary between church and environment is widening, and it is clear that we live in a mission field. Therefore, a corresponding shift in our understanding of the church and its ministry is necessary. The church must enter the culture, learn its language, understand its ways, discover its thought patterns, know its heart, and then bear credible witness.

Park Street Church recently surveyed its nearest neighbors. About a hundred thousand people live within walking distance of the church, and they are the church's primary Christian responsibility. Canvassers discovered that the vast majority of Park Street's neighbors barely knew the church existed and really didn't care that it did. Organized religion is simply not part of their consciousness. I suppose Boston is a case of advanced secularism, but that is the direction of our culture. God seems to be part of the culture but hardly the God of the Bible. The church is marginal at best and more so all the time.

Some churches deny reality and continue business as usual. Failing to understand the times, they just keep talking to themselves and, consequently, make less and less of a dent in their world. They simply don't understand the times and thus can't do anything about them. Other churches curse the moral and spiritual failure of our time and work furiously to turn back the tide of time. But the sheer numbers of non-Christian people, along with the pluralist and tolerant mood of the times, seem to make that a futile battle. Moreover, how can one win a battle against principalities and powers with the very human weapons that people try to use to replace the power of the Christian gospel? There is a difference between knowing about the times and understanding the times and knowing what to do.

Again, other churches adopt a defensive posture in the laudable effort to protect the truth and themselves from the secular onslaught. They build the walls thicker and make the moat deeper to somehow keep the deadly perils of our time outside the church and, hopefully, outside their lives. In protecting the past and present they mortgage the future by leaving it to modernity. Defensive Christianity is a death trap that not only fails to engage the world Christ commanded us to win but inevitably produces malformed Christians turned in on themselves with little or no vision for their lost neighbors. They refuse to understand the times. It's too dangerous.

A new breed of church and pastor have determined that being the salt of the earth and the light of the world demands that the people of God enter into modernity in order to transform it. They take the Incarnation as the model and firmly believe that since the gospel is the power of God, we need not fear any adversary. These sons and daughters of Issachar determine to understand the times. They listen more than they talk, and they take their neighbors' doubts and fears seriously. They love this culture in spite of its sin because Christ does. They know who sits on the throne and are convinced, therefore, that all history is heading for its proper conclusion in Christ. Above all, they long for Christ's reign to expand here, there, and everywhere. Like David's warriors and the wise men of Issachar, they live to make Christ King.

SIGNS OF THE TIMES

I recently attended a gathering of church leaders from New England. We met to discuss ways in which we could work together to make a greater impact for Christ in our region. We started by listing the changes we saw in the larger culture; consequently, the list was similar to most lists describing the changes in American culture. We discussed the following ten changes.

1. *Internationalization*. One form of internationalization is the emergence of the global village created in part by modern communication systems. In an instant we know what is going on all over the world.

Another form is the migration of huge numbers of people. Many of these immigrants are coming to America and thus creating a new political equation. Some analysts project a pattern of immigration and population growth that by A.D. 2050 will create an America in which European-Americans will be a minority. Latinos will soon be the second largest minority group in America. In Boston, for example, the Latino population grew 72 percent between 1980 and 1990. Presently, there are almost as many Latinos as African-Americans in Boston. The implications for the church and society are enormous.

The religious scene is deeply affected by internationalization. Non-Christian religions are taking their place on the American religious map. If present immigration patterns continue, there will be more Muslims than Jews in the United States by the late 1990s. Again, the political and religious implications are huge.

Churches that fail to take cities, immigrant groups, and minorities seriously will be increasingly irrelevant. Evangelical Christianity is overwhelmingly white and middle class.

Our strength is in rural and suburban America. We won't disappear in the next decades, but unless we change the way we see the world, we will become a marginal movement with little to say to the larger culture. We need pastoral leaders who understand the times and know what to do.

2. *Urbanization.* The world is moving to the city. By A.D. 2000, by one estimate, 50 percent of the world's population will live in cities. By A.D. 2000, seventeen world cities will have populations of over 10 million, seven of them in the Muslim world. Poverty and hunger is now greater than at anytime in world history, and some suggest that 900 million people will be living in poverty by A.D. 2000, 100 million of them in utter poverty. The challenge for the missions movement will be so overwhelming that missions will have to be reinvented.

According to the 1990 census, more than half of all Americans live in the thirty-nine American metropolitan areas of one million or more. Ninety percent of all growth in the decade of the 1980s was in cities. Because much urban growth is due to immigration of minorities, the social, political, and religious implications are great. Urban poverty and crime alone frustrate the persistent efforts of the best minds and hearts available. There seem to be very few solutions to a thousand diagnoses. Even the suburbs offer no escape from the sins of the city. The power of drug and alcohol abuse, violence, and moral decay differ only in style not substance. The city seems to bring out the best and worst of any culture at the same time. We need pastors who understand the times and know what to do.

3. *Secularization.* American culture has moved the Christian God out of its consciousness. The cultural assumptions on which the opinion makers operate begin and end with humanity. The media portrays a culture devoid of any religious content or practice. The ascendance of science and technology has created a people who assume that the empirical world of objective objects is the only reality.

The companion of the secularization of America is relativism, the conviction that no absolute truths exist or, if truth does exist, it cannot be known. On campuses and in the media, the only absolute these days is that there are no absolutes. Morality is radically individual, persons autonomously deciding what is right or wrong with little or no reference outside themselves. The result is pervasive moral and intellectual apathy.

Not too long ago I was talking with a group of college and university ministers. They told me that they cannot work with the same assumptions they held just a few years ago. While most students are open to discussions about spiritual things, few care. One veteran of campus ministry recalled how he used to set up a Christian book table next to the Marxist book table. Students then debated great "truths" about life and its meaning. "Now," he said, "nobody sets up book tables. Few are interested in what's true, because even if there is some truth out there, no one can find it."

John Stott's book *The Contemporary Christian*[3] is written against this background. Stott notes that the truth of Christianity is seldom the issue these days. Now people are much less interested in the truth claims of Christianity than in whether or not this ancient faith can possibly be relevant in the twenty-first century.

If the church will minister to this generation, it must find a way to hold fast to the truth that holds our faith together while creating ways to answer the questions raised by a generation void of Christian assumptions and content. Christian demonstration of the love command and the transforming character of the gospel is the crying need of the hour.

A while ago I was asked to present an introduction to Christianity before a group of interested but skeptical young adults. I worked hard at preparing it and gave a fairly traditional presentation providing evidence that Jesus is who he claimed to be and that the Bible tells the truth. The audience was polite but very restrained and apparently not very impressed. The next week I talked about the church and told stories of the power of the gospel I have seen and experienced myself over the years. The discussion afterward was electric. These young skeptics were greatly interested in a community of faith that demonstrated the grace and power of God. My own church needs pastors who know the times and know what to do.

4. *Technology.* Our world and lives are driven by technology. Our young adult ministry at the Park Street Church had a retreat in the woods. The topic was being a Christian in the technological age. The dominant discussion topic was the loneliness produced by a world in which machines are often valued more than people and in which people interface with machines rather than relate to people. Many live most of their days alone with a machine. Increasingly people prefer to communicate electronically because it is safer and very controlled. Life is impersonal and often empty.

Technology can be a wonderful gift, but is it congenial to the gospel? God became flesh and lived among us, and the church is people living in transforming relationships. Congregational life is people in relationship with God and people. Therefore, television church is an oxymoron.

When I called one of my favorite Christian organizations, a machine answered. After several minutes of waiting and finally more minutes lost in a phone-mail wilderness, I gave up. I'm sure the motive behind the answering system is good—to save staff time and to control incoming calls—but the outcome is contrary to the nature of the gospel. The church is, by its very nature, a people place. Human voices and real presence are the very stuff of our life. Technology must be subordinate to and the servant of the real flesh and blood people of God.

5. *Individualism.* When Alexis de Tocqueville described America at the time of the Revolution, he had to invent a new term, *individualism.* The individual and his or her happiness and rights lie at the heart of the American character. Robert Bellah's *Habits of the Heart*[4] is a powerful critique of this

national characteristic. He maintains that ultimately individualism destroys persons and culture. Individualistic and self-serving modern Americans are cut off from community, family, and traditional interpersonal systems that nurtured the heart and soul for all of human history.

Psychologist Martin Seligman documents the consequences of individualism in the young adult population in his often-quoted "Boomer Blues."[5] Seligman and others note that the rate of clinical depression in younger adults is up to ten times greater than the rate of their parents' and grandparents' generations. His diagnosis is telling. The younger generation is cut off from the safety nets that cared for people for all of history. They no longer trust the government or any public institution. For millennia, people trusted their tribe, their people's system we call "government." When trouble came, you could count on your people for help. No longer. Time after time young adults tell me that they have a very difficult time with the church because they just don't trust institutions.

Young adults wonder about the family. Everyone knows someone who's family was broken, and many, if not most, know firsthand the devastating consequences of divorce in their own family. How can a person believe that someone will love him or her forever? And who can trust God? If there is a God, young adults believe, God doesn't seem to be able to do much. And if God is a father, how can a generation with absent or nonfunctioning fathers understand this God?

My daughter, now a member of the so-called twenty-something generation, came home from school when she was in third grade and told us that her classmates played "divorce" at recess. Even in our rural and very traditional community broken families were "normal." Years later, in high school, she asked my wife and me if we would ever divorce. Her good friend, "Vicki," had been devastated by her parents' divorce. After our firm assurances that that was not a possibility, she responded, "Sure, that's what Vicki's parents told her, too." For my daughter's generation, broken marriages and broken families are part of the framework of expectations. The result, Seligman says, is a generation cast back on themselves, a hope that is slender indeed. Americans feel alone before a hostile universe and on their own morally, emotionally, and relationally.[6]

Again, the implications for the church are obvious. The church and its pastors must feel the pain of a broken generation and provide communities of faith in which healing is an essential part of the framework of expectations.

6. *Materialism/consummerism.* Materialism takes many forms, but beneath them all is the belief that the tangible stuff around us is all there is. Material things have the highest value; hence, stuff gives satisfaction. The material motivates because it is a measure of worth. He or she who accumulates lots of stuff is successful.

Consumerism naturally follows. It's the great engine that drives our culture. We are urged to buy things we really don't need, because those things will bring us everything we do need for the good life. In America material things have often replaced God as the source of life and health.

While the perils of secularism are more obvious, the dangers of materialism/consumerism may be the most deadly enemies of the church, because most of us unthinkingly accept their grip on our lives. The inevitable consequence is that God is reduced in importance, consigned to the realm of the invisible matters of the soul. We judge our own worth and that of others by signs of material success. In churches we assign value according to financial worth and material possessions. Money talks—very loudly.

A Christian woman who assigned enormous worth to the signs of success once suggested to me that one of the problems with our church was that we didn't have enough doctors in the congregation. She meant that they would bring necessary prestige and money to our rather humble congregation.

We allow the affluent to assign their good fortune to the "blessing" of God without asking if that means that the poor somehow miss God's "blessing." Jesus' teaching about wealth and poverty (Luke 6:20–26) is turned on its head in our time. Like the men of Issachar, do we understand the times?

7. *Rootlessness.* Long ago Vance Packard called America "a nation of strangers."[7] Our unprecedented mobility has destroyed the sense of community that held society together throughout history. Add our rootlessness to our individualism, and the result is great numbers of people who are utterly alone in the face of a vast and lethal universe that seems out of control. That sense of doomed isolation sits heavily on the souls of men and women in our congregations.

The Park Street congregation had a large number of young adults. Nearly all of them lived far from home and were temporary residents of our city. A survey of the congregation indicated that half of our people had been part of our church for less than two years. No wonder relationships ranked as the highest value of our young adults. A few of them even moved home for more than economic reasons. They longed for roots, home, and stable relationships. Park Street's turnover rate is, no doubt, exceptionally high but marks a growing trend in our time.

Churches and pastors who know what time it is will feel the ache of loneliness in their people and their neighbors and will know what to do.

8. *Moral breakdown.* In a secular world there are no moral authorities outside ourselves. Day in and day out we hear that we are autonomous and free moral agents who should not judge the moral choices of others nor allow our own choices to be informed by anything other than our own self-interest.

The tragic societal consequences of free choices surround us. Pastors see the effects of moral breakdown every day in broken people. As in the book of Judges, we live in a time when everyone does what is right in his or her own eyes with equally tragic results. Each Sunday, the pews are filled with people whose lives are twisted by the consequences of their own sin and the sin of others.

Sadly, many Christians justify their moral failure in a variety of creative ways. Pastors are finding that most of the couples who come to be married are already living together or are sexually involved. Inevitably, they seem surprised and often take offense when we inform them that the Bible clearly says that they should abstain from sex until marriage.

More tragically, the moral crisis strikes at the heart of the church. The moral collapse of pastors and church leaders is frightening. While we are properly shocked by clergy misconduct, a more insidious moral erosion is eating away at the character of the church. The very pragmatism that makes evangelical Christianity vibrant at the same time tends toward a loss of integrity. Some lay leaders have counseled me to play games with the truth if telling the whole truth may negatively affect the church or some of the people in the church (usually people with money or influence!). Ironically, one of the finest church leaders I know tells me I'm too honest to lead a church. If only he knew the deep self-interest that tempts me to pull punches when I preach and manipulate the truth and people when I lead.

In a market-oriented world like ours, pastors are continually tempted to play to the audience and tell the people what they want to hear. Because pastors are agents of the peace of Christ, we are tempted to keep the peace at all costs, even the cost of truth-telling, so we often just let things go. We fail to distinguish the difference between peace keeping and peace making. The latter is always costly but inevitably better.

If the Lord's servants are tempted to blunt the truth for the sake of an organization, no wonder our laypeople long for ethical help in the work world. Nearly every day I talk to men and women in the marketplace who live under enormous pressure to lie or cheat for the sake of their company or for advancement in the company. One of the greatest challenges in our time is living authentic Christian morals in the marketplace.

We need a generation of pastors with clear vision, straight moral spines, and deep and empathic understanding of the times to lead the church toward the twenty-first century.

9. *Conflict/Culture Wars.* The book *Culture Wars*[8] describes the battle for the soul of America. That battle, however, is only a small part of a larger descent into chaos. Back in 1963, Daniel Patrick Moynihan and Nathan Glazer predicted the present crisis. Their celebrated but ignored book, *Beyond the Melting Pot*, maintained that the Marxist claim that this would be the century of "class struggle" was dead wrong. It would be, they insisted, a century of increased ethnic tension, the recovery of tribal consciousness.[9] In 1993 Moynihan told *Newsweek* magazine, perhaps with tongue in cheek, that his next book would be titled *Pandemonium*. He reminded the interviewer that in *Paradise Lost*, Pandemonium was the capital of hell.[10] If that is what politically astute observers predict, the church desperately needs more of the men of Issachar, wise leaders who know what the church should do.

The larger cultural conflict is echoed in a variety of smaller but very real conflicts. Racial, ethnic, gender, generational, family, and political battles dot the cultural map of our time. This is an adversarial world, and all of us take the conflict home and to church. We have a new profession to match the spirit of the age—"conflict resolution" management.

Our churches are filled with people living in deep personal, moral, and relational conflicts. The church itself, intended to be the demonstration of God's peace, lives in far too much conflict. "Holy wars" are fought in denominations, seminaries, and local congregations. In our time one can make a living by traveling around and dispensing conflict resolution advice and training to churches. The fact is, Christian conflict is a denial of the power of the peace of Christ. But chances are that conflict will continue to escalate in society and in the church. Therefore the church needs leaders who know what time it is and what to do.

10. *Descending quality of life. Fortune* magazine claims that we are living through four business revolutions simultaneously.[11] Together they are larger than the Industrial Revolution that shaped the modern world. Downsizing, reengineering,

and an obsolescent workforce are creating insecurity that has many younger Americans thinking they will experience downward mobility.

Single parents, usually women, are becoming a new class of the marginally poor. The underclass in America seems to be growing, and no one has answers. Add growing violence, crime, and social unrest, and the result is a pessimistic culture. The seventy-fifth anniversary issue of *Forbes* magazine sums it up in its issue theme, "Why We Feel So Bad."[12] It is a collection of essays by prominent Americans led by an article titled "Oh, Our Aching Angst." The diagnoses differ, but all agree that the American people are increasingly pessimistic as our culture seems to disintegrate.

How can a culture move upward when its morality is spiraling downward, conflict is escalating, relationships are weakening, loneliness is intensifying, families are breaking, violent crime and poverty are increasing, and the rising generation has little hope? This century has demonstrated that government by itself can do little to reverse cultural decline. The church stands in the midst of this culture and offers hope, power, and home. In times like these the church must be led by pastors who understand this culture incarnationally and who know how to lead redemptively.

THE NEED OF THE HOUR

As our group was discussing the state of our culture, it dawned on me that each of those ten cultural markers is powerfully addressed by the gospel. In fact, ancient Israel and the early church went up against forces greater than these and prevailed. The church need not be afraid, defensive, or hidden. If the gospel is the power of God, we should be on the offensive with a message of hope—not despair, a positive word—not a pessimistic message, a redemptive offer—not a hostile rejection.

Consider the list again with the Christian message added.

1. *Internationalization*. The Christian gospel is designed to be international and speaks powerfully to an

international reality. Acts 13:1 describes an international and multicultural church that reached the world. The names of the church leaders variously indicate Roman, Greek, and Jewish backgrounds. This diverse congregation sent the first missionaries out into the Roman world. The great theological statement of the universal kingdom of God is Ephesians 2:11–22. By the power of the cross Christ smashed the walls that separate God from humanity and humans from each other: "For he himself is our peace" (v. 14). The result of Christ's work is the church, where human distinctions no longer matter and Christ's peace unites fractured humanity. "Here there is no Greek or Jew, circumcised or uncircumcised, barbarian, Scythian, slave or free, but Christ is all, and is in all" (Col. 3:11).

That vision is no mere ideal. Even in Christ, human realities mar the redemptive work of Christ. The early church wrestled long and hard against cultural division, and so will the contemporary church. However, no organization on earth is better equipped to meet the challenge of an international world.

2. *Urbanization.* The early church didn't seem intimidated by the collective evil of the great urban centers of the Roman world. In fact, Paul's mission strategy featured ministry to the large Roman cities, and cities such as Philippi and Ephesus became strategic centers for outreach to entire regions.

More than ever, cities are strategic locations for Christian ministry and influence across the world. In our own country the future of Christianity is in the cities. The suburban captivity of the church must give way to a partnership with urban churches as a demonstration of the culture-defying nature of the Christian gospel. Evangelical Christianity is uniquely equipped for ministry to the city. We believe God is larger than urban ills and suburban corruption. We are convinced that the gospel transforms lives from the inside out and that communities of transformed persons profoundly alter the nature of larger communities.

3. *Secularization.* Secular humans long for spiritual reality, as the rise of New Age and other exotic contemporary religions indicates. Christian faith declares that it is the final reality and that God can be known. The church offers precisely the supernatural reality denied by much of modernity. We are a company of people who live in the presence of God. We meet each week in the presence of the transcendent Christ who comes to transform people. The love of God, the ultimate supernatural reality, fills our hearts and forms our relationships. Our life in Christ is a demonstration that eternity exists in time and space.

The more secular the culture becomes, the greater the opportunity for the church to demonstrate the reality of a transcendent God who has chosen to live among us in order to change us. The church should leap at the opportunity not run from it. The world is waiting for Christian demonstration.

4. *Technology.* The harsh, impersonal, and lonely character of a technologically driven world meets a God who loves the world, knows our names, and counts the hairs on our heads. God wants us to know we are his dearly loved children. God places us in a new community that bears his gracious, loving character. There, in the church, the love and mercy of God take on flesh once again, and ordinary humans can know and experience the warmth of the heart of God.

In the church, if nowhere else on earth, people count for something. Every Christian bears God's name and is accepted for that reason alone. What we produce counts for nothing with God, and the church that knows God treats people with that kind of grace.

The more that technology captures our world, the more the church must bear the interpersonal and gracious character of the gospel. Churches and pastors who know the times and know what to do will capitalize on the warm and personal power of the gospel to touch lives left cold and alone by a world that doesn't care.

5. *Individualism.* The church, by its very nature, is communal—the opposite of individualistic. The very name "body

of Christ" given to the church in the New Testament indicates the interdependent character of the church. It's a place where people care for each other, live for one another, and share a common life. God dispenses his grace, love, and mercy through gifted people in the church.

The New Testament church is most certainly sacramental. It is a vessel bearing the grace of God to people. And people in the church are likewise sacraments. They bear gifts of grace to each other. I am a recipient of gifts of grace borne by the people of the church. Most of what I know of the Christian faith has been mediated to me through humans who taught me, loved me, challenged me, encouraged me, and helped me grow.

Churches that know what time it is will determine to make the communal character of the church strong and vibrant. No Lone Ranger pastors need apply!

6. *Materialism/consumerism.* The Bible declares that ultimate reality is spiritual not material, that real significance is found in matters of the heart, and that we are whole when we love God and each other. Whole people are driven by a passion for God and a love of neighbor—not by acquisition of things.

The church needs to learn that lesson fast. Christians know better, but we often act as though we believe that those who have accumulated the most material things have the greatest significance. We even talk as if they have special favor with God. The twenty-first-century church must demonstrate otherwise. We must develop a spirituality that is in touch with this world but is driven by the values of gospel and eternity.

7. *Rootlessness.* Our God is the God of Abraham, Isaac, and Jacob. Therefore, men and women of God have roots as old as the world. Further, our rootedness extends into eternity, where the saints, prophets, and apostles worship God. And geographically we belong to a community that wraps around the world. Most significantly, however, this community of faith is local. Through participation in a local congregation, I

am part of a worldwide body that has a history extending all the way back to Abraham and Sarah.

Churches that know what time it is will find new and creative ways to teach and help others experience the rootedness that is central to the Christian faith. Biblical education teaches us about our ancestors in the faith, while worship links us to the church around the world that joins us in song and prayer as well as to the eternal church gathered at God's throne in ceaseless praise.

8. *Moral breakdown*. The gospel offers recovery more powerful than any human recovery movement. Scripture declares that the gospel is the power of God, and Jesus Christ offers to transform all who come to him in faith. The church is designed to be a place of moral development in the midst of moral decline.

Contemporary Christians need not fear the moral anarchy of our time. Jesus certainly wasn't intimidated by evil spirits, disease, hostility, and indifference. If the gospel is God's power and the church is a redemption center, what better time to be alive than now? For the church, the present crisis is the greatest opportunity for outreach and ministry ever.

Churches that know what time it is will create powerful ministries of recovery for those crushed by the consequences of sin and evil. Pastors who know what time it is will lead their churches toward authentic encounter with this evil world in whatever ways are appropriate to their gifts and opportunities.

9. *Conflict/culture wars*. In the Old Testament, salvation is described by that wonderful and rich Hebrew word for systemic peace, *shalom*. In the New Testament, Jesus the Messiah and Prince of Peace comes to establish peace between tribes, races, and peoples (see Eph. 2:14). Paul draws a beautiful picture of God's peace that is wonderfully experiential: "And the peace of God, which transcends all understanding, will guard your hearts and your minds in Christ Jesus" (Phil. 4:7). It's part of God's amazing grace.

How dreadfully ironic that for centuries Christians have declared wars of various kinds in the name of the Prince of Peace. How alienating that in our time some of God's people have declared war on our culture in the name of God. It is time to cease fire! Grace, mercy, and love, which make up the central character of the gospel, must also mark the character of God's church. Peace-making churches are the need of the hour. When pastors who know what time it is lead their congregations toward God's *shalom* and God's people find resolution for their own inner and outer conflicts, the world will sit up and take notice.

10. *Descending quality of life*. The truth and power of the gospel and therefore the quality of life for Christians are not dependent on economic, political, or social factors. To hear some Christians talk, God is bound to the "American way," and anything less than that is destined to be disaster for the work of God. But in reality the destiny of the people of God is independent of national and international success or failure. Further, the quality of life for Christians is determined on other grounds. Upward mobility is not necessarily Christian destiny. In fact, it may be the worst curse of all if it makes one proud and independent of God. Jesus put it powerfully: "What good is it for a man to gain the whole world, and yet lose or forfeit his very self?" (Luke 9:25).

The present hour is a moment of opportunity for the church. What better time could there be to demonstrate to the rising generation the power of our convictions? Our hope is in God and not in America and its moral or economic fortunes. Churches and pastors who know what time it is will, in the name and power of God, create communities of faith where the values of the gospel are embraced, taught, and lived out.

CONCLUSION

We need missionary churches and missionary leaders. We need pastoral leaders who understand this culture with deep pathos and who know the power of gospel well enough to create redemptive congregations.

Many Christians will reject this vision for the church and its ministry. They will prefer comfort over engagement with our world. There is, however, a growing cadre of pastors and leaders who are willing to take the times seriously in the name of Christ.

Some of the enlistees in this new force for God surprise me. Russell is retirement age. He is as traditional, in the best sense of that term, as any Christian I know. He called me recently to encourage me. He told me that he was glad that I am his pastor because I haven't let him be comfortable. "I'd prefer being comfortable," he said, "but you've forced me and the church to face the needs of the nineties. That's hard for me, but thank you."

Russell is a man of Issachar's tribe. He knows the times and wants to do something about them.

4
Whose Church Is This? The Question of Ecclesiology

I will never forget my first night with the Single Parent's Fellowship at Crystal Evangelical Free Church. They invited me, their new pastor, to meet them. They met every Thursday night at the church for Bible study and conversation although most of them didn't regularly attend our church. They had heard about the fellowship from friends. I had heard that the group was doing powerful ministry for very special needs. I also knew that many of the single parents had come to faith in Christ through the ministry of the group. I knew their leaders and was eager to meet the group.

When I walked into the room, I immediately felt pain in the air. I had never experienced anything quite like it. These single parents, male and female, old and young, knew a pain so deep that it has no name, so powerful that it permeated the space. I was overwhelmed.

After the introductions were finished, I gave a short talk and opened the meeting for questions. They had only one question for me, though it came in different forms. "Is there room in this church for people like us?" they asked. "Do you accept us?" "Does God offer any hope for me?" "Will you as our pastor help us find a future?" "Can this church be a safe place where we can heal and grow?"

One of those single parents was a pastor, another a high-profile pastor's ex-wife. Both of their lives were in ruin and their ministries effectively destroyed. Like many of the others in the room, they couldn't see much hope for today or tomorrow. For some the issue was whether or not their spouse would let them see their children. For others it was living hand to mouth on the edge of poverty. For all of them the greatest adventure in their lives had come to ruin and they felt utter failure. There, in a setting full of mercy and love, many met Jesus Christ and experienced the sheer grace of the gospel.

That night I learned another dimension of the gospel's power. When the church reaches out with compassion to the wounded, many come and find substantial healing in the body of Christ. Broken people often see their spiritual need and turn to God or the church for help. When they know that God's people genuinely care, when we welcome them in their need, when they see that we really want to love them and help them, they will come—I've seen it. The word travels quickly.

For some time I had known the power of grace and gospel among God's people. One Sunday morning I studied the congregation during the offering. As my eyes made their way over the people, I recalled the depth of needs they had shared with me. I had walked through deep waters with nearly all of them. The pastoral prayer came next in the service, and I could barely make it through as the accumulated burden of these dearly loved children of God rested on my soul.

I don't think I was ever again the same. And I determined that worship would never be the same either. From then on I realized that public worship was a God-given opportunity for the power of the gospel to do its work. And it did. Not just through preaching and teaching, but also through the mutual ministry of the people of God gathered to meet him. And during the week the work went on. Life was shared, grace and gospel were offered, and transformation came.

But that night at the Single Parent's Fellowship, I learned that the church can be a place of healing for outsiders. If Jesus' incarnation is our pattern and reaching the lost is his mission, we must find ways of bringing mercy and good news to lost and needy people. A passion for people must accompany our passion for truth. It must.

Recently I heard a campus pastor tell of a special answer to prayer. For several years he had been praying that God would give him a love for homosexuals. It was a struggle, he confessed, to care for and minister to gay men. He wanted us to know that God answered his prayer and his ministry focus expanded dramatically. Will the twenty-first-century church pray that way?

Scores of special needs surround us. Each is an opportunity for gospel outreach and Christian caregiving. Will the church be there with God's good news for people who have no earthly hope, with tender mercies from a God who never created a person he didn't love with an endless love? Support groups for a mind-boggling number of ills created by the modern and postmodern world are already springing up as God's people begin to seize this moment for Christ's kingdom. The immense destruction modernity will surely bring must be matched by a church full of grace upon grace that spills out into a society dying for it.

Cultural sensitivity and outreach are essential in any age, but particularly ours. However, they also create a grave danger in any time and, most especially, our own. In our concern for the lost and our adapting of method and structure for outsiders, we risk letting modernity define the church's agenda, and, if we're not careful, create our identity. We risk running in so many directions at once and becoming so busy doing what we think is God's work that we forget who we are, whom we serve, and what our mission is.

In other words, staying on the fine line on which the church must run is difficult. How can we be as sensitive to our world and its brokenness as Jesus was and at the same time be as churchy and as different as Scripture demands us to be? Or, to turn it around, can we be the church—one, holy, catholic, and apostolic, grounded in Scripture and two thousand years of accumulated wisdom—and not lose touch with our neighbor? Paul Tillich said it well a generation ago: "For the last two centuries, the perennial question for Protestant theology has been, 'Can the Christian message be adapted to the modern mind without losing its essential and unique character?'"[1] Tillich was right—that is the question for theology and, more important, for the church. The church is, after all, where the Christian is most often seen by modernity. How do we adapt the message to post-Christian America without losing our unique biblical shape?

It is not enough to be culturally sensitive or even to have an overpowering passion for the lost. We need pastors who understand the times and biblical norms. In particular, we need pastoral leaders with a profound understanding of the biblical idea of the church. Adjusting the church for a new era is not a simple matter. It is, in fact, the continuing problem of the church, at least for the empirical, objective churches of which we are a part. Surely the gospel must be contextualized; Paul taught us so. He was all things to all people in order to win some. But, at the same time, the church is the church. It bears witness to eternity, is governed by values alien to this world, and is distinguished by Christlike members, something utterly unlike modernity.

We are in the middle of a reformation. Regardless of what any of us may think of it, the church is being reinvented. Or, more specifically, evangelical Christianity is being redefined by its churches. The older evangelical centers of influence, such as The National Association of Evangelicals, *Christianity Today*, the Billy Graham Association, and the evangelical seminaries, simply do not shape the movement as they once did. No one I talk to considers those older power centers as influences in their lives or ministries.

The centers of influence in this generation are large churches, thousands of them, most of which did not exist twenty years ago. I would venture a guess that Bill Hybels, the pastor of the best-known and largest of these churches, Willow Creek Community Church, in South Barrington, Illinois, is one of the most influential leaders in American Protestantism. I have not been in a Christian gathering of leaders in five years in which he and his church have not been a topic of discussion.

Networks of pastors and leaders, not organizations, are also centers of influence. The Leadership Network, with headquarters in Tyler, Texas, is a case in point. The Network was formed to provide an informal system of support for pastors of large churches. Originally, ten to fifteen pastors would gather for several days with no agenda simply to form relationships and learn from each other. More recently the Network has been offering new forms of continuing education called summits. Significantly, the teachers at summits are practitioners not theoreticians. As a participant in both a forum and several summits, I can say that I have learned more about being a pastor and Christian leader there than in any other setting except my own experience. Networks and workshops exert enormous influence in and through large churches in our time.

Large churches are a fact of life in America. Please note that this is a movement that did not begin with church-growth theory, leaders, and literature. In fact, large churches were springing up across America long before church-growth theory was taught. God raised up a new breed of entrepreneurial pastors who created a new kind of church. I recall from back in the 1950s the excitement and wonder I heard in my father and his friends when they discussed some of the first large churches. We even visited several to check them out. Since then thousands of churches of unprecedented size, at least in Protestantism, have emerged to create a new force in American Christianity. Os Guiness suggests that the rise of large churches is the most significant church movement in the twentieth century.[2] The trend is not likely to be reversed in the near future.

Whatever anyone may say about large churches, one thing is clear: They moved mission back to the center of the church. The result is that churches large and small are increasingly asking themselves how they can reach their unchurched neighbors. Evangelism is back in the churches.

An accompanying shift of consciousness is equally, if not more, significant. Whether intentionally or not, the exponential increase of large churches in America is moving ecclesiology to the front burner of evangelical consciousness. The size, complexity, and strategic focus of large churches are forcing pastors, church leaders, and theologians to think creatively and biblically about the nature of the church, especially the local church.

A young theologian complained to me that her theology faculty has fundamentally opposing visions for the church. I trust that the doctrine of the church will receive a thorough workover by those theologians, and I implore them to include pastors in their dialogue.

All these changes represent a fundamental and necessary paradigm shift in ecclesiology and pastoral theology. Both the church and its ministry are being rethought in terms of the mission of the church in a post-Christian society. The notion of the church as a safe haven from modernity and the ministry as a chaplain-like preoccupation with the organization is giving way to a church with its doors flung open sending its people out into modernity to change it.

THE ECCLESIAL CHALLENGE

In my judgment, the shift we are witnessing is a movement born of God and a *kairotic* moment to be seized. My primary concern is that the movement recover a biblical understanding of the church to accompany its proper sense of mission.

What Is the Church?

Somewhere along the way ecclesiology, the doctrine of the church, got lost. I suppose the struggle for theological integrity early in this century forced an unreflective interdenominationalism that simply didn't have the time or energy for ecclesial thinking. Denominational lines blurred in the battle while a plethora of parachurch organizations took up parts of the church's mission. The doctrine of the church was placed on the theological back burner.

Regardless of the cause or causes, evangelical ecclesiology has become fuzzy at best and more often than not is ignored or misunderstood. And where there is fuzzy thinking about the church, there will be no clear thinking about the ministry of the church.

Where Is the Doctrine of the Church?

Modern ecclesiology wears a very human face. The reason is uniquely American. American Protestant theology has for some time been more interested in matters of polity than fundamental ecclesiology. American ecclesiological thinking tends powerfully toward matters of organization, polity, offices, and officers. Definition is important but seldom gets beyond the nature of the universal church or, at the local church level, the meaning of the word *ekklesia*. In the Bible, however, the doctrine of the church is far larger and profoundly deeper. Biblical ecclesiology features the distinguishing *character* of the people of God. The longest sections of recent ecclesiologies are nearly always matters of polity. Theological discussion is usually restricted to that larger invisible or universal church. This break between earthly and practical matters, the local church, and eternal and theological matters, has worked enormous mischief in the church. Theological reflection or, more particularly, integrative theological thinking about the church, especially the local church, is missing. Ecclesiology has been marginalized and detheologized. It is less "theological" than the body of theology.

In today's evangelical circles, theological focus on the church has virtually disappeared. In popular thought, evangelicalism itself or some fuzzy Calvinistic notion of the invisible church became the church. The local church is a matter of organization, and any ecclesiology is at best an abstraction divorced from the function of particular churches where real ecclesiastical life does take place. The recovery of ecclesiology must include a powerful *functional* side, the life and ministry of a local congregation in theological-biblical reflection.

The absence of evangelical thinking about the church has been observed. The most visible notice given is Robert Patterson's article, "In Search of the Visible Church," in *Christianity Today*.[3] Patterson claims that evangelicals have weakened and even abandoned ecclesiology. He notes the neglect of articles on ecclesiology in *The Journal of the Evangelical Theological Society* and the remarkable absence of statements on ecclesiology in two major theological documents, "Evangelical Affirmations" and "The Manila Manifesto." I would add the equally remarkable absence of an ecclesiological article in the original National Association of Evangelicals statement of faith. Where do the theologians think they should live out their work? Of what value is theology if it does not point in some way to the local church where faith and life occur? Does anyone remember that the New Testament is written to churches?

What About the Local Church?

A corresponding neglect is clear in ordinary church life where faith and theology ultimately reside. Patterson detects a certain "McChristian" mentality that brings consumerism to the church.[4] The church is often seen as a place to receive goods and services rather than as a body whose purpose it is to serve. Church is one of the options in the cafeteria of the Christian life. Consumers of religion decide church affiliation on the basis of the best services available. I seldom hear prospective members say they are joining our church because they sense God leading them to us. Most come to us because one or some of our ministries meet their needs. That is certainly not wrong, but it does leave out much of the biblical doctrine of the church.

Modern evangelicalism tends toward the neglect of the sacraments. We live with the specter of large numbers of unbaptized Christians (a historical and theological oxymoron) and huge numbers of professing Christians with no relationship to a local church and no sense that they need one.

The Central Significance of Ecclesiology

The loss of ecclesiology at any level is no small matter. It could be ultimately fatal. After all, ecclesiology is the place where all theology finally takes on life. Some would even claim that the single most informative and revealing element of any theology is its ecclesiology. Evangelical theology is increasingly remote from the life of the church, perhaps in part because it neglects the place where proper theology comes to rest—the church. Instead, our theologians tend to point their work at themselves and their academies.

Because of neglect, the practice of the church has become ecclesiology. Most ecclesiological conversation and theology is largely descriptive. There doesn't seem to be a lot of biblical and theological reflection about the local church. The stakes are quite high, especially if ecclesiology in a very real way is the place where all theology finally rests. The implications for a church and its ministry are enormous.

The disengagement of the doctrine of the church from the body of theology inevitably creates ecclesial thinking along human organizational lines. Needless to say, the Christian ministry suffers as a result. The practice of ministry, the human work of pastors, is the focus. The practice of ministry is now the theology of ministry. Pastors live with a diminished understanding of themselves as Christian ministers and conduct their work without a clear biblical and theological vision for the church and their ministry.

It seems clear that pastoral ministry takes its meaning from ecclesiology. The church is the house in which that ministry takes place. The shape of the house forms the character of the ministry. Without a clear doctrine of the church, there is no real Christian ministry, only imitations. Pastoral ministry, therefore, must properly begin with a powerful, even transforming, ecclesiology.

What, then, should the church look like? That is certainly the right question, and it demands the proper starting point. The movement of this conversation is critical, and it is a matter of theological integrity. Discussions and conclusions depend on proper starting points. Our environment, this world, this tumultuous time, is absolutely the wrong place to begin. We inevitably end up with a descriptive ecclesiology that falls short. Description is proper, but it comes at the end. It is a conclusion, the proper end of a very important discussion that must occur first.

THE ECCLESIASTICAL QUESTION

Millard Erickson notes that Protestant ecclesiology has not received sustained theological inquiry.[5] That is not to say that there is little writing about the church. Since the 1960s there has been a flurry of ecclesial writing, but nearly all of it has been descriptive.

The Core of the Question

Erickson rightly points out that the real ecclesiological issue is far deeper. Ecclesiology must begin with the essence of the church, for what the church is precedes all other discussions. He correctly notes that our increasingly pragmatic culture is impatient with discussions about essences.[6] We much prefer description. We like building theology from the ground up. Hence, theological reflection, especially at the popular level, is difficult. But essence is precisely where we must start—in theology and at church.

We err in two directions. It is possible to accuse evangelical ecclesiology of a form of Docetism. A semi-Calvinist and quite popular view of the "real" church as the universal invisible church tends in that direction. This kind of thinking keeps the local church in a secondary position and keeps us from a real or functional ecclesiology—the nature of the local church. And it is in the congregations that Christianity is lived out.

Or, on the contrary, we can be equally Ebionite.[7] Our preoccupation with the historical church, with pragmatic matters, the nitty-gritty running of the church, the human face of much American ecclesial thinking, forces our ecclesiology to suffer from a lack of transcendence. The church is or becomes strictly human. In our time this Ebionite-like ecclesiology is dominant. In light of the New Testament, an immanence ecclesiology is utterly deficient. What, then, is the church?

Hans Kung states is nicely. In ecclesiology, "a fact precedes the explanation.... The church is an essence that took on historical form."[8] Unless that essence is the starting point of all ecclesiological and ministerial discussion, the church becomes the prisoner of its own theories rather than subject to its Lord.

The Church Is Defined by Its Lord

Sound ecclesiological thinking begins with Christological thinking. That seems obvious, but it is a point modern evangelicals seem to forget. The church with its roots deep in the doctrine of Christ is foundational Christian theology. A century ago P. T. Forsyth, a Congregationalist theologian, lamented the loss of power in the church of his time. It was, he said, the result of the loss of the power and presence of Christ in his church. The church must have, Forsyth went on, a Lord big enough to oppose the demonic powers unleashed by the twentieth century.[9] He went on to say that when ecclesiology is cut off from Christology, it is cut off from Christ's power, and the church inevitably becomes little more than a social club, a mere religious society.

Karl Barth agrees. "Ecclesiology is given firm root in the one reconciling work of God in [his Son]."[10] He adds that "the Christological question cannot be avoided."[11] Jürgen Moltmann joins the Christocentric ecclesial chorus, "If Christ is the foundation of the Church, Christology will be the dominant theme of ecclesiology."[12]

This Christological essence is not, however, mere theological reflection, some remote doctrinal touchstone. Thielicke says it best: "The ground of the church is the presence of Christ."[13] This is no mere theological nit-picking nor just an assumption on which to build a grander church practice. The ground and center of a transforming doctrine of the church of Christ is the very real presence of its Lord.

Nothing could be more necessary (or should I say "relevant") in a time like this. The fact and experience of Jesus Christ, his presence in and lordship over life and his church, is the ground and being of the church of Jesus Christ. That alone guarantees transcendence, a supernatural dimension that is precisely what people in our world are searching for in all the wrong places.

The Lord Is Alive in His Church

The New Testament is built is on a powerful assumption, which is, in fact, a living reality. The powerful word and deed of the church at Pentecost, the impact of the Pauline mission, the dynamic spiritual life of the churches, and the substance of the epistles—all of it presupposes a living reality. Kung says that the historical fact of the church assumes a prior essence.[14] New Testament ecclesiology is not a reflection on mere ideas, discussions of abstract principles, or the creation of interesting theology. The early church was in touch with a reality that created ideas, principles, and theology.

The early Christians were convinced that the risen and glorified Christ was present with them. For them that presence was and is the essence of the church. That fundamental reality, Christ's powerful presence, created the fact of the church and all the descriptions of it in the New Testament. The entire New Testament is written out of that Christological experience. It is that core that must be the theological center as well as the experiential defining factor in ecclesiology. Transcendence, eternal presence, is the starting point of a biblical ecclesiology. It begins in empirical history and continues to live in ordinary time. But its essence is the eternal Lord who enfleshes himself once again in his church.

"Where two or three come together in my name, there am I with them" (Matt. 18:20), was not a Scripture verse to them— it was living reality. They knew Christ's magisterial promise that he would build his church and the gates of hell would not prevail (Matt. 16:18) in a larger and transcendent context.

Matthew begins his gospel with "Immanuel," God with us (1:23). He ends with a summary of this ecclesiological foundational essence, Jesus saying, "All authority in heaven and on earth has been given to me" (28:18). Think that over for a minute: Christ is Lord of time and eternity and therefore of his church in history. Then he commissions the church to make disciples everywhere and always. The Great Commission ends even more magisterially than it begins: "Surely *I am with you always*, to the very end of the age" (v. 20). Here is the focus of all ecclesiological reflection and activity! This is the beginning of an ecclesiology big enough for modernity.

The New Testament is full of images and metaphors for the church. Each in its own way drives the same point home: The church belongs to Christ and is therefore defined by his presence. Paul speaks often of a local congregation as the body of Christ (1 Cor. 12:12–31). The church is also described as Christ's bride (Rev. 21:9), a strikingly powerful picture of possession and participation. Christ's possession of and lordship over the church could hardly be more specific. Paul reminded the church at Corinth that it (of all churches!) was the temple of God (1 Cor. 3:16), the place where the Holy Spirit resides. The whole Trinity is involved in ownership, lordship, and personal participation in the local church.

Since the Reformation we have been taught to think of the church in terms of Word and sacrament. Too often we flatten out both and humanize them, even when we are sacral. We need to rethink Word and sacrament. The Word stands at the center of the church's life and teaching. Supremely, the Word is Jesus, the living Word of God who dwells among us (John 1:14). Paul boldly states that the proclamation of salvation in Jesus is itself "the Word of God" (1 Thess. 2:13). Scripture, the written Word of God, is his Word and therefore the living and active sword of the Spirit, which never fails to accomplish its purpose (Heb. 4:12).

The sacraments are equally powerful because they, too, belong to Christ and find their reality and meaning in him. Paul says that the Lord's Supper is a "participation" (*koinonia*) in Christ's body and blood (1 Cor. 10:16–17). Regardless of one's understanding of sacraments, a participation in Christ's body and blood is at the very least a powerful presence of the risen Christ.

According to the apostles, the existence of the church is the result of the Resurrection. Christ is now the exalted Lord who lives in his church (Rom. 1:4). The ecclesial experience of the early church is centered in the presence of the Lord in his church.

First Corinthians contains two references to Christ's presence in corporate worship that indicate the early church's belief that Christ really stood in their midst. Because the Lord was present, things happened. In the first passage Paul explains what is to happen at a meeting. "When you are assembled in the name of our Lord Jesus ... *and the power of the Lord Jesus is present,* hand this man over to Satan ..." (5:4–5, emphasis added). What an awesome presence and power—and responsibility.

The second reference is in Paul's discussion of spiritual gifts. However we might interpret some of the more controversial gifts and their expression in public worship, one thing is certain: Their power flows from Christ's presence in people.

Prophecy, for example, doesn't seem to be a spectacular gift; it is the orderly and rational gift of someone speaking under divine direction. Yet unbelievers will be so convinced by the words of the one prophesying that they will fall on their knees in repentance and exclaim, "*God is really among you!*" (1 Cor. 14:24–25, emphasis added). This is the essence, the definition, of the Christian church: "God is really among us."

Hebrews 12:18–29 is a classic text on Christian worship. It compares the frightening experience of Israel's worship at Mount Sinai with the church's joyous worship at Mount Zion. The author confidently proclaims that when we worship we enter into eternity itself, linking our experience with saints, angels, and the throne of God where Jesus himself meets us.

Our Puritan fathers were wiser than we are in many ways. The distinguishing mark of their ecclesiology was remarkably apostolic. Their battle was against an Episcopal church that claimed that the real church existed only where there was an authentic bishop in residence, for his presence validated and empowered a local church. Others claimed that a real church existed where an ordered clergy was in office. This Presbyterian viewpoint declared that a legitimately ordained minister validated and empowered a church.

The Puritans thought otherwise. They taught that the presence of Christ created a genuine church and that his presence was so real and powerful that each church could, therefore, rightly make its own decisions and determine its destiny. But this is far more than church polity. Most significantly, Christ's presence empowers his church. No wonder Puritan preaching was described as "hissing hot." And no wonder their "experimental religion" boiled over into life-changing and society-altering churches.

An Authentic Church for Modernity

The Word is truth to build on and live by. It is the foundation of ecclesiology and ecclesial thinking and planning and of any theology of the ministry. Nothing could be in greater contrast to modernity. We stand before a faithless generation that believes nothing on the grounds that nothing can be known with absolute certainty. God was pushed to the margins a generation ago, and all that's left is flat and immanent human experience. Sadly, the church has offered little more. In part, it's a failure of ecclesiology. Stanley J. Grenz and Roger E. Olson summarize twentieth-century theology as the struggle for balance between transcendence and immanence.[15] That is certainly true of evangelical thinking about the church. Unfortunately, in our concern for the transcendent at other levels, we forget about it in the church, where ordinary Christians live and learn. The larger battle against modernity is fought in the trenches at the ecclesiological center where the struggle is great.

Ecclesiology is obviously more than disembodied theology. It is the guarantee that real churches like yours and mine have a supernatural center. The essence of the church, the fact on which all else depends, is the presence of the transcendent Lord. All descriptions of the church must flow from that reality.

It is far too simple, even reductionist, to presume that the presence of the transcendent Lord in power translates into "signs and wonders" as the term is currently used. At its crudest, that would mean that all Jesus was about was miracles and thus would empty his teaching of its power and the cross of its place as the defining event of history and theology. The presence and power of Christ is far wider in the New Testament.

An incarnational faith takes the Incarnation seriously. We believe that the eternal Word became flesh. The living Lord of history brought eternity into time and space. When he spoke, those who heard in faith were never again the same; when he touched people with grace, they were transformed; and when they followed him, their lives were eternally reordered.

The New Testament epistles tell us the apostolic experience of that transformation. Ephesians 5 describes thieves who quit stealing, liars who began to tell the truth, speech that began to build rather than destroy, marriages made whole, and families formed in faith. It describes communities of faith in which the healing of wounds caused by hate, prejudice, abuse, and other things took place. We believe that the gospel is the power of God—really. The gospel is powerful enough to turn back principalities and powers, to transform twisted lives, and to heal minds, souls, and bodies. The gospel creates congregations that hold eternity in their hands. There, in the congregation, the power of eternity takes on flesh in transforming fashion.

I shall never forget the time I realized this truth for the first time. It happened during seminary chapel when Clark Pinnock was giving a talk on some theological aspects of prayer. His point was that prayer is the experiential side of the ontological reality of God. Brilliantly, he sketched the transcendent reality of God. More brilliantly, he turned that ontology toward life and faith. That application got my attention. He said that God has an easy way of checking on what we really believe: He listens to our prayers. Dr. Pinnock noted that individuals or a church can claim to believe that Christ is present when they meet to worship but never experience anything beyond ordinary human experiences. He spoke of the irony of a movement that claims transcendent reality but experiences little of it. Eternity does not touch time, at least not at eleven o'clock on Sunday morning! It is possible, he said, to be a so-called great church yet be little more than a humanistic plant. We can run things well without the living God. After all, we have our ways.

Then Dr. Pinnock asked what we expected in our pastoral ministries. Did we expect people to be converted? Did we really think God's Word would transform stubborn sinners? Did we believe God would heal the sick and mend broken individuals and families? By the time he was finished, we felt as if we should fall on our faces to weep and pray. Of course we didn't—we were middle-class evangelicals.

I didn't have a name for it then. Now I do: *the church,* the living reality of the living God. I've seen it too. One Sunday I went back to a church I once served. God was still at work. They had knocked out a wall to make room for the people God was touching. I didn't know half the people, but the man who led the worship had been a high school student when I pastored there. God had snatched him and the girl he married from the ordinary and created a son and daughter. They had been part of a revival among the youth of the community. Now the man is a leader in the church and a model of faith in the community.

We sang that song that says, ". . . for those tears I died." The man singing right behind me was a former colleague in ministry. I had seen some of his tears as he had struggled fiercely against his homosexual desires. I saw one of the first men I baptized. His marriage had been a terrible mess. In fact, I've never seen a marriage that seemed more hopeless. I remembered feeling so helpless trying to minister to them. But there they sat—together after all these years.

After the service a woman dying of cancer whispered in my ear, "In life and in death, it is well with my soul." Another man, the first board chairman I ever had and a mentor in many ways, grabbed me, wept, and said he thought he would never see me again. Another man, a local businessman who had had a reputation so bad that the local gossip said he would rob his mother to make a buck, told me that I had been the most influential man in his life. He had come to faith in Christ in those days. We used to study Scripture, and he would ask God to change his mean heart. God did! I saw people whom I had led to faith and for whom I had performed marriage ceremonies. Now they had children and were still growing in Christ.

Why had this congregation flourished? Because Christ stood in the midst of them. I remember services where Christ's presence had been so powerful that I could scarcely breathe. From house to house we prayed and studied. I even took Christ with me into some bars and surprised some people on the inside and the outside. A bar maid believed and was saved.

People came to see what was happening. They came to my office and asked how to find this Christ. They came to church and were stunned by a presence beyond themselves. The city sat up and took notice. All this happened because some people simply believed it when Jesus promised to be with them in transcendent power. They really believed that conversions would occur, that marriages would be healed, that people would be transformed, and that a town would never be the same. Christ was as good as his Word. Everything rests on whether we believe the Word or just think it's true.

Pastoral ministry in a church effective enough for the twenty-first century will be ministry owned, operated, and inhabited by the living Christ. It will be ministry that exists in supernatural power and demonstrates the power of the gospel to change lives. It will be ministry that builds itself from eternity down. Each form of ministry will take that powerful reality with it wherever it goes. Addicted people will be touched by the living Christ. Sexual deviance will retreat before the living Word of God. Families will find their center in the Lamb of God. Ministries of which we have not yet dreamed will arise and will be used to change lives. All this is possible because the living Christ stands in his church ready to empower his people to touch their world with his presence and power.

Part 2

A Portrait of a Pastor

5

CHRIST'S PRISONERS: THE PASTOR'S CALL

But thanks be to God, who always leads us in triumphal procession in Christ and through us spreads everywhere the fragrance of the knowledge of him.
—2 Corinthians 2:14

When I was a student, my wife and I spent a week on the beach in Florida. We were the only "young" adults at our hotel, and we became objects of curiosity and conversation. One day a group of us was sitting under a beach umbrella, and one of the women asked me what I was studying. She was clearly puzzled by the idea of studying theology and preparing for pastoral ministry. "Why do you want to do that?" she asked rather incredulously. The very strong implication was, "You seem to be perfectly normal."

"The Call"

I stumbled about for an appropriate answer that the woman could understand, and utterly failed. I don't recall what I said, but it wasn't the real reason I was studying for the ministry. The truth was, I was in seminary because I felt "called" to the ministry. I had a hunch that she couldn't understand my rather vague sense of "call." I wasn't sure I did either.

I did know when that sense of call had first come to me. It was when I was twenty years old. I had taken a year off from college and was working in a factory. I was saving money to finish school and trying to figure out what to do with my life. I worked alone from 4:00 P.M. to midnight and spent a good deal of that time thinking about my future and my faith. Somehow I had a deep sense that I was wrestling with God in the struggle of my life. One night as I was pulling switch #3 on the monorail, I gave in and said, "Yes, Lord." I knew exactly what that meant, although I don't know how it came to me. God wanted me in the Christian ministry, and I said yes.

Part of the struggle was very personal. I was deeply in love and knew for certain that the love of my life did not want to be a pastor's wife. With great sadness but with greater peace in my soul, I went to a phone in an empty office to call her and tell her the bad news. To my surprise she not only accepted the news, she told me that she would accompany me through my life wherever ministry took me.

Now I sat with her on a beach in Florida trying to put words to that experience that seemed so vague upon reflection. Later that afternoon I took a long walk on the beach, thinking about my very poor answer to a very good question. I walked and walked and thought and thought. *How does one explain flashes of spiritual insight? Can God's call be described? Why was I entering this profession that seemed so foreign to these new friends?* As I walked, suddenly it seemed as if a light went on and God said, "If the gospel is true, then it's the answer for all of life and death. Somebody must tell the world. That's you!"

I was compelled to Christian ministry by two overlapping and profound issues. On the one hand, I was convinced that the gospel is the power of God, and on the other hand, I sensed a deep concern for people to know that transforming truth. I suspect the call of God to any form of vocational ministry is some combination of conviction about God's truth and concern for people. The great nineteenth-century evangelist Charles Finney was a lawyer before he entered the ministry. He put his call in graphic terms: "I have a retainer from Christ to plead his cause."[1]

The Pastoral Call

The call to pastoral ministry, however, must be even more specific. While a vague call to Christian ministry may lead to the pastorate, it will not sustain a pastor through the harsh realities of church life. My call to ministry needed specific pastoral content.

I wandered through my first two years of seminary, knowing that I was called by God to the ministry but hoping against hope that my call was not pastoral. I wanted to teach, be a missionary or campus worker—anything but be a pastor. After all, I grew up in a parsonage and knew what I was in for! My third and last year in seminary forced me to decide. I determined I would go on to graduate school and prepare myself to be a theologian. I applied to several schools and was accepted. My mind was at ease, but my soul was restless.

In the sequence of theology courses the doctrine of the church came in the winter quarter of that final year. I came face-to-face with the biblical witness about the living church for the first time in my life. I was stunned and intrigued. I had never really thought about it before, but it seemed that in the Bible the church is at the very center of God's plan for the universe. I began to have a nagging suspicion that my future lay in a different direction.

That same quarter, the seminary president, Dr. Harry Evans, preached in chapel, and it seemed he was talking directly to me. He conceded that many forms of ministry appear quite attractive, especially academic work. "But," he added, "if you want to be where the action is, go into pastoral ministry." He illustrated his point from his pastoral experience. He told of lives changed, relationships restored, people healed, and communities of faith built.

I knew he was right, and God grabbed my heart. I knew I must spend my life and gifts pastoring God's people in a local church. A settled conviction crept into my soul: *God had made me to be a pastor.* Over the years that conviction has been inescapable. Now I am convinced that being a pastor is simply what God made me to do. I can't imagine doing anything else.

That is certainly not to say I don't want to do other things. Pastoral ministry can be harsh, and every pastor I have ever talked to wonders if it is worth it or if he or she should do something else. That kind of doubt is part of the cost of doing pastoral business. But in the long term, when doubt fades and calm returns to my heart, I know this is what I ought to do.

Timothy George, now a seminary dean, grew up in Bible-Belt fundamentalism. He was a boy preacher in the South who did the unthinkable: He decided to attend Harvard Divinity School. There he met the cold winds of modern theology that rocked him to the depths of his soul. He was also pastor of an inner-city church in Boston with only a handful of parishioners. He spent his days studying strange theologies and his nights wrestling with massive discouragement. He says that his constant prayer in those days was the cry of the prophet Jeremiah, "O LORD, . . . we are called by Thy name; leave us not" (Jer. 14:9 KJV).

For seven years George battled for his soul and his vocation as a pastor of Christ's church. He nearly gave up both. When the war in his soul was fiercest, he presided over a Eucharist attended mainly by new believers. He says that they were street Christians who looked and smelled more like the street than the church. It was a pivotal moment. George writes:

> No silver chalice, no lengthy liturgy, just the simple words of institution, "This is my body, this is my blood." But in my mind the words of [the Nicene Creed] rang out like a peal of bells shattering all the revisionist Christologies I had been taught. "God from God, Light from Light, true God from true God . . . who for us and for our salvation came down and was

incarnate." In that moment, I knew as never before, *the grip of a call from beyond myself.*[2]

Inner and Outer Call

Every pastor I know senses that "grip of a call from beyond myself." It's what the older pastoral literature calls the "inner call." But our inner call, this godly grip on our souls, must be affirmed by an "outer call." In time, God's grip on my soul was shared by a congregation who called me to be their pastor. Their outer call affirmed my inner call. My call to pastoral ministry took specific form in the call of a congregation. They listened when I preached, they responded to my pastoral work, they told me I had the gifts necessary to be their pastor. They provided outside evidence that God's grip on my soul was genuine.

Over time, the call from a congregation may fade or be replaced by another call to serve a different congregation. I have been "called" by five congregations. But that inner call, the inescapable conviction that I am called by God to pastor his people, remains. Often God's grip on my soul takes the form of Jeremiah's call. He tried to escape God's prophetic call but couldn't. The word of God was in his heart like a fire, a fire in his bones. It forced him to speak the word of the Lord and would not go away (Jer. 20:9).

The Power of God's Call

I understand that inescapable fire that lives in the heart and settles in the bones. My call, that grip on my soul, is the sustaining power of my pastoral ministry. I have doubted every outer call I have received. The pressure of ministry tends to deafen the soul, and quite often I wonder if God really called me to a certain place. When my leadership is doubted or criticism drips like acid on my soul, I argue with God about my outer call. Sometimes I have begged God to move me. The only reason I stay in this work is the call of God that grips my soul and won't let go. When the outer call is in doubt, this calling sustains my heart and mind.

I was asked to give the charge to a pastor at an installation service. Fresh from seminary and recently ordained, it was his first call. After the service he said to me, "Thanks, I needed that. During the morning service today, I was thinking that this is really a lousy job."

It doesn't take long to discover the realities of congregational life. Quite often pastoring is a lousy job. Leading isn't easy. Preaching can be excruciating. Pastoring reluctant sheep is crushing. Being a public figure under scrutiny and living with unnamed expectations will shrink your heart.

My first pastoral friend was a lot like Jeremiah. The pastorate was his second vocation, and the local Methodist Church was his first congregation. He constantly argued with God about his call. We had known each other only weeks when he asked me if it was possible to get out of God's call. He was hoping that his call was temporary! Like Jeremiah he agonized with God about his vocation, begging for release. But also like Jeremiah, God's word was like fire in his bones, intense and inescapable. My friend became a powerful evangelist and effective leader. His church grew, and people grew with it. He was very good at his work. God's grip on his soul never let go, and neither did he.

I don't know if God's call to pastoral ministry is permanent for all God's pastors. I don't know if God will ever release his grip on my soul. But I do know that as long as I have the conviction that being a pastor is what God made me to do and as long as some congregation will affirm that call with theirs, I am bound to God and this work. And if that sense of call ever leaves me, if God's word is no longer fire in my bones, I will leave my work and find another.

PAUL'S CALL TO MINISTRY

Paul clearly was gripped by a call from beyond himself. He begins most of his letters by declaring that he is an apostle by the will of God (1 Cor. 1:1; 2 Cor. 1:1; Gal. 1:1; Eph. 1:1; Col. 1:1; 1 Tim. 1:1; 2 Tim. 1:1; Titus 1:1). His introduction of himself in Romans 1 is even more specific: "Paul, a servant of Christ Jesus, *called* to be an apostle and *set apart* for the gospel of God. . . . Through [Christ] . . . we received grace and apostleship to call people . . . to the obedience that comes from faith (Rom. 1:1, 5, emphasis added). Paul' sense of identity flowed out of a deep conviction that he was called and set apart by God for apostolic work.

Paul's introduction to Galatians uses the same vocabulary in an expanded version of his apostolic call. Notice the deep sense of call, his settled conviction that apostolic work was what God had created him to do. "God . . . *set me apart* from birth and *called* me by his grace" (Gal. 1:15, emphasis added). Paul was gripped by a call from beyond himself that encompassed his entire life and pointed him toward his destiny in apostolic ministry.

That sense of call comes straight from the prophet Jeremiah's call:

> *Before I formed you in the womb I knew you,*
> *before you were born I set you apart;*
> *I appointed you as a prophet to the nations. (Jer. 1:5)*

In Romans 1, Paul links his call to apostolic ministry to the person of Christ. Likewise, all Christian calling must be centered in Christ. Paul uses an early Christian confession of faith, perhaps an ancient Christian hymn, to describe the Christ who calls people to ministry. He is the Son of God, "who as to his human nature was a descendant of David, and who through the Spirit of holiness was declared with power to be the Son of God by his resurrection from the dead" (Rom. 1:3–4).

It was through this exalted Christ that Paul received his call (Rom. 1:5). Paul was stunned by Christ when he first saw him on the road to Damascus. Christ wasn't a peasant prophet from Galilee now; he was the Lord of glory. The sight of Jesus knocked Saul off his horse. He landed on his knees, where everyone lands—and belongs—who is struck by the glory of Christ. There on his knees before the Risen One, Paul received his call to preach to the Gentiles. It was the defining moment of his life. He repeats the story twice in the book of Acts and alludes to it in his letters whenever he speaks of his ministry.

The pressure of apostolic and pastoral ministry weighed heavily on Paul, and he grew weary and discouraged like all of us. Second Corinthians is a monument to Paul's difficult ministry. But he kept moving because, as he puts it in 2 Corinthians 5:14, "Christ's love compels us."

CHRIST'S CAPTIVE: 2 CORINTHIANS 2:14

Paul was quick to say that he was a man under orders. His sense of servanthood was so intense that he often described himself as Christ's servant (Rom. 1:1). Such labor was costly and nowhere more so than in the church in Corinth. Second Corinthians, in particular, gushes with Paul's anguish with himself and the church. Early in the letter, Paul confesses to the Corinthians the deep pain he felt regarding the poor relationship between himself and the church.

Pastoral Ministry in Corinth

The church rejected Paul's leadership, impugned his motives, mocked his preaching, and refused every attempt at reconciliation. He had written them two letters and had made several visits. Nothing seemed to work. Now he writes to tell them that he has determined not to make another painful visit that would merely increase his distress (2 Cor. 2:1–2). He had written them a letter "out of great distress and anguish of heart and with many tears" but to no avail (v. 4).

Finally, in a last-ditch attempt at peace, Paul sent Titus to Corinth on his behalf and waited in Macedonia for word from Titus. Paul's distress was intense. He writes that his body had no rest while he waited and that he felt harassed at every turn. Life became "conflicts on the outside, fears within" (2 Cor. 7:5). But the church listened to Titus and repented. Second Corinthians is Paul's written response to Titus' good news. He wrote that his joy knew no bounds (v. 4).

Clearly, Paul wrote out of a pastoral context. His testimony reflects the two sides of pastoral ministry, anguish and joy. He wraps up that pastoral reflection in a metaphor in 2:14: "But thanks be to God, who always leads us in triumphal procession in Christ." His pastoral life was like a victory parade, but the joy of victory was woven into the fabric of pastoral anguish.

Roman Triumphal Processions

Newer translations make clear what the King James obscures. Paul is not talking about mere triumph; he is referring to the Roman army's triumphal processions. Being a Christian is like marching in one of those great celebrations. More specifically, by using this metaphor in reference to his apostolic and pastoral ministry, Paul is emphasizing that pastoral ministry is a unique way of marching in Christ's triumphal parade.

The citizens of Rome did not see the battle of the legions as they carved out an empire. Therefore the military held parades in Rome so that the Romans could share in the army's far-off victories. The Greek word *thriambeus* (Latin *triumphus*) was used to describe the victory parades. It is a technical term that Paul uses in this metaphor.

The purpose of the triumphal processions was clear: communication. The Roman historian Polybius summed up the triumphs this way: "The Senate can add glory even to successes of generals by bringing their achievements in tangible form before the eyes of the citizens in what are called 'triumphs.'"[3]

These triumphal processions were times of joyous celebration and civic pride. The victorious generals and their troops marched through the city leading their prisoners of war. In fact, the triumphal processions featured the defeated foreign kings and military leaders. Often these very significant prisoners of war were held in confinement for years until the conquering Roman general returned to Rome for his triumphal procession. Julius Caesar, for example, held the defeated Gaulic chief Vercingetorix for six years before putting him on display in a triumphal procession.[4]

The triumphal processions were also deeply religious affairs honoring Jupiter for victory in war. The triumphant general rode into the city in a victory chariot pulled by four horses. He was dressed in a purple toga decorated with symbols of Jupiter, and his face was painted red to resemble Jupiter. The citizens shouted *"io triumphe"* as he rode through the city leading his captives.[5]

The entire scene—soldiers, weapons, chariots, and captives—made the might and splendor of Rome quite tangible to the citizens. Like all parades, it created a fellowship of joy among the Romans. People of every culture are impressed by a military parade, and the Romans specialized in them.

One of the most moving moments of my life was my only visit to the Vietnam Memorial in Washington, D.C. I went there for one reason: I had unfinished business. In seminary I served as a youth pastor on Chicago's north side. The president of that youth group was drafted and sent to Vietnam. I graduated and went to the Pacific Northwest. Nearly two years later I received word that Bill had been killed by a sniper the last week of his tour of duty. I sent my love and condolences to his parents but was left with a hole in my heart. Bill was a great kid with much to give. His life and death seemed so far away, almost unreal.

I went to the memorial to say good-bye to Bill. I looked up his name in the register and then found his name on the wall. Suddenly, the reality of his life and death crashed down on my soul. The remote became intensely real. I stood and wept for my lost friend.

To me, the Vietnam Memorial is more than a monument. It is a stark reality. The triumphs in Rome served precisely the same function. They made war dramatically real. For the citizens of Rome, the experience was the polar opposite of my hour at the wall. The triumphs brought far-off victories into the streets of their city. The iron might of Rome marched right in front of them. They cheered the generals, praised Jupiter, and sensed the power and glory of being part of the most powerful empire in history.

Paul suggests that his pastoral ministry is like a military parade in Rome. The context makes it clear that he is celebrating a victory. He begins, "Thanks be to God. . . ." Titus has brought good news: The gospel has triumphed again. Paul's battle with the Corinthians is over. Paul stands and cheers for the Corinthians, blesses Almighty God, and revels in the transforming power of the gospel: "I have great confidence in you; I take great pride in you. I am greatly encouraged; in all our troubles my joy knows no bounds. . . . God, who comforts the downcast, comforted us by the coming of Titus. . . . He told us about your longing for me, your deep sorrow, your ardent concern for me, so that my joy was greater than ever" (2 Cor. 7:4–7).

The Pain of Pastoral Ministry

The triumphs also demonstrated another reality. The prisoners from the great battles were part of the parade and were being led to their executions. Scott Hafemann demonstrates this grim side of the triumphs in his groundbreaking interpretation of 2 Corinthians 2:14–3:3.[6] For the Romans the triumphs were a lavish and joyous celebration. For prisoners the triumphs were death marches.

Hafemann notes a long section in Plutarch describing one of the triumphs, a victory over Perseus in 167 B.C. It was a three-day ostentatious demonstration of Roman power, pagan religion, and wealth. On the third day King Perseus, his family, slaves, and attendants were marched through the city on their way to the execution site. Plutarch notes that the entourage, especially the children, extended their arms and pleaded for mercy. They walked along, bewildered and grief stricken, following the king to their deaths. "The

Romans, moved by compassion, kept their eyes upon the children, and many of them shed tears, and for all of them the pleasure of the spectacle was mingled with pain, until the children had passed by."[7]

The triumphs featured the shame and humiliation of defeat that led to execution. Both joyous celebration and grim weeping make up the picture of the triumphs. Paul wants his readers to know that his ministry bore the grim reality of a death march. The New English Bible translates 2 Corinthians 2:14 with both sides of the metaphor in view, "But thanks be to God, who continually leads us about, *captives in Christ's triumphal procession*" (emphasis added). Victor Paul Furnish's translation is even more specific, "To God be thanks, who in Christ always puts us on display (*as if we were prisoners in a triumphal procession*)" (emphasis added).[8]

Obviously, Paul's view of the ministry is paradoxical. He was Christ's captive, and that was a matter of both celebrative joy and excruciating anguish. His defeat at the hands of the Lord Christ was total. A soldier of Christ's enemies, Saul was, as the King James puts it, "breathing out threatenings and slaughter against the disciples" (Acts 9:1). On the road to Damascus Christ captured him and called him to Christian ministry. A captured enemy general, Paul joined Christ's victory parade to the cheers of saints and angels. Second Corinthians is a long cry of victory celebration. Christ's slave, Paul, is the instrument through which humans are reconciled to God and the Corinthians reconciled to each other and him. "Thanks be to God . . ." (2 Cor. 2:14).

But woven through the epistle is a deep sense of anguish and suffering. Apostolic ministry hurt deeply, and the Corinthian church was killing Paul. Immediately following the triumph metaphor, Paul adds another picture of ministry, the *aroma* of Christ. It is a sacrificial metaphor picturing the smell of the animal offered to God on the altar: "For we are to God the aroma of Christ among those who are being saved and those who are perishing. To the one we are the smell of death; to the other, the fragrance of life. And who is equal to such a task?" (2 Cor.2:15–16).

Paul had just escaped what he calls "a deadly peril" in 1:10. He was quite conscious of the danger associated with his apostolic ministry. A death theme runs through the epistle. But it is more than physical death that characterizes his ministry. Paul makes a remarkable statement in a few chapters later (4:10–12): "We always carry around in our body the death of Jesus, so that the life of Jesus may also be revealed in our body. For we who are alive are always being given over to death for Jesus' sake, so that his life may be revealed in our mortal body. *So then, death is at work in us, but life is at work in you*" (emphasis added).

Paul's conclusion is equally remarkable. Christian ministry is a life-and-death struggle. Though he is wasting away, dying, if you will, his spirit is constantly renewed. Therefore, he never loses heart (4:16). Paul refers to the hardship of ministry several times in this epistle, the most compact and well-known passage being 4:8–9: "We are hard pressed on every side, but not crushed; perplexed, but not in despair; persecuted, but not abandoned; struck down, but not destroyed."

Excruciating physical pain was another aspect of Paul's ministry. He lists some of his hardships in 2 Corinthians 11:23–27. But he also experienced psychological anguish caused by the inward pressure of his ministry. In chapter 6, after listing some of his physical trials (vv. 4–5), Paul adds that he also commended himself "through glory and dishonor, bad report and good report; genuine, yet regarded as impostors; known, yet regarded as unknown; . . . sorrowful, yet always rejoicing" (vv. 8–10). Later in the epistle Paul adds to his list of hardships and includes the anguish every pastor knows: "Besides everything else, I face daily the pressure of my concern for the churches. Who is weak, and I do not feel weak? Who is led into sin, and I do not inwardly burn?" (11:28–29).

Pastoral ministry, whether in the first century or the twenty-first, requires those of us who have been captured by

Christ to lead God's people by climbing up on an altar as a way of life. It is the call given to all God's people but uniquely experienced by Christian leaders, especially pastors. Our master also calls us to carry his cross (Luke 9:23). By the use of this double sacrificial metaphor Paul indicates that our pastoral ministry, like his, is uniquely sacrificial and therefore painful.

I have never found God's call to be easy. I am regularly tempted to crawl off the torturous place of sacrifice. But Paul says that surveying life from the perspective of the cross is worth the pain. And I have seen the gift of a pastoral life produces divine life for others. It does hurt when people reject us, our ministry, and the gospel. I bear scars on my heart and deep in my soul. Paul asks a rhetorical question with which we all can identify on a daily basis, "Who is equal to such a task?" (2:16). No one. But there's a wonderful and divine side too. God's people let us into their hearts with the gospel. And neither we nor they are ever the same. A I write these words, I see a long line of men, women, and children who let me into their lives to share the grief and the joy. By God's grace they were changed, and in turn I am transformed. Paul is right: "When I am weak, then I am strong" (2 Cor. 12:9–10).

PASTORAL CALL AND PARISH REALITY

My seminary teachers never suggested that ministry would be a death march or life on an altar. We all thought we would leave the seminary and preach, teach, and pastor people, living happily ever after. After all, they told us, the Bible has all the answers. The problem is, my academic mentors didn't know what the questions were. We soon discovered the reality of life in Jesus' triumphal army.

Our Intense Struggle

Like most pastors, my call to ministry included a burning conviction that the gospel is the answer for the needs of all people. I think the intensity of that conviction is, in fact, my call to the pastorate. I was, indeed, gripped by a call from beyond myself. That call and my decision to follow it was deeply idealistic as well as profoundly real.

My seminary education fostered the idealism of that call because my training took place under the tutelage of men as idealistic as I. They were men shaped by the academy who lived in the world of ideas and who passed that idealism on to their students. I learned theology and ministry in highly theoretical forms. Ironically, I learned about the church in a classroom. It was antiseptic, critical, abstract, and very idealistic. I graduated an advanced idealist. The old fire in my bones still burned but less fiercely.

I learned quickly that parish life is not a set of ideals, nor is it neatly theological. Instead, the issues I faced were real and personal. Theology and exegesis had to learn to serve reality. I moved quickly from classroom discussions about the ubiquity of Christ and the *ordo salutis* to board meetings, funerals and weddings, telephone interruptions, dysfunctional people, needs deeper than I had ever imagined—and yes, mimeograph machines.

Real issues emerged quickly: immoral church officers, board members who didn't attend services, an openly immoral choir member, church business meetings where I was personally attacked, and indifference to the Word of God on a level beyond my imagination. It hurt.

My first Sunday I stood at the door to greet my new flock. A nicely dressed man introduced himself and said that he had come to town to start a new church—with some of our members. I almost fell down.

My ideals were quickly tempered by church and community realities, and my big ideas were significantly altered to fit the context of ministry. Today I still struggle. I proclaim and teach the greatest ideal in the universe—that men and women can be significantly altered by the gospel. I am equally convinced that God does that profound work in the church and that the church can be the very body of Christ. If I lose that ideal, which is the substance of my call, ministry has no

transcending power and is little more than the cynical acceptance of the status quo.

Yet ministry takes place in a fallen world and addresses
people who are inevitably sinners and who are taught and led
by another sinner, namely me, who obscures the divine ideal.
The church is not what it should be, and neither am I. We all
fall woefully short of the glory of God.

I have a theory about starting out in a ministry. We all
begin with high ideals and expectations. It takes about three
years for me to offend everyone (although some pastors can
do it a lot quicker). By then I've failed to meet all the impossible and unspoken expectations of the congregation. And by
then they've disappointed me and failed to live up to my unreal
expectations. Then, and only then, can real pastoral ministry
begin, for it is then that we have to decide if we will love one
another and believe the gospel. But too often we can't make
that decision. Far too many of us are wrecked on the shore of
harsh reality. Pastors inevitably report a high level of frustration in their vocation. We are frustrated about conflict in the
church, futility in our labor, and failure in our people.

Ministry just plain hurts most of the time. I weary of
rumors and of unrelenting criticism by people who should
know better. I'm tired of blame and misplaced anger. I wonder if anyone hears and obeys the Word of God. I have spent
more hours in nonproductive board and committee meetings
than I can count. I am all too aware that I am not fit for this
work, and I'm tired of people telling me that or implying it.
The truth hurts. I want to quit more often than I want to
admit. With Paul I cry, "Who is equal to such a task?"

Besides, this business is spiritual warfare. Fiery darts come
from directions seen and unseen, making pastoral ministry a
wearying task. Once when God was working in power in our
congregation, several dramatic conversions led to two marriages being healed and a sense of God's presence in our
church. People began to visit to see what God was doing. It was
a small revival. And it was a struggle. Evil gives up reluctantly.

After a month I simply ran out of gas spiritually and physically. I couldn't take any more. My wife came home to find me in bed with a pillow over my head. It was too much for a mortal soul to bear. We laugh about it now, but then I thought I would die.

When I said yes to God's call, I had no idea it would be such a struggle. But as long as humanity is sinful and the church is full of and led by humans doing God's work, ministry will be war. That's my calling. I am Christ's captive in the midst of a cosmic war. Of course it's intense!

Living out our call responsibly means accepting both the ideal and the real in joyful embrace. The struggle and pain are real. After all, we are in a war. But, according to Paul, that is precisely where we find the power of God. The joy of the ministry is in the very midst of the struggle in our own souls and in the church of Christ. Indeed, the battle in our souls demonstrates that God is at work in and through us. How tragic if our ministry causes no divine-human encounter.

The Gospel Assures Triumph in Ministry

Paul was gripped by a call from beyond himself as are all of Christ's ministers. We march as Christ's captives in his victory parade. Being Christ's captive is reassuring because the progress of the gospel and our success are ultimately Christ's responsibility. If my ministry is part of Christ's parade, it must succeed even when appearances suggests the contrary. God is sovereign, and Jesus is Lord of history. The gospel is the power of God, and it will prevail. Consequently, Paul received great assurance at Corinth when Christ told him, "I have many people in this city" (Acts 18:10). Paul didn't know who they were, but he preached in confidence knowing that the gospel was doing its work.

Not only is God sovereign, the victory of the gospel is assured because the Cross and Resurrection decisively won the victory against demonic forces that oppress our fallen world. The picture Paul draws in Colossians 2:15 is dramatic. Christ is defeating principalities and powers in the cosmic battle with the power of his cross. From God's point of view, the battle is already over. Christ is victor. We are simply workers for the Lord of Lords. He has given us divinely powered weapons (2 Cor. 10:4–6) by which he is overthrowing the existing order (1 Cor. 1:18 NEB). Hence, we work with confidence because the outcome is assured.

Locked in time and space, our perception is easily clouded, and we fail to see reality from God's point of view. Sin appears to reign in and out of the church. God's people seem to be molded by the values of this world and often appear indistinguishable from their pagan neighbors. The press of time and ecclesiastical necessities,—meetings, administration, assorted pastoral duties—rob us and the church of our most precious assets, and we despair of progress. Yet the image of Christ's triumphal march reminds us of the truth. The parade and we captives in it are led by the eternal Son of God who wields a holy cross. The battle is his, not ours.

Scripture says that the just shall live by faith—and that includes the clergy. Faith is dependence on divine realities and promises in spite of contrary human appearances. In the ministry it is easy, even natural, to live by works that can be seen. But Paul states clearly in Romans 1:16–17 that salvation (and pastoral ministry) is a matter of faith from start to finish. Christ's captives live out of resources beyond ourselves.

Occasionally we are given glimpses of the divine side of our work, although that may mean seeing results long after we have ministered to someone. Recently I went back to a former church to celebrate an anniversary. I was stunned by what some people told me. One young man told me that the year he was in my leadership study group was the pivotal event of his Christian life. I had forgotten he was in the group! A teenager remembered a children's sermon I had forgotten. She said it changed her life. And on the stories went. What often appeared to be empty acts of ministry were, in fact, the power of God changing lives before my very eyes. I just couldn't see it. If we could see, really see, what the work of the gospel is doing in people we love, we would complain a lot less and rejoice more.

Ministry Is Joyous Labor

Here is the divine irony: Being Christ's captive is being truly free. Participating in Christ's death march is, in fact, to participate in divine life itself. A metaphor that seems to emphasize pain and suffering is actually a picture of joy. Second Corinthians, written out of Paul's excruciating pastoral pain, is a long shout of the triumph of the gospel.

Philippians, a letter written by Paul from prison, features the joy of pastoral ministry in the very worst of circumstances. Paul's mind fills with nostalgic recollections of persons he loved back in Philippi, many of whom were his partners in ministry (1:7; 4:14). Long ago he had tucked a long list of people deep into his heart, where he nurtured them and cared for them. Now, under the pressure of prison and possible death, his heart swells with the same love grown stronger in adversity.

Pastors can identify with Paul's feeling of satisfaction at being Christ's captive and seeing Christ's work progress. What brings more joy than seeing some spiritual movement in those we are called to love and serve? What offers more confidence to wavering pastors than the certainty that God is at work? Often silently, always mysteriously, certainly more slowly than we would like, but always powerfully, God changes people through our labors. I am stunned by that truth known and experienced again and again.

I recall the first public response to my preaching. I called for decisions, and to my utter surprise people responded. I was so awestruck that I scarcely knew what to say. Equally satisfying are the many times more personal pastoral ministry changes lives. I remember the first time a couple told me my ministry saved their marriage. Another time a strong but quiet man, a leader in the church, confessed that I was the most significant man in his entire life. I was, to borrow a phrase from C. S. Lewis, "surprised by joy." That conversation got me through a month of the ordinary and the awful.

Years of ministry and repetition of labors tend to blur our vision. Institutional management, ecclesial routines, personal agendas, and a thousand other ordinary matters cloud our perception. We fail to see what God is doing and even demand more from God than we see. And, of course, we want the battle to be less than war. Christ's prisoners of war cannot escape the harsh truth that we battle against principalities and powers. Yet Paul's deep joy in 2 Corinthians is the result of his deep anguish over the Corinthians. Joy works that way. The greater the peril to life or ministry, the greater the thrill of victory.

And it will be a struggle. A major function of the Word of God, and therefore of pastoral ministry, is critique. Biblical preaching and counsel will trouble many. We are called to lead God's people as they follow Christ, yet many would rather stay comfortable where they are. Leadership, by its very nature, will alienate some people, and we will be pitted against our predecessors as well as our neighbors. Party spirit is an unfortunate fact of church life, and misunderstanding is as natural as hearing.

Several years ago the ministry struggle became particularly intense for me. I was young and inexperienced, and the situation was desperate. Lives, families, and a church hung in the balance, to say nothing of my resume. Two prominent leaders in the church were having an affair. It had gone on for nearly a year, and it seemed that everyone in town knew about it but me. I found out about the affair when the people suddenly repented, confessed publicly, and asked for forgiveness. It was a powerful moment for the church and the community. People looked up and took notice. God was at work. We thought two families would be restored and the church order restored. And it was almost true. One of the marriages was transformed. The other marriage was more fragile.

The husband of the guilty woman would have none of it. A church leader himself, he was wounded too deeply to forgive so quickly. He had known about the affair and had done everything he could to stop it, including threats of bodily harm to his wife's boyfriend. In fact, the reconciliation seemed to embitter him rather than bring relief.

His wife and children were torn apart by his bitterness. The church was, too. What could we do? On the one hand, God was using this reconciliation in a powerful way. People all over town were talking about it, and several came to see me about their spiritual condition. On the other hand, the church was deeply affected by the hurt in this man whom we loved. His hurt and anger cast a shadow over the congregation. I didn't know what to do. I loved all four of the people involved but understood his anger toward this brother in Christ who had stolen his wife.

Two older women in the church set out to pray for me and for these four people. They didn't tell anyone but me. They prayed day and night.

One Sunday night all four of the people involved in the scandal came to church. The reconciled couple sat in the back on the left side of the church. The angry man and his wife came in at the last minute. I was standing at the door of the church, and he rushed past me, his face set in anger, without a word. He and his wife sat toward the front on the right.

Since the confession and reconciliation, the congregation had had long and powerful times of personal sharing on Sunday nights. God was working in all our lives, and we came to tell about it. That Sunday night we started telling what God was doing in us and through us. I watched the angry man out of the corner of my eye. He kept his head down and scowled. But he was listening.

After nearly an hour of testimony, he suddenly leaped to his feet and began to talk. His speech was interrupted by tears that came from deep in his soul. I'll never forget his words, "I came in here tonight hating [the man who'd loved his wife]. I wanted him to die. But I want you to know something. God has changed my mind." He turned around and said to the offending man, "I love you and forgive you."

The two men left their seats and met in the middle of the church. They embraced and cried. We joined them! We were looking at the grace of God at work. We shared a joy beyond words. My pastor's heart has never been the same. That's a very dramatic illustration of what I have seen in a hundred lesser ways. I have a file folder five inches thick that contains the letters and cards I received when I left Park Street Church. Each item is a testimony to the way God used me to be his instrument in lives of his children and my parishioners. It's a wonder—a joy beyond words.

More often, the struggle is more subtle and the enemy more cunning. Sometimes sheer indifference can destroy a pastor's heart. A friend of mine pastors a church that never learned how to say thank-you. I can see the progress of the gospel, but he is often reduced to depression because in the midst of the battle his vision is blocked by the struggle. He wonders if he is making any difference at all. I tell him it's worth it, but I know his pain.

I heard a pastor say once that all God's servants have a "wilderness experience" like Moses and the children of Israel. There are times when our ministry seems empty and barren. People are not responsive and sometimes hostile. Our words and labors fall on hard soil, and nothing happens. In these wilderness experiences, our souls are barren and empty too.

I had my wilderness experience. In fact, I have had more than one. But one of them lasted nearly five years. The church didn't grow. The people seemed disinterested and distant. The "spirit" of the congregation was dead. It seemed as if I was preaching into a dense fog. My relationships seemed per-functory and seldom touched the soul. I thought I would die.

One Sunday my wife and I came home from church, sat in our living room, and wept. On and on it went. Desert days and barren nights, dead souls and empty relationships. We poured out our hearts to a fellow pastor and wife. They promptly told a couple in our church, who became very angry with us. Then we felt betrayed and misunderstood as well as empty and barren.

I know God worked in some lives during those years—a few people told me so. But that did not take away the sense of futility and my empty soul. And sometimes that's the way pastoral ministry is. Now I understand that the wilderness experience was part of the journey and worth it. If nothing else, my own pastor's heart took on new shape, and my understanding of pastoral ministry was reformed. And God was in it all.

In any case, dealing with human hearts, including our own, is difficult. But the deeper the struggle, the sweeter the victory. We are captive to Christ, the Lord of life and of his church. We march in his parade, and we know where it is headed. And once in a while we get a glimpse over our shoulder and see fellow prisoners following us in the parade. It's worth it.

6 JARS OF CLAY: THE PASTOR'S BURDEN

But we have this treasure in jars of clay to show that this all-surpassing power is from God and not from us.

—2 Corinthians 4:7

Recently I talked with a pastor friend. He has served the same congregation for twenty-eight years and is two years from retirement. He said that he had thought about working beyond age sixty-five but decided that pastoral life is too intense. He added that most of the time he felt like the teddy bear Winnie the Pooh dragged down the stairs, its head banging on every step. "It's too intense. I can't take much more," he said.

JOYOUS BURDENS

The Burden of Ministry

Every pastor can identify with my friend's feelings. The business of caring for eternal souls is wearying as is the job of pastoral leadership in a world and church where leaders are under suspicion and institutional religion is under attack.

My pastor from seminary days is one of my models for ministry. Successful, skillful, and pastoral, he was my mentor and advisor. He had a friendly manner and easy laugh. But there was a certain seriousness, even sadness, about him. One day as we talked, I observed his heart. He was deeply burdened for his flock. Their lives, faith, and struggles weighed heavy on his soul. He toiled on their behalf and labored in prayer for them. He worked hard at leading a somewhat backward church toward its destiny, yet met resistance at every turn. In fact, the board finally forced him to resign. I'll never forget his face the Sunday morning he announced his resignation. I'm sure there is more to the story than I know. But I watched a man I respected and loved live through profound pain. It took a long time for the church to recover. I'm not sure my pastor ever did. He had experienced the burden of the ministry.

Like all Christian pastors, I quickly felt the weight of that burden. It arrived in a variety of shapes and forms. Part of it was the growing awareness of the responsibility of speaking and acting in God's behalf. I was God's steward entrusted with Holy Scripture and Christ's church, the people of God, and would some day give an account of myself to God. I experienced another part of the burden as I learned to lead God's people from where they were to where they ought to be. More often than not, churches resist movement out of the comfort zone. Leadership is lonely.

Any theological or theoretical awareness can grow dull from time and routine. It is easy to forget the weight that accompanies the care of souls. Sometimes I take pastoral leadership far too lightly. But there is something about the daily experience of caring for the people's souls that is powerfully intense. From the first day of my ministry I was swept up in the lives and faith of God's people. Their joys and pain became mine. They included me in their lives and looked to me for a word from the Lord to explain things. Even when they resisted the changes my leadership brought, they still looked to me to care for their souls and our church.

One morning during my first year in ministry, I jogged up a hill outside of town to see the spectacular view of the snow-capped Cascade Mountains from the county fair-grounds. As always, I was stunned by God's creative handiwork. The rising sun cast a pink glow on the sides of Mount Adams, Mount Hood, and Mount St. Helens. It was an unforgettable moment.

As I turned and headed back to town, I looked down on the rooftops and thought about my work, Christ's church, and that town full of needy people. What a contrast between the beauty of God's creation and the tawdry mess we humans make. I had been in town long enough to know what was under some of those roofs. I had seen the power of evil up close. I had learned that life doesn't get easier with time; it gets more complicated. The placid exterior of village life was, in fact, a collection of very human people living experiencing life in all its pain and glory.

The Joy of Ministry

Rising above the trees on the west side of town was the steeple of the church I pastored. The cross atop that steeple cast a shadow across the village. Under that steeple beat the life of a Christian church. In many ways it reflected the ordinary life of our community. We were a collection of humans with all the sins and shortcomings of our neighbors. The pain of life in a fallen world pressed down as hard on each of us as on everyone else. Suddenly, I felt the collective weight of that human experience with a new intensity. Yet under that steeple and in this village, God was at work. The faces of God's people rose up in my memory as I recalled how the gospel was really becoming good news in these children of God. As never before, I was aware of the call of God to Christian ministry in this town and in this church. My heart soared with joy and at the same time felt the burden of that call.

The tension of that moment is summed up in Paul's picture of his own pastoral ministry in 1 Corinthians 4:7: "We have this treasure in vessels of clay." Our calling offers us the glory of working with the inestimable treasure of the gospel and the infinitely valuable people for whom Christ died. It's enough to make an apostle—or a Christian pastor—shout for joy!

But we are all too aware that we are nothing better than clay pots. We crack, chip, break, and wear out. We are expendable, fallible, and sinful. It hurts to be a clay pot. The church is equally human and sinful—pews full of clay pots—and the mixture of all that humanness inevitably creates tension, escalates depravity, and hurts both pastors and parishioners. We are responsible for it all, and that is the joyous burden of the ministry.

THE WEIGHT OF GLORY: GOD TRUSTS ME!

Rick Warren, the pastor of the Saddleback Valley Community Church in California, has a wonderful definition of the grace given to pastors: "God knew every sinful and stupid thing I'd ever do and chose me anyway." That is a staggering reality too often forgotten in the press of ministry and the passing of time. The other side of that grace is the equally staggering truth that none of us is sufficient for the task nor worthy of the trust given us.

A young colleague in ministry asked me how to keep from getting cynical. I suppose that question came from reflection on the clay-pot side of ministry. She felt betrayed by the church, used by people, and short of resources necessary to keep going. In fact, her vocational crisis was at the same time a deep crisis of faith. How do any of us keep from being overwhelmed by our own humanness, let alone the collective depravity of our congregations?

The Glory of the Ministry

There are no simple answers to that question. Ministry is an inescapable burden, and that can be lethal to both faith and joy. One way to deal with our "clay potness" is to focus on the treasure inside all of God's clay pots. C. S. Lewis suggested that all humans carry "the weight of glory." Christians, in particular, bear that alien dignity, for the Lord Christ himself lives in us. Christian pastors not only bear that weight, the very currency of our work is that weight of glory, the treasure of the gospel and grace entrusted to us.

I knew about the glory of the ministry. I had studied about it, believed it, and observed it growing up in a pastor's home. But I'll never forget my first experience of it. The memory stands at the very center of my pastoral formation. It was a Sunday worship service in which God was powerfully present. From the opening hymn to the benediction every act of worship carried the "weight of eternity." I led the worship and was overwhelmed by the experience. I sensed both God's presence and the burden of being part of a sinful collection of people at the same time. The sermon seemed to come from a deeper source in my soul than I knew existed. I said what I planned to say but with energy and fluency not my own. I recall the excitement as I wrote my dad and told him I had preached "in the Spirit" for the first time. God's strength carried me beyond my ability, and my human words struck hearts with the power of God.

Several key people were transformed that hour. None of us was ever the same. All we could say was "Wow!" God took a very human moment in time and transformed that hour and most of those present. Eternity entered time. The kingdom of God encountered human reality, and everything changed. And wonder of wonders, God let me be part of a divine moment.

I have never recovered from that experience. None of us deserved that season of grace, least of all me. I was young, inexperienced, and ignorant. The church was old, tired, and in need of mercy. Together we were without merit. Yet the glory of God came to this mixed mess of humanity. All we could do was stand before the mystery of it and give thanks.

Through the years, I have known larger and smaller moments of that weight of glory. Each confirms the original message. We pastors are privileged to stand in the center of God's work on earth. It is a sheer gift for which I am profoundly grateful. And that grace has another and equal side.

Being an instrument of grace among God's people is also profoundly humbling. I know the difference between my power and God's. My human resources simply cannot touch eternity. When God takes my acts and words and changes lives and forms his church, the best I can do is humbly stand back and cry, "Glory to God in the highest!"

A Biblical Theme

This glory of the ministry is woven through all Paul's letters. The introductions to his letters overflow with his profound joy that God was at work in his ministry. He begins 1 Thessalonians by reminding the church that his ministry among them was marked by "power, with the Holy Spirit and with deep conviction" (1:4–5). Paul's love for the Thessalonian Christians and his awe that he was one "entrusted with the gospel" (2:4) permeate the entire epistle.

Despite the discouragement and pain of ministry in Corinth, Paul's letters to that rebellious church reflect his wonder that God used him as a pastor and apostle. The clay-pot metaphor of 2 Corinthians 4 is a case in point. We pastoral clay pots hold an imperishable treasure. It is ironic and quite humbling to realize that ministry is given to us independent of any achievement or value inherent in us. God simply chooses us for his own reasons. Though we are clay pots that crack and break, God chooses to make us the instruments through which the treasure of the gospel does its work. A. T. Robertson was so struck by that recurring theme in the early part of 2 Corinthians that he titled his book on that section *The Glory of the Ministry*. God's using clay pots like us is a breathtaking reality that ought to straighten the drooping pastoral spine of the most discouraged minister of the gospel.

Nevertheless, there is always the danger of forgetting the privilege of working for God and the inherent dignity that accompanies God's servants. That is certainly true in our secular world, where the church and its ministry are pushed to the margins of culture. Even God's people tend to trivialize the work of Christian pastors.

And even ancient Israel, a people who had experienced the Exodus and the mighty works of God, needed to be reminded of the glory of the ministry. So God instructed that the priests at his altar wear elaborate and expensive vestments to give them "dignity and honor" (Ex. 28:2, 40). Because their ministry at the altar was divine work, their appearance was required to bear witness to eternity. God's servants bore an alien dignity that spoke of the glory of God. Their vestments never let them or the people forget it.

A Historical Reality

Christian history bears witness to the weight of glory borne by ministers of the gospel. For centuries pastors were called "curates." Their task was the "cure of souls" (from the Latin, *cura animarum*) or, when anglicized, "care of souls." Their role as curates was as physicians of the soul.

Few traditions took the care of souls more seriously than the Puritans. Their ministers were entrusted with the spiritual health of the entire community, and their task was to heal all ills of the soul, mind, and heart. They took their office as physicians of the soul most seriously—some suggest, too seriously. Nevertheless, they knew who they were and what they were called to do. Seventeenth-century Puritan scholar Richard Baxter's classic pastoral theology, *The Reformed Pastor*, describes the entire work of the ministry as the diagnosis and healing of the spiritual ills of the congregants.[1]

Until recent times the respect offered God's doctors of the spirit was similar to that given physicians today. I have yet to meet a physician who doesn't have a firm sense of identity and often a firmer sense of dignity. Their work is a matter of life and death and health. Until recently, the work of the cure of souls carried even more dignity, for the clergy deal with living souls, ultimate health, and heaven and hell.

A Lost Art

One of the great pastoral theologies of the past century is W. G. T. Shedd's *Homiletics and Pastoral Theology,* first published in 1867. For Shedd, the foundation of pastoral theology is the moral and religious character of the minister. He argues that the pastor "by his very vocation is the 'sacred man' in society." He is the "parson," a term derived from the Latin *persona.* The title means the pastor is "The Person" in the community.[2]

Quite clearly the days of "The Parson" are long gone, but the inner truth remains. Even in a world that marginalizes the church and devalues the Christian ministry, the church believes, or at least ought to believe, that its ministers are entrusted with and carry about in their very persons the glorious gospel of Christ. Pastors are a depository of the truth of God. Our work is the intersection of time and eternity. We hold in our hands the transforming power of the Christian faith.

A Transforming Truth

It is easy to forget the glory of the ministry in the barrage of tasks that we face every day. Sometimes, amid all the business, I can scarcely catch a glimpse of eternity. Budgets, meetings, committees, duties, and problems, along with destructive criticism, negative people, and the sheer humanness of the whole enterprise, disguise the reality we serve. Even holy things tend to become common over time.

I am horrified by my ability to trivialize the glory of God. Recently a new member of the congregation took me out for dinner. During the meal, he shared with me the account of his pilgrimage toward Christian faith. It was a remarkable story—the kind preachers love as illustrations of the prevenient grace of God. This man is the kind of lay leader pastors long for. Yet in the middle of his wonderful story I found my mind wandering as I teetered on the edge of boredom. I had heard it all before in one form or another—same song, different verse. On my way home I repented with bitter tears. I had demeaned one of God's beloved sons. I had looked straight into the face of God's grace and yawned.

I long for some of Aaron's vestments to remind myself—and others, too, I suppose—of the "dignity and honor" inherent in my calling. Instead, I settle for the trappings and symbols of human power to find my significance. Too often I take myself more seriously than the gospel that is entrusted to me.

With longing I recall the wonder of those early days of ministry when every experience was new. Like the early Christians, I depended on God for most everything because I had nowhere else to turn. I had no experience, very little wisdom, and a church full of people hungry for the reality of God. It was exhilarating! I saw God at work everywhere, even when that vision was only hope. I lived in awe of the task to which I had been called and of the God who had called me.

As I write this book, I am completing my twenty-fifth year as a Christian pastor. It seems that only yesterday I stood behind a Christian pulpit for the first time. It was a bright and sunny July Sunday and, like Paul, "I came in weakness and fear, and with much trembling" (1 Cor. 2:3). I knew that that pulpit, like every other one on earth, was exactly what my forefathers called it—a "sacred desk." I stood there that day and feebly, yet somehow confidently, spoke a word from the Lord. I entered into the miracle of the Word unleashed among God's people.

Days tumbled over one another as I visited the homes of families in the congregation; listened to stories of faith and failure; studied hard; learned much; and, Sunday after Sunday, stood behind that old pulpit and watched God work. I was marked for life. Now it seems that the years run together as I think back over a quarter century of life, ministry, and churches. It is hard to believe that I am better than halfway through my ministry.

I never quite recovered from that first Sunday behind the sacred desk. I am still a bit shocked that God trusts me with his Word, sacraments, and church. My pulse still quickens when I create sermons. My heart races when I stand before God's people to speak on behalf of the Lord of the church. I am deeply honored that God's people listen, follow my leadership, and invite me into their lives. My life is still a story being written one day—one Sunday—at a time.

THE INTOLERABLE BURDEN: WE'RE ALL CLAY POTS

I don't know why God chose to bless those early days. It was certainly not any reward for my good efforts or the church's excellent record. Nevertheless, God visited us in a remarkable way. It seemed that every Sunday was another transforming moment. The church became vibrant with the power of God. People came to see what God was doing, and many came to Christian faith. I don't think anyone there was transformed quite as much as I. Here I was, a child, it seemed, and I was handling the power of eternity. I figured this was how it was supposed to be—and would be.

The Mystery of Grace

It wasn't, of course. Movements of the Spirit ebb and flow outside human control, and I have known more ebbs than flows over the past quarter century. Nevertheless, God has blessed it all, every single day.

I don't know why. I don't understand how I have survived when so many of my contemporaries haven't. I am not sure why I have had the inestimable privilege of serving wonderful congregations. And I am still surprised when God uses what I say and do to change lives and touch souls. It is a deep and wonderful mystery. I only wish my heart and soul were as conscious of the glory of the ministry as my head—then, maybe, being a clay pot wouldn't be so difficult.

Inevitable Pastoral Reality

Back in the glory of those early days, reality set in quickly. I recall with equal vividness the first sting of criticism. God was blessing, people were trusting Christ, the church was growing, and everyone seemed pleased—but we were still very human.

One evening just before the midweek service, I got a frantic phone call. The caller told me to get over to the church quickly. There was a rumor going around that I was going to take the church into another denomination. I was stunned. Nothing was further from my mind or intentions. In fact, I was arguing hard with some people to keep us in our denomination. There was little I could do. Rumors have a life of their own, and most attempts to stifle them simply serve to fan the fire.

The rumor died out, but the pain remained. I was sadder but wiser. Some people in the Christian church love to spread untruths, and even more people enjoy hearing bad news whether it is true or not. More rumors, some silly and others harmful, followed. There was always somebody who believed the rumors and passed them on. My journal from those days drips with self-pity as I wondered why some people preferred the dark side of humanity over the glory of God.

Of course, some criticism hurts intensely because it is at least partly valid. My predecessor's widow was a member of that same congregation. She was a wonderful woman of faith who was unceasingly supportive. However, she was bothered by the volume of my preaching. She thought I might preach with a bit less vigor. Bless her heart, she came and told me and didn't share her criticism with anyone else.

I knew this woman was still grieving for her husband, who had been dead for only a year. I understood that he was a gentle and quiet man who had been her pastor for forty years. I was young, brash, and loud. I did need to slow down and turn down the volume. I can still remember her criticism as a good but painful moment.

I have wondered why criticism seems to hurt pastors even when it is constructive. I guess it is because we are people of deep, even passionate, conviction and tender hearts. Consequently, we don't like to be wrong, and we really can't stand rejection. Criticism, even at its best, threatens our convictions or our pastor's heart.

We pastors and our congregations are unrelentingly human. Paul calls it living with a heavenly treasure in a jar of clay. That's annoying, even maddening. I have tried to wish it away, prayed it weren't so, and avoided it when possible. But it is a fundamental fact of pastoral life.

I have never tired of reading about the life and ministry of C. H. Spurgeon, the great London preacher of the last century. His two-volume autobiography is a treasure-house of pastoral wisdom. This "heir of the Puritans" certainly understood the glory of the Christian ministry. In fact, he was so intensely aware of the weight of his responsibility, that he staggered under the awesome burden of a ministry to growing thousands of listeners. His reflections on his pastoral ministry emphasize the glory of Christian ministry.

An American journalist visited the Metropolitan Tabernacle, Spurgeon's church in London. The visitor was seated in an overflow section where he couldn't see the pulpit. It was, however, near the vestry door. At the time the service was to begin, he witnessed Spurgeon and some of the deacons coming out of the vestry and waiting at the bottom of the stairs to go up to the pulpit. He later reported that Spurgeon was so overcome by the size of the crowd and the weight of his ministry that he collapsed in the arms of the deacons. Only after prayer and reassurance from his deacons, did Spurgeon enter the pulpit to face the people in the name of God.

Of his phenomenal early success, Spurgeon wrote, "My success appalled me; and the thought of the career which it seemed to open up to me, so far from elating me, cast me into the lowest depth, out of which I uttered my *miserere* and found no room for a *gloria in excelsis*. Who was I that I should continue to lead so great a multitude? I would return to my village obscurity, or emigrate to America, and find a solitary nest in the backwoods, where I might be sufficient for the things demanded of me."[3]

The great man of God was a jar of clay incapable of bearing the weight of the burden of Christian ministry. He was very aware of his human inadequacy. In his *Lectures to My Students* he tells how he was oppressed by occasional periods of depression. His autobiography reveals a man fully conscious of his tendency to pride and vanity along with a weak body that helped keep him humble. It appears that he never lost his sense of wonder that God trusted him with a huge church and a ministry to the world. That spirit is the glory and burden of the ministry.

PASTORAL REALITY: WE'RE CRACKED POTS

Paul uses a metaphor to describe how God's preachers bear his glory: "We have this treasure in jars of clay" (2 Cor. 4:7). To put it in more contemporary language, we're cracked pots who bear the weight of glory. God does his divine work through fallen, fallible, and sinful human instruments. God puts the gospel in clay pots that crack and break.

I suppose all pastors wish, even yearn, that we could somehow bypass our own humanity. Some even act as if they have. And congregations love it! Many want to put us on pedestals hoping, I suppose, that our pastoral perfection will somehow deny the reality of sin somewhere on earth. We all love pedestals because they make us feel special. But they evade humanity, and eventually they all fall down.

A Biblical Reality

The Bible, from beginning to end, highlights the humanity of God's leaders. Moses, the greatest leader of them all, was full of self-doubt and begged God to excuse him from having to lead the Exodus from Egypt. Later he thought he was indispensable as a judge and decision maker, and his father-in-law had to tell him how to delegate such responsibilities. Another time, when he was angry, he disobeyed God and struck a rock instead of speaking to it, as God had instructed. Because of that sin, God prohibited Moses from leading the people into the Promised Land. Moses was no different than the last person who crossed the Red Sea—just another human. Yet God chose Moses to perform the most important job on earth.

King David's sad story needs no repeating. Suffice it to say, this great man, "a man after God's own heart" and one of the great leaders of history, had a very dark side. His sexual misconduct and subsequent criminal cover-up mar his brilliant leadership of Israel. His sin cost him dearly. His humanity destroyed his family and finally divided his kingdom. The glorious king of Israel was a jar of clay no different from any man in his kingdom.

Peter, the first great leader of the Christian church, apostle and martyr, leader and probably an outstanding bishop, was not just impetuous and often stupid, he denied Jesus when his master needed him most. Later, in Antioch, when he was a "pillar of the church," he turned away from the truth he knew and had to be rebuked by Paul. Even the great ones are made of the same stuff as all of us. We all are jars of clay and are cracked and marred, and sometimes we break.

Paul, too, was limited by his humanity. His "thorn in the flesh," probably a physical or psychological malady, struck him down repeatedly. During those dark days, he learned an important lesson: The very point of his human weakness was precisely the place of God's power and grace. Paul knew he was a jar of clay and a cracked one, at that.

Human Experience Confirms the Biblical Truth

Experience confirms the biblical witness. Despite the front we may present to our congregation and the world, we know what we really are deep inside, and God knows even when we deceive ourselves. We are common sinners like everyone else, though we and our churches may like it otherwise. We don't know everything. In fact, we don't know most things. Despite whatever success we may have, in our more honest moments we know it is all in spite of our humanity.

Add the complexities of our modern world and the crisis of today's church to our inherent inadequacy, and the results can be devastating. Simply put, contemporary pastors were not trained adequately for ministry in a world like this. Leonard Sweet suggests that one of the problems of the ministry in our time is that we were trained as "typewriter repairmen for a computer age."[4] At this turning of the ages, the church is, as Sweet suggests, "quaking," and the Christian ministry is standing on the fault line of history and eternity. And none of us is equal to our task.

One of the best Christian leaders I know said to me one day, "If I'm so successful, why do I feel so inadequate?" Then he added, "And if I'm so successful, why is it destroying my soul?" Those are my questions too. In fact, the more I experience what is ordinarily called success, the more I feel inadequate for the task. That sense of failure is often accompanied by a deep feeling that I have somehow cut corners and blunted the truth for political expediency or personal advancement. If it is true, as someone has suggested, that the birthright of every American male is a chronic sense of inadequacy, the male-dominated clergy has a problem. And if, as Scripture and experience teach us, we all are moral failures, how dare we lead God's people or speak in his name? It is part of being a cracked pot in our time.

To put it another way, I asked a friend of mine, a successful pastor by any standard of measurement, if he ever felt like he was a flash in the pan and that someday the success would retreat before reality. He smiled and said, "Every day of my life." We do have this treasure in cracked pots.

I don't suppose many pastors want to risk the honesty of one pastor I know. He openly tells his congregation that all the horrid things they may think about him don't even begin to describe the evil that lurks in his soul. If they really knew what was in his heart, they would be horrified.[5] His point is clear. We need to get the clergy off their pedestals and admit that the glory of the ministry sits in the midst of depraved human servants.

Hope for Clay Pots

We should be encouraged to note that one of the glimpses we get of the working pastor in the New Testament is a powerful description of a vessel of clay. Toward the end of his life Paul wrote to young pastor Timothy two letters filled with pastoral concern for his young friend who was failing in health and courage. Throughout the letters Paul alludes to Timothy's timidity (e.g., 2 Tim. 1:7); and encourages him to stand firm in the Lord and not quit or despair. Paul calls Timothy to be courageous, to remember his calling, to recall his ordination, to press on. Interestingly, Paul doesn't argue that Timothy's shortcomings invalidated his ministry or that they should be eliminated from his personality.

Like most of us, Timothy didn't need reminding that he was a cracked pot in danger of crashing into a thousand pieces. Rather, he needed the encouragement of a mentor who reminded him that the glory of the ministry finds its context and its power in human servants who are by their very nature inadequate for the task. Paul told Timothy that despite Timothy's personal failures, he should continue his divine task.

Even as the Old and New Testament giants of the faith were flawed, so, too, were the giants of Christian history. Spurgeon and Luther suffered from depression. Calvin's physical maladies were legion and overwhelming. He once said that every day was a death struggle.

The giants of the faith are not the only ones who were prisoners of their own humanity. Their story is our story. We all are jars of clay, chipped, cracked, and liable to break.

A young colleague of mine recently left our staff to take up his first solo pastorate. When I talked to him a year later, he said he was tired, lonely, and discouraged. He had discovered weaknesses in himself and flaws in his congregation. If we ever doubt our humanity, our congregation will confirm it. No matter who we are or what we accomplish, some people will not like us, won't follow us, and may even reject our ministry. None of us are exceptions to that rule. And in the meantime, there are some people, even churches, we don't like, don't respect, and wish would go away. In attempting to serve them, we make mistakes, sin gravely, fall short, and otherwise fail our divine calling. If we would admit it, much of the conflict between church and clergy might be resolved.

INEVITABLE TENSION

Every Christian pastor lives with the inevitable tension inherent in a life lived between heaven and earth. We work for God and deal with holy and eternal issues every day of our lives, being ever mindful that we are fallen and fallible human vessels. Our pastoral identity includes both sides of what is, in fact, a paradox. God does heaven's infinite work through earth's finite creatures. It's a mystery, a wonder, a glory—and an intolerable burden. And, as Paul says, none of us is adequate. He wasn't, neither was Timothy, nor are we.

Divinely Productive Tension

A couple of years ago the distinguished English theologian and pastor John Stott came to preach to our evening congregation of university students and young professionals at Park Street Church. We were thrilled to have him come because he has spoken at university missions all his life. Our students and young adults invited their non-Christian friends, and the sanctuary overflowed with people.

I had told Dr. Stott who would be in the audience: young Christians and their seeking friends. He commented that such an audience was intimidating. I was a bit surprised, since he had spoken in similar settings so many times before. I left Dr. Stott in my office before the service so that he could collect his thoughts and prepare. I came back to the office and found Dr. Stott on his knees with his face toward heaven, pleading with God for sufficient grace for the hour. The image is forever etched in my mind.

After I introduced Dr. Stott to the throng, our paths crossed as he made his way to the podium. He grabbed my arm and whispered, "Please pray for me, dear brother!" He preached with confidence and power born of deep and humble dependence on God. His young audience loved him and received his message. It was a great night, and lives were changed by the power of the gospel.

Dr. Stott's example was a vivid reminder that no matter how skilled or experienced we may be, in the final analysis the Christian ministry is God's work, and none of us deserves our calling nor are any of us adequate for the task. As the *New English Bible* translates 1 Corinthians 4:7, "We are no better than pots of earthenware to contain this treasure."

Clay Pot Pastors in a Pot-Smashing World

Christian pastors in the late twentieth century face a world of ministry with gigantic intimidation factors added to the already intolerable burden of bearing God's truth in our human packages. Postmodern America is creating a world that is hostile to Christian faith and that is forming a church in many ways in its own image.

When I was finishing my doctoral work, my supervisory professor counseled me strongly against pastoral ministry. "These are bitchy times," he said. "The church will destroy you." He thought teaching and seminary administration were safer alternatives.

Perhaps. Certainly the times are exposing the "clay pot-ness" of the ministry in ways not experienced for centuries. Pastors are quitting the ministry, and churches are firing them in unprecedented numbers. Moral failure among the clergy seems epidemic. *Leadership* magazine found it necessary to devote an entire issue to marital infidelity in the ministry.[6] The clergy have fallen off whatever pedestals we once inhabited. There is no more avoiding the obvious truth: We're just as human and sinful as the people we serve!

Everywhere the clergy are reported to be discouraged, depressed, or frustrated. Management consultant Peter Drucker says ministers are in "the most frustrated profession in the nation."[7] In the March 1995 issue of the *Clergy Journal*, pastoral counselor Lloyd Rediger sums up his twenty-year study of the clergy. He reports that "high levels of stress" are pervasive along with a "growing level of depression," which is accompanied by increasingly vocalized "internalized anger." Perhaps more significantly, the church does not seem to hear the cries of its clergy, and denominations are increasingly seen as part of the problem rather than the solution.[8]

A young colleague of mine recently left our staff for his first solo pastorate. I invited him back to report on the experience to our seminary interns. He talked about the joys of ministry but spent much more time sharing his sense of loneliness, isolation, and frustration. He said that he had recently attended a regional gathering of his denomination's clergy and couldn't find a single happy pastor.

It takes a while, but most of us learn that there is no greener pastoral pasture on the other side of the fence. Ministry is always and everywhere a combination of soaring joy and excruciating pain. "We are no better than pots of earthenware to contain this treasure."

RESOLUTION

For Paul, however, the stark humanity that rendered him inadequate to his calling was not something to bemoan. In fact, the clay-pot metaphor is an expression of exaltation and thanksgiving. The conclusion to be drawn from the image of clay pots, Paul says, is profound and transforming: "this proves that such transcendent power does not come from us but is God's alone! (1 Cor. 4:7 NEB).

Here is a vision that transforms all of pastoral ministry, including its pastors. While our gifts and calling demand that we work hard and give God and Christ's church the very best we have to offer, in the final analysis, all of our ministry belongs to God and is empowered by God.

Clay Pots Are God's Opportunity

Our inadequacy is the opportunity for divine power. Paul learned that the hard way, and so do we. His thorn in the flesh, whatever that malady may have been, was a painful reminder to the apostle that "power is made perfect in weakness" (2 Cor. 12:9), and when we are weak we are, in fact, strong. At the moment Paul depended on God in his inadequacy, God's grace invaded and transformed Paul's humanity. Paul sums up that gracious moment by saying, "I shall therefore prefer to find my joy and pride in the very things that are my weakness; and then the power of Christ will come and rest upon me. Hence I am well content, for Christ's sake, with weakness, contempt, persecution, hardship, and frustration; for when I am weak, then I am strong" (2 Cor. 12:9–10 NEB).

Lost Opportunities

If our pastoral shoptalk reveals the state of our hearts, not many of us understand the profound power of being clay pots. Most of our conversation focuses on our frustration and is often laced with cynicism or even self-pity. I can't remember a pastoral conversation that featured the triumph of being contented with weakness, hard times, frustration, and contempt. Nor do I remember telling a colleague that God's grace is sufficient for my weaknesses and that I, therefore, glory in the difficulties and burdens of the pastorate. In fact, I suspect that most of my professional frustration is the direct result of depending on myself and my own abilities to get the job done. I also suspect that the better we get at it or the more success we have, the more difficult it is to live in dependence on God's power.

If, on the other hand, Paul is right and God entrusts humans like us to do his work "to show that this all-surpassing power is from God and not from us" (2 Cor. 4:7), the implications for ministry are indeed profound and transforming.

A Word for the Church and Its Ministry in Times Like These

The Christian ministry and the Christian church must rest on a *theo*logical foundation. This century has witnessed the emergence of a doctrine of the church and a practice of ministry that is anthropological. American pragmatism has captured ecclesiology, and the practice of the church and ministry has become the theological base. By nature such thinking is centered in human ingenuity and ability. Note the pervasiveness of "how-to" books and seminars. Success, as humans measure such things, has become the implicit and often explicit goal of the church and pastors. Our thinking about the church or the ministry centers in accomplishing great things for God, but we easily substitute techniques and programs for the power of God.

One of my brothers-in-law is a member of a very conservative church that called a new pastor. This pastor guaranteed that if the church would follow the program that he had instituted in his other pastorates, the congregation would double in size in five years. They followed the program, and the growth didn't come. The disillusionment is great and the pastor's future uncertain.

One of the defining moments of my early ministry was the sudden realization that I wasn't the Holy Spirit. My job as a pastor was not to convict people of sin nor to turn their lives around. I didn't need to struggle against people nor manipulate them into doing the right thing. My role was to be a faithful witness to the truth of the gospel and to leave the results to the work of God's Spirit.

I recall the relief I felt at that moment of discovery. Suddenly the pressure was off. This was God's work, not mine. This was Christ's church, not mine. The Holy Spirit is sovereign, not me. I am responsible, for God trusted me, a clay pot, with his church and his truth. But if anything divine is to occur, it will be the gracious activity of God.

Over the years I keep forgetting what should be an unforgettable reality: I continue to find myself depending on my own work and energy and failing to trust the Lord of the church. It is a miracle whenever the gospel does its work. I just happen to be the clay pot in the right place at the right time by divine appointment.

In an age of superchurches and megachurch leaders we need a wake-up call from God. In fact, maybe the crisis of the clergy and the church in our time is precisely that wake-up call. The distress of the moment may be a call back to a church and ministry radically based on the sovereign power of God. "We have this treasure in jars of clay *to show that this all-surpassing power is from God and not from us*" (2 Cor. 4:7, emphasis added).

A Word to Proud Churches and Pastors

Believing in our own abilities is easy for us clay pots. Before long we trust in ourselves rather than in God. Those whom God trusts with impressive gifts and ministries are most prone to fatal self-confidence. When large numbers of people flock to hear us, follow our leadership, give their dollars to accomplish our vision, and trust their souls to our keeping, we tend to get puffed up. Success is intoxicating— we become full of ourselves. Successful techniques and programs can be idolatry—we depend on the golden calves we erect and even take credit for the worship of God's people.

I learned that lesson the hard way. My first church was a delightful series of successes. I was loved, followed, and trusted. The power of God was part of our corporate life. Nearly everything I tried worked. The ministry was fun from sunup to sundown the year round.

I went to my next church full of myself. I didn't realize it, of course. Pride is far too subtle for that. I said that all that success was from God and really believed it. But I was equally certain that all I had to do was give a repeat performance and the same good things would happen again.

I was dead wrong. I was the same person, preached the same kind of sermons, and led the same way. In turn, no one listened and no one followed. They really didn't like me much, and before long I returned the sentiment. It was awful. I woke up one day and realized that without the hand of God on my ministry I was utterly helpless. I began to learn how to take the truth of God with the greatest seriousness and not to take myself very seriously.

The ancient Greeks had a saying that adapts quite well to Christian ministry: "Those whom the gods would destroy they first make mad." Peter Drucker has a modern turn of phrase on the ancient wisdom: "Those whom the Gods would destroy, they first give ten years' success." The Bible is filled with even more powerful warnings against pride.

One of the most pointed warnings against the pride of success is the story of King Uzziah in 2 Chronicles. A good and godly king, he reigned for fifty-two years. Uzziah built up the nation, constructed great buildings, defeated Judah's enemies, and established the worship of God. Nevertheless, the chronicler sums up the end of Uzziah's reign in these powerful words, "His fame spread far and wide, for he was so wonderfully gifted that he became very powerful. But when he grew powerful his pride led to his own undoing" (26:15–16 NEB). Lest we forget the lesson, a few chapters later the chronicler reports on one of the greatest kings of all, the great Hezekiah, "Being a proud man, he was not grateful for the good things done to him and Judah and Jerusalem suffered for it" (32:25 NEB).

We live in a time of exceptionally gifted pastors. In fact, leadership in the evangelical world has passed from Christian organizations and institutions to the pastors of large churches. The entrepreneurial spirit that once built great schools and parachurch organizations now seems to rest on gifted pastors who are redefining the doctrine and work of the church. I suspect this is a movement of the Spirit that will not only create a new evangelism but will also force theologians and pastors to focus once again on the neglected doctrine of the church.

I fear that the so-called great churches of our day are far too dependent on the great men who lead them. Extraordinary leaders generate large crowds. Whether or not we intend to, churches become overly dependent on good or great leaders. Inevitably, pastors and people forget that we all are just clay pots and that all real success (and there is little doubt that we need to redefine success along biblical lines) depends on God. In fact, it is possible that what passes for churchly success is little more than human ingenuity and organizational techniques applied to church life.

When churches need to take out key-man insurance on their pastors, they have lost proper focus. When the successors to great leaders are usually "unintentional interims," it is clear that churches are more dependent on people than on God. When we think that our success can be cloned and we offer seminars that seem to guarantee similar success to whoever will pay the money, we have lost sight of the most fundamental fact of Christian ministry: All ministry is a gift from God, and everything depends on him. In fact, we may be flirting with an idolatry of techniques.

We can't imagine Paul or the other apostles offering church-growth seminars and charging people money to learn the apostolic techniques for outreach. I have no quarrel with seminars. I have learned more from them about pastoral ministry than I learned in seminary. But they tend toward the same fatal disease that afflicts seminary education: pride. Theological education tends toward dependence on knowledge while church seminars tend toward dependence on human techniques.

All of us so-called successful pastors need a good dose of humility. Perhaps the moral fall of so many of our colleagues is a wake-up call for us. Because nothing is so repellent to the non-Christian as spiritual pride, especially in Christian leaders, our ministries will be ineffective if we appear haughty. Our churches need to learn humility too. Church pride devastates ministry and generates a certain arrogance that is obvious to people in other churches as well as to non-Christians. But some church people can't seem to help finding their significance in their participation in a well-known church. The result is an inability to evaluate the life and ministry of the church.

Large churches naturally generate successful programs that easily become golden calves. Suddenly, what was once a means to a larger end becomes the end itself. Golden calves, pastoral or otherwise, generate pride in the clergy and lay leaders. Some of my most painful pastoral moments have occurred when I challenged golden calves. Even when the program no longer works, some of its devotees simply cannot stop worshiping at the shrine. My first church had a chapter of the Women's Christian Temperance Union (WCTV). In its heyday, the WCTV worked powerfully, but that time is gone. This chapter consisted of eight elderly women—all in their eighties—who still sang the old songs and even marched around a table, singing while putting their offerings in a little basket. They had no effect on the church or in the community, and they couldn't understand why. Peter Drucker says, When the horse is dead, dismount.[9] That's easier said than done. I know.

It is more than interesting that Paul begins most of his letters with a commendation to the addressee. Those commendations are worth noting, for they define a great church. The common theme that runs through Paul's commendations is "faith, hope and love." Needless to say, Paul elsewhere adds that the greatest of these three is love. Imagine how refreshing it would be for great churches today to be so designated independent of size, budget, and the other signs of ecclesiastical greatness in our time. Rather, a great church would be a congregation notable for its faith, hope, and especially love. After all, everything else will pass away.

A Word for Downcast Pastors

Working for God has never been easy. The prophets, apostles, and martyrs bear witness to the painful reality of ministry. Today is no different. Ministry is difficult in churches both large and small.

Pastors of large or growing churches know that the larger the church, the more difficulties there are. Sometimes it seems that all we do is negotiate between special interest groups, including our own staff. On the other hand, pastors of small gifts or small churches suffer from the terrible tendency to compare. Your congregation compares you to the big boys in the big churches, and you probably do too.

A friend of mine is a district superintendent for his denomination. He spent an early Sunday morning with a layman delivering the Sunday paper from a van. As they drove throughout the early morning they listened to John MacArthur, Chuck Swindoll, and Chuck Smith on the radio. Later, they arrived at the layman's small church. The pastor there hasn't a fraction of the gifts and skills of the radio preachers to whom his congregation listens daily. And because many in the congregation got ready for church, listening to the same trio of marvelously skilled communicators, their poor pastor didn't have a chance that morning. In fact, he loses the battle of comparison every time he enters his pulpit. He probably wonders why God called him into the ministry.

I spent a decade in small churches in small towns, and I know the power of comparison, the envy that hides behind insecurity, and the feeling that the big boys could not care less about the rest of us. I also know the seduction of unfulfilled ambition and how blinding it can be. To my everlasting shame, I also know how seemingly small ministry can erode the excellence necessary to gospel work. It is easy to be lazy when the stakes seem small.

Every small-church pastor knows the power of extended families and meaningless traditions. Leadership is often impossible. Evangelism is painfully slow because everybody knows everybody and small towns have few secrets. You can't hide church depravity behind anonymous numbers.

Paul doesn't seem to distinguish between the so-called successful and the rest of Christian pastors. All of us are clay pots entrusted with precisely the same treasure. There is no distinction between the pots; all of us are made of the very same stuff. We crack, chip, and break. And every pastor in Christendom works with the very same material: God's people and Christ's church. And in every single case we are inadequate, but God works through our feeble efforts anyway.

If you are downcast and weary, remember that all of heaven breaks into song when one sinner repents. Your work, whether large or small, bears the eternal weight of glory. If your labors produce but one transformed life, it is more than worth the struggle, and heaven sings.

A Final Word to All God's Pastors

Being human hurts and being a human pastor hurts intensely, for we bear the weight of people's lives and eternal destiny. Since we follow One who calls us to bear a cross, we shouldn't expect otherwise. Paul certainly didn't. With breathtaking honesty he bares his soul and reveals his pain in 2 Corinthians.

But Paul never tells of the hardships without relating another and more powerful truth. In the verses that follow his clay-pot metaphor he shows that the metaphor has meaning for the day-to-day labors of God's pastors: "We are hard pressed on every side, but not crushed; perplexed, but not in despair; persecuted, but not abandoned; struck down, but not destroyed. We always carry around in our body the death of Jesus, so that the life of Jesus may also be revealed in our body. . . . So then, death is at work in us, but life is at work in you" (2 Cor. 4:8–12). The triumph of the gospel is assured to all who labor for the Lord of the church—that is, if we believe that the gospel is indeed the power of God for us, for the church, and for the world.

7

God's Penmen: The Pastor's Impact

Are we beginning to commend ourselves again? Or do we need, like some people, letters of recommendation to you or from you? You yourselves are our letter, written on our hearts, known and read by everybody. You show that you are a letter from Christ, the result of our ministry, written not with ink but with the Spirit of the living God, not on tablets of stone but on tablets of human hearts.

—2 Corinthians 3:1–3

The phone rang during breakfast one Sunday morning. I knew it wouldn't be good news. I have learned that phone calls at odd hours usually mean bad news. In this case it was the worst news possible. A young godly and gifted woman from the congregation had been killed in an auto accident. Her boyfriend, another church member, was seriously injured and in the hospital. The woman's family had attended our church for years and served in leadership positions.

I have also learned through the years to say little and listen lots in the face of tragedy. I said about all that could be said: "I'm so very sorry. . . . God loves you. . . . I'm with you."

Then I hurried off to church for a long day of worship, ministry, and meetings.

I don't recall exactly what I said that morning when I announced the tragedy to the congregation. I was nearly overcome by my own emotions. What I do recall is that I chose my words very carefully. Public moments like these are profound pastoral and church opportunities for grace, and I wanted my words and manner of speech to be gracious and pastoral. The assembled people of God gasped in unison at the news.

What I didn't know was that the family was listening to the radio broadcast of our second morning service. I called after the morning services to see how the family was doing. All the mother wanted to say was how much my words to the congregation had been the grace of God for them.

Over the next week I talked to the family in person and on the phone and conducted the funeral. Each conversation was another powerful moment for all of us. The God who understands the death of a dearly loved child reached into this tragedy with amazing grace.

The next week I received this thank-you note from the mother:

> Mere words can never begin to express our appreciation for the way you have walked through the fire with us during these days. . . . Your love and concern and prayers and support have touched us deeply and helped to begin the healing of our hearts. Thank you for [conducting] the committal service. . . . It was just right. Your words, the Scriptures, and prayers touched us all.

As long as I live, I am bound to each member of that family with cords of love. The extreme moments of pastoral ministry do that kind of binding. But the ordinary moments are part of the binding too.

At the end of my first pastorate I did a little calculating. I had preached or taught nearly eight hundred times. I had attended approximately 250 board and committee meetings. I had visited in every home, and I had been to the hospital and nursing home nearly every week. I had also presided at the high moments of our common life: baptisms, weddings, and funerals. I had been there through the ordinary. And in all of it—nearly every minute—I had been talking! I realized that my ministry was a blizzard of words. Pastors talk all the time. That is what we are trained to do and often do very well. We always seem to have something to say.

At the end of my calculations another thought occurred. After I am gone, no one will remember much of what I said over those years. I am pretty sure that not more than one or two could give the outline of a sermon. I doubt if anyone could now remember the theme of any of those finely tuned messages on which I worked so long and lovingly. But they would never forget that I had been there. For better or worse, I had helped them write a chapter in the life of that church. I wondered what they would remember.

Just as powerfully, my first church had written a chapter in my life as a Christian pastor. It was there that I learned most of what I know about pastoral ministry and there that I formed my pastoral identity and my understanding of a Christian church. I don't remember much of what anyone said to me in those years, but I do remember a congregation who loved me, listened to me, and followed me. They still live in my heart, speaking volumes and ministering to my soul.

AN APOSTOLIC PENMAN

Paul used a metaphor to describe this relationship. He told the church at Corinth, "You yourselves are our letter, written on our hearts, known and read by everybody. You show that you are a letter from Christ, *the result of our ministry*, written not with ink but with the Spirit of the living God, not on tablets of stone but on tablets of human hearts" (2 Cor. 3:2–3, emphasis added).

God's Penman in Corinth

As in any church, there was more than enough mistrust and suspicion at Corinth. It soured the relationship between

Paul and the congregation. Some mistrusted Paul's motives and doubted his sincerity. Thus the church apparently wanted some of Paul's character references to write letters of recommendation to the church. His response was a lovely picture drawn in a metaphor: The church at Corinth was his letter of recommendation. Could the other apostles add any word to that letter? What more powerful recommendation could there be than the life of their church? After all, he writes, this churchly letter was "the result of our ministry" (2 Cor. 3:2). Paul was God's penman who, with the ink of the Holy Spirit, wrote lines on the hearts of each of them and, at the same time, penned the first chapter of that church's life.

Paul went on to say that being God's penman is a "glorious" ministry (v. 9). Each epistle written, whether personal or congregational, moves steadily toward its final goal under the power of the Spirit. The conclusion to each epistle is, in fact, a benediction. Each of us is "being transformed into [Christ's] likeness" (v. 18).

Pastor, Pen, and Ink

Each pastoral act, each word spoken, every Lord's Day and every other day, every relationship, conversation, meeting, or chance encounter is the pastor's opportunity to write the larger story of God's purpose for the universe. Paul writes elsewhere that at the end of time when God sums up all human history in Christ, Paul will stand before God and present every one of his parishioners "perfect in Christ." That is why he worked diligently at preaching, "admonishing and teaching . . . struggling with all his energy, which so powerfully work[ed]" in him (Col. 1:28–29). Much was at stake in Corinth. The heresy, division, and rancor that were destroying the church all served to erase the lines Paul had carefully traced on their hearts. Paul's letters and trips to Corinth each served to rewrite the story in that wandering church. And in all his writing Paul was conscious that while he held the pen and made the lines, deep in the soul it was the Holy Spirit writing in permanent ink.

PASTORAL PENMANSHIP

The penman/epistle metaphor loses much of its force in the modern world since we don't take penmanship or letter writing very seriously. But for most of history people took both with great seriousness. Penmanship was an art form for centuries, and letter writing served as the primary means of communication until very recently.

My wife has a box of letters written to her great-grandmother in the 1890s. Most are from her sisters who lived far from home and a brother in college. The letters are works of art. The penmanship is flowing and easy to read. Some of the capital letters have flourishes that set off the whole page. It is obvious that the words were chosen with care and phrases shaped with precision. Even the letters that seem to be written in a hurry bear signs of careful composition.

The content of the letters is the very stuff of life, from the weather and the crops to adjusting to marriage and the births of firstborn children. One sister writes of the trials of starting a family business. The other tells of their mother's regret that the sister lives so far away she may never come home. Brother writes about calculus class, a new girlfriend, and a classmate who died suddenly. The letters also bear news of other tragedies. One winter, four cousins died from diphtheria. Another letter was filled with grief. Their father died, and one sister couldn't come home for the funeral. Even religious humor creeps in occasionally in jokes about a rival denomination.

I had heard about these relatives for years. But after spending a few hours reading their letters, I felt like I knew them. Those letters are epistles from the heart, and they reveal the content of life and the character of the writers. Letters from the heart are revelatory.

That's Paul's point. Pastoral work is a form of letter writing that reveals the nature of our work and our character. The letters we write in the hearts of people, the chapters we pen in the lives of churches are far more than idle chit-chat. Our writing with the Holy Spirit's ink reveals the character of the gospel and Christ's church. Our work bears the marks and the weight of eternity. We make marks in permanent ink—for better or for worse.

Pastoral letter writing bears a certain beauty when crafted with care and undertaken with divine power. We should never be satisfied with anything less than our very best in any pastoral task, for we are marking God's people for life and eternity. We must never settle for mere human excellence in our labor. Any pastoral work, excellent or otherwise, not accompanied by the divine power will, in fact, fade from the page very soon. Pastoral work, by its very nature, is a work of grace and therefore must be conducted with all the character and beauty of the grace of God.

Pastoral Prose

Most homiletics texts suggest that sermons should be written in full whether delivered from a manuscript or from memory. Writing forces precision in thought, compactness of language, and careful vocabulary not present in extemporaneous speech. Writing is an act of mental and verbal discipline that is reflected in our preaching, our thinking, our conversations, and all our work.

The work of a pastor in the pulpit, study, or in the neighborhood is a matter of words and language. From our prayer to our preaching, we do our work in thoughts and words. Undisciplined preaching and pastoral work is an offense against the very nature of our work and the One who calls us to it. There is no substitute for clarity of thought and speech in pastoral work.

Paul's penman/letter metaphor raises the significance of fitly framed communication to a higher level. All our work with words in conversation and teaching is part of a larger act of communication: We are writing lives and churches. Our work includes all the elements of composition. In general, we must labor to be clear, precise, and correct. In particular, we are engaged in writing the story of faith. The smaller stories we pen are part of the larger story God is writing in the universe.

Like any story, our writing includes characters, plot, and movement. The cast of characters is diverse, and like good authors, our ministry is, in part, the development of these characters toward all God wants them to be. The plot is infinitely complex since it is the collective story of a community of fallen creatures. All plots are driven by tension that escalates until finally resolved at the end. The stories we write overflow with tension. The cast of characters alone, fallen people bent in the wrong directions, manufactures enough tension in our work to provide job security until the end of time. Add to the cast of characters that plot-twisting antagonist Satan and his hellish horde, and the plot certainly thickens.

The tension would be unbearable were it not for the ink of the Holy Spirit. God provides sufficient grace in the gospel to resolve the most twisted plot and to heal the most shattered character. Just when the tension takes us to the breaking point, grace and gospel break through, lives are transformed, and the peace of God guards lives and the church. Our work does not end with "And they lived happily ever after." We Christians always live "in the meantime" between the beginning of faith and its finish in eternity. God's sufficient grace provides everything necessary for all our "in the meantimes."

Not everybody can write a novel, and not every Christian can pen epistles. God calls and equips some of us to be his pastor-writers as he sees fit. Not all writers—or pastors—have equal talents and abilities, but God does expect us to develop the gifts he has given us. Rewriting, editing, and shedding sweat and tears are part of a good writer's work. Writing involves the continuous honing of one's skills. Writers work hard at finding just the right word. They live themselves into their characters. They continually search for ideas and plots. They even write when they don't feel like it. Their goal is to keep tightening their prose into more powerful vehicles of communication.

Pastors work the same way. We design our ministry especially for this church and that person. We continually analyze our work and our church in order to better develop the characters and move the plot along. We live ourselves into our people and communities in order to understand them and minister to them. It's the pattern of the Incarnation. All of this activity is part of God's movement in the universe. Our little stories are part of the great story God is writing.

Susan was only fifteen when I first wrote a line in her soul. She and her future husband, David, were among fifty high school kids won to faith in Christ through a youth ministry in our town. A bunch of those brand-new Christians renewed our aging church with their fresh faith and enthusiasm for Christ. They were incredibly teachable and open to whatever God wanted for them—Susan, perhaps, more than any.

I didn't know it until years later, but it seemed that nearly every word I said she remembered or wrote down. I have kept in touch with Dave and Sue over the years. Each time we are together, Sue tells me something else I once said that I don't remember saying but that changed her life. Dave and Sue are leaders in their church in a community far from where their Christian walk all started many years ago. But lines written in two lives and in a little country church took on a divine life, and now Dave and Susan write their own lines in another church—and in me.

Ralph and Kathy were two other teenagers in my first church. While in high school, they fell in love. One night the doorbell rang, and there stood Ralph and Kathy. They came in, and Ralph blurted out, "How can we control our sexual urges? It's driving us nuts!" I don't, for the life of me, remember what I said. All I remember is profound gratitude for their honesty and desire to obey Christ. But we have had lots of laughs since then as we recall their youthful passion.

They are now married and are leaders in their church and community. We see each other occasionally and talk about life and faith. This year Ralph joined Dave and me on our annual motorcycle trip. The three of us talked a lot about those early days of faith and ministry. Day after day I listened to these men talk and thanked God for the lines I was permitted to write on their lives then and the continuing writing ministry we now have in each other's lives.

Writing for God is a frightening and wonderful task. When Sue reminds me of things I said, I am grateful to God. I am equally aware that my pastoral writing needs editing and rewriting since it still falls far short of the character of the gospel I proclaim. I am still in God's writing school!

The Pastor as Poet

The artistry inherent in the penman/letter metaphor is extended a bit in Ephesians 2:10 where Paul says, "We are God's workmanship, created in Christ Jesus." The word translated "workmanship" is *poiema,* from which we get the English word *poem.* God is the poet, and we are his poems.

Just as God took the primeval world that was "without form and void" and created a universe of spectacular, infinite, and intricate beauty, he is in the process of turning this twisted, fallen mess of humanity into beautiful poems. Christ's church is a collection of poems in process, and pastors are God's co-workers in this great creative task.

I never understood or appreciated poetry until I got to know a poet. I have always been in too big a hurry to listen to poetry. I like fast-moving fiction, and I lack the patience necessary to appreciate the pictures and images formed by a poem. Recently, however, I have listened to my poet friend enough to know that I have missed a lot. I have slowed down and begun to appreciate the labor and artistry necessary for poetry. Poets work for weeks to find just the right word. Words and phrases must not only be precise, they must sound just right too. The right combination of sounds and meanings paints the desired picture. In fact, poetry is meant to be heard not read. In the end, the grace and beauty of the completed work conceal the long labor that created it.

Quite often, poetry is born out of pain and darkness. The skilled poet can create a work of beauty from the deepest tragedy. The hearer not only enters the poet's world of pain but stands aside to see the beauty created out of the darkness. Likewise, pastors help to create beauty out the ashes of life. The work of the gospel is always transformation, and we are the servants of that creative power of God.

Since it is an art form, our work must reflect the care and craftsmanship characteristic of artists. Texture, form, and beauty should characterize our words and our work. More important, our work must reflect the beauty of the gospel we serve.

This is far more than a lesson about preaching, though the woeful state of pulpit ministry certainly suggests that preachers can learn from Paul's metaphor. Rather, the metaphor speaks powerfully to the whole of our work. The work of the ministry should be as finely crafted as the best literature in the world. All we do should be the continual process of making our penmanship beautiful, the plot fascinating, and the characters fully developed. Our work as God's authors using the Holy Spirit's ink should always bear the character of the One who commissioned us to do the work.

LETTERS IN THE HEART:
THE WORK OF A PASTOR

The first time I thought of myself as God's penman was at my ordination. My father was the preacher, and his message was from this text in 2 Corinthians. I don't recall what he said, but I remember the image vividly. After all, I was seated in front of my congregation as he spoke. I visualized my hand reaching out to write God's lines in their hearts. My hand trembled as I extended it toward God's people. I knew I was an unskilled writer and feared lest a slip of the pen damage one of these people, the congregation, or misrender the truth entrusted to me.

Over the years I have never forgotten that moment and that image. I have since reflected long on it and continue to see my hand reaching out to the people of God. And still my hand trembles before the task. I trust that it always will. Paul's picture of pastoral ministry has shaped my own identity and my understanding of Christian ministry. Two theological principles along with two principles for pastoral practice emerge from the penman/letter metaphor.

Theological Principles

1. *Pastoral ministry is sacramental.* A sacrament is an earthly vessel that bears divine grace. God has marked off two sacraments, baptism and Holy Communion, as official church sacraments. While the various denominations of the church differ (often profoundly) on the nature and number of these gifts of divine grace, the whole church does agree on the principle. God's grace comes to us in earthly packages.

The Incarnation is the great and central sacramental model. God wrapped himself in human flesh and came to seek and to save us. He was, as John puts it, "full of grace and truth" (John 1:14). And Jesus, later in John's gospel, said, "But I, when I am lifted up from the earth, will draw all men to myself" (12:32). He draws us to himself because he is full of grace and truth.

The Christian church is an extension of the Incarnation. We are the body of Christ. Not fully divine like our Lord, but fully human, the church has the grace and truth of God in its hands and in its heart. Once in a while, in flashes of brilliance, we are even "full of grace and truth." We are in the process of becoming like Christ.

Christian pastors are called by God and gifted by the Holy Spirit to direct the life of Christ's church. Under construction ourselves and being filled with grace and truth, God builds people and the church through our work. We bear God's grace to God's people. We are not sacraments, but our work is sacramental.

The penman/epistle metaphor dramatically pictures our sacramental work. We are instruments whose lives and words make God's marks on souls as we act out and speak forth God's Word. While our hands must tremble as we grasp the pen of pastoral work, we work with the assurance that our feeble marks become the very etching of God on the soul. Since we are God's artists and our work is divine art, we must take great care in our work.

It is said of the great Scottish preacher Arthur Gossip that as he walked down the pulpit stairs at the conclusion of one of his masterful sermons it seemed as if God said to him, "Arthur, is that the best you could offer me?" The best we offer falls short of the divine standard set by the grace and truth of Christ himself. We dare not be satisfied with our work, for it bears God's name.

But, at the same time, we dare not become morose over our inadequacy. God loves us infinitely regardless of our performance, and God will bless our work because it is his Son's work. Our satisfaction rests in what God has done and not in what we do or how we do it. A holy discontent is inherent in pastoral ministry. We are proud and satisfied that God uses us but humbled and impatient that our best can never be fully grace and truth. All of this suggests that we take our pastoral work with divine seriousness without taking ourselves very seriously. Everywhere we go and whatever we do we bear God's grace in a unique fashion. We are writing epistles in divine ink, yet all the while we are very human instruments. That should make us smile at the irony and laugh joyously at the beautiful lines we write.

2. *Pastoral ministry is revelatory.* From the beginning, God revealed himself in human forms and language. The prophets and apostles were human voices speaking in language understandable to ordinary people in ordinary time. The fully human is God's form of presentation. Jesus Christ is the final and complete Word of God (Heb. 1:1–4). The church and its ministry bear witness to its Lord.

While the Christian church is not revelation, it is revelatory, because the empirical church reveals the grace and truth found in Jesus Christ. As the body of Christ, our message is the Word of God, and sometimes our very human forms bless the communication of the gospel and at other times inhibit it. The church is often an offense to its Lord and keeps many from clearly hearing and receiving the gospel message. Yet the very humanity of the people of God draws people to Christ. Nearly every Christian comes to faith through the witness of another fallible human being. The ring of truth that attracts us to Christ is the evidence of the gospel in another person.

Since our work writes divine lines in the hearts of God's people, pastoral ministry is revelatory. The letters we write are full of grace and truth and show the power of the gospel. The church as the great sign of the kingdom of God on earth must bear witness to the values of the gospel. The pastoral task is to bring the core values of very human churches into line with the character of the kingdom of God. The closer the correspondence the more revelatory the church.

Therefore, the integrity and character of Christian ministers cannot be overestimated. In order to write straight lines for God, our soul must be straight with God. Our writing, in itself, is revelatory. Pastors should be shaped far more by the values of the kingdom than by corporate America. Success in God's kingdom is measured in dramatically different fashion than in a corporate boardroom. The numbers of bodies, buildings, and budgets are not God's bottom line.

Jesus' great pastoral question to Peter after the Resurrection was not one often heard in pastoral shoptalk these days. "Peter, do you love me?" Jesus asked his great apostle. Three times he asked him the same question (see John 21:15–17). In the final analysis, that was what really mattered. Peter answered yes all three times. Then, and only then, did Jesus say to his pastor-apostle, "Feed my sheep."

The central value of the kingdom of God and, therefore, of the Christian church is the love of Christ. It is the standard against which our character is measured. If our letter writing for Christ does not flow from a heart passionately in love with

Jesus and God's people, it is little more than a clanging cymbal or the fading sound of brass.

Recently, I have added another image to my trembling hand outstretched toward God's people. Standing before the congregation is the risen Christ, who looks straight through my eyes and into my soul as he asks, "David, do you love me?" Before I dare answer, I remember that I cannot feed his sheep unless I love him and them with the same love. With repentant voice I answer, "Yes, Lord, I love you." He smiles and says, "Feed my sheep."

Back when I discovered that all my words, even those messages I thought brilliantly conceived, were or would be forgotten, I stumbled on to another and more profound truth. If they couldn't forget that I had been there, what would they remember? I hoped they would remember that I did my best, told the truth, and respected them. Above all, I hoped they would remember that I loved them. If all they recalled was my skills and theological acumen, as important as those may be, my ministry would be a waste of God's time and ink. If they remembered I loved them for Christ's sake, it would make all of it worthwhile.

I suppose I learned this lesson from being a father too. At the end of my life, when all is said and done and my children gather at the funeral to remember me, their walk down memory lane will not be about my fame, fortune, success, and ecclesiastical prowess. They will recall matters of the heart. They will know I was a man of Christian character and remember how I loved and nurtured them. In fact, I hope they will put something about my heart on my tombstone.

Only love for Christ who first loved us will ever make our letter writing both sacramental and revelatory. In the depth, width, height, and breadth of Christ's love the church and its pastors become full of grace and truth.

The Pastoral Practice of Letter Writing

1. *Letter writing is done with the language of affection.* If the character and integrity of the gospel demand a ministry

that flows out of divine love, it follows that the practice of ministry is, in fact, writing a love letter. We write God's lines because we have begun to grasp the magnitude of God's love, and we do our writing lovingly because God's people are the apple of his eye and ours too.

I am continually amazed at Paul's affection for the Corinthian church. They annoyed him, exasperated him, and even depressed him, yet he never stopped loving them and telling them so. After telling them how much they tried his apostolic soul, Paul writes, "We have spoken freely to you, Corinthians, and opened wide our hearts to you. We are not withholding our affection from you, but you are withholding yours from us. As a fair exchange—I speak as to my children—open wide your hearts also" (2 Cor. 6:11–13).

I find Paul's pastoral love quite convicting. My annoyance with the church quickly turns to anger and its sophisticated evil twin, cynicism. I tend to close my heart to people who have hurt me or despitefully used me. I want my ecclesiastical enemies to go away. I want to win more than I want to do the right thing.

Then I remember Philippians 1:7 where Paul says to the church in Philippi, "I have you in my heart." Novelist Frederick Beuchner suggests that all of us need "a room called Remember"[1] in our hearts. It is a place set aside for people we love and who have loved us. There we hang pictures on the wall and stroll through thinking about our loved ones. Paul had room in his heart for the church at Philippi. The walls were full of pictures: the Philippian jailer and his family and probably a few prisoners from the jail, too, Lydia, Euodia, Syntyche, Epaphroditus, Clement, and other loyal yokefellow to name a few. In the dark moments of Paul's imprisonment he wandered through the room called "Philippi" lost in wonder, love, and praise.

I keep reminding myself to tuck all my church folk deep into that room in my heart called Remember. Some of them keep escaping and running up to my mind where they argue with me and mess with my soul. But I have to put them back. I tuck them back into my heart where by God's grace I love them with the affection of Christ, for I cannot serve those whom I do not love.

2. *Pastoral ministry is personal.* It goes without saying (or does it?) that ministry in Christ's church is, at the bottom line, working with people and not with buildings, budgets, and other institutional matters. After all, the church is no more or less than the people organized to serve the gospel. Paul and all other pastors write chapters of a church's corporate life by writing on the hearts of the people.

That truth is easy to forget, especially in a large or traditional church where institutional values loom so great in ministry. Big churches are incredibly complex social organisms that can marginalize ministry to people. My life sometimes seems like a series of meetings that accomplish little except to serve the values of the institution. Preaching is reduced to mass communication in the hope that some word will find the anonymous souls gathered to hear from the Lord.

But I also remember the complicated nature of the small churches I pastored. There I looked every person in the eye each Sunday. I knew everyone quite well—perhaps too well. I knew about frustrating, even sick, family systems; long-lasting personal feuds; and old sins that kept on hurting; and I knew enough gossip to last a lifetime. All of it hindered the progress of the gospel and the work of the church. I also remember small-town pettiness, meetings without leaders, lack of excellence, and hidebound traditions. I remember wondering if God would ever break through all the human junk.

Then I take a stroll down from my mind to that room in my heart full of people sent into my life. I wander around smiling, remembering and thanking God for each of them. Some God transformed; others transformed me by frustrating me. All of them are dearly loved children of God.

I remember the Thanksgiving service when we all took turns telling what we were thankful for. Suddenly, it had dawned on me what a gift this church was to me. I had chosen to come there rather than to pursue graduate studies. I second-guessed myself when the realities of pastoral life hit me. But like a light that flashed in my heart, I realized that I loved these people and that they had begun to reshape my heart. It had shrunk from so much education, and these simple and sinful people had stretched it in every direction. I stood before them and told them I loved them and was thankful that God had sent me there. They opened their hearts wide, as their beaming smiles revealed. We had discovered together the heart and soul of Christian ministry in the church of Christ.

Perhaps the real bottom line of pastoral ministry and epistle writing is my heart. After all, Paul introduces the metaphor by saying that the Corinthians were a "letter, written on [his] heart." The churches I have pastored have given me as much or more than I have given them. Each in its own way has tugged at and shaped and stretched my heart, filling it with love and grace and bestowing on me the benediction of God.

I have had the wonderful opportunity to be God's penman. Some of the marks I have been privileged to make are remarkable indeed. A teenage girl told me that a children's sermon I had given when she was nine years old was the slender reed of hope to which she had clung through years of sexual abuse by her father. Now she is recovering by God's grace. My marks on her life are the work of God. Wow! But when she told me that story, she in turn wrote a deep and permanent line on my heart.

I have a file in which I keep letters and notes from parishioners. Each is testimony to the epistle-writing nature of the Christian ministry. Each letter tells of a line God drew in one of his children through my words or pastoral acts. Occasionally I browse through that file to remind myself of the power of the ministry. That file is supplemented by a vault in my mind where I store pastoral conversations. I remember words and acts in which I have been God's penman and marked one of God's children with grace.

My prayer is that slips of the pen in my trembling hand will be fewer and farther between. I ask God to make me a more skillful and creative author, even a divine poet, so that my pastoral life will increasingly fill God's people with grace and truth, and so that the world will see the beauty of the Good News I proclaim.

8

Both Mother and Father: The Pastor's Heart

We were gentle among you, like a mother car-
ing for her little children. We loved you so much that
we were delighted to share with you not only the gospel
of God but our lives as well, because you had become
so dear to us. Surely you remember, brothers, our toil
and hardship; we worked night and day in order not
to be a burden to anyone while we preached the gospel
of God to you.

You are witnesses, and so is God, of how holy,
righteous and blameless we were among you who
believed. For you know that we dealt with each of you
as a father deals with his own children, encouraging,
comforting and urging you to live lives worthy of
God, who calls you into his kingdom and glory.

—1 Thessalonians 2:7–12

A veteran pastor, Malcolm Cronk, came to speak to my
seminary's married students fellowship. I was busy holding

down three part-time jobs while studying full-time, but because it was Malcolm Cronk who had touched my soul, as my pastor, my wife and I went to the meeting.

I'm not sure what I expected, but I got what I needed. Toward the end of his talk, Dr. Cronk admonished, *"If you don't love people, stay out of the pastorate!"* I was stunned into consciousness. Deep in my soul I knew he was right, but my head argued violently against the point. I was in love with ideas. Daily I soared into the stratosphere of disembodied concepts wrapped tightly in books and encoded by scholars. It was a very safe world. I loved every minute of it. But people! That was a different story.

I grew up in a parsonage and knew about people. I knew from bitter experience that church people were every bit as cruel and hurtful as people in the secular world. I had seen my parents' pain, and as a result, I carried a load of unresolved anger and resentment. I really didn't want to love people. I wanted to teach them, scold them, change them, perhaps even hurt them, but I did not want to love them.

Yet deep down inside I knew Cronk was right. And when I landed in a small-town church surrounded by very ordinary people full of delights, difficulties, and pains, the pastoral instinct to love people took on flesh and blood. In the process that instinct became profound conviction. I discovered a pastor's heart. The people of that little church were my first teachers. They loved me and my family. They gave us their lives and along the way gave me their souls. The experience was overwhelming and transforming. I fell in love with that church and its people.

Scripture came alive in ways I had not imagined. First it lived in me, and then I delivered it to my people with enthusiasm. All of us changed—me most of all. Like all fledgling pastors, I was wrestling with my new identity as a Christian pastor. I longed to discover who I was in this new role. One morning I was reading 1 Thessalonians. As I was reading, suddenly a metaphor leaped out of the text and grabbed my soul, and my life has ever been the same. I read, "But we were gentle among you, *like a mother caring for her little children.* We loved you so much that we were delighted to share with you not only the gospel of God but our lives as well, because you had become so dear to us" (2:7–8, emphasis added). I had never in my life thought of myself as a mother. But Paul had! My pastoral identity took a surprising and radical new shape. I was a church mother!

But the text wasn't finished with me yet. I read on. Another metaphor in verse 11 jumped out at me. "For you know that we dealt with each of you *as a father deals with his own children,* encouraging, comforting and urging you to live lives worthy of God" (emphasis added). Certainly this was an easier metaphor to grasp for a male, but it was equally transforming. I was also a father to God's children!

I recall looking up from the biblical text with lights going on all over in my mind. Here was a biblical model for pastoral identity. I was a parent in God's house, and I knew that I had some changing to do. I had to develop a feminine side of myself that I had never considered—a gentle mother. And I had to be a father to the church too. Both roles would be difficult. Being a male mother is no small feat! And being a father to people more than twice my age would be a challenge. But there it was—a strategic model for pastoral identity in a double metaphor, a model that was biblical, apostolic, theologically fertile, and rooted deep in human experience.

I realized the powerful implications. If the pastor is like a parent, the church is a family. It is a place to grow. It is where people love you simply because you belong to them. There you are always welcome and are cared for and kept safe from harm. Family love is foundational and is so deep in us that it defies description. But we sure do know it when we have it! If anything is certain on this fallen planet filled with uncertainties and broken promises, it is that my mother and father love me.

Sadly and tragically, families can be very dangerous too. Families can twist the soul, torment the mind, and ruin lives.

We have all seen the damage, and some of us have experienced it. Even churches can be dangerous, especially when they pervert the good news into bad news in people's lives. The church can turn the liberating grace of God into a tyranny of the soul. Pastors, therefore, as parents in the house of God, bear a deep parental responsibility. God trusts us to care for his children in his house.

As parents in God's household, we exist to grow God's children to maturity. Leadership is fundamental to parental guidance. In God's house, pastors are called to move heaven and earth into the lives of God's growing children. We are called to lead the people and the organization they form toward God's goals and objectives. Like Moses leading the children of Israel toward the Promised Land, we must be strong and wise to lead God's children through this life and onward to God's heavenly home.

But more than anything, the mother/father metaphor describes a pastor's heart. Being a mother and father to God's children demands a proper heart, yet at the same time continually and powerfully molds the heart into precisely the right shape.

A MOTHER'S HEART: GENTLE GRACE

Like all leaders, including pastors, Paul faced false accusations. People tend to judge the motives of their leaders without sufficient evidence, especially when another leader suggests that the leader is devious. Some of the Christians in Thessalonica listened to false accusations against Paul. He wrote 1 Thessalonians, in part, to defend himself against rumors that he didn't tell the truth, was motivated by money and glory, used trickery to deceive them, and probably would never come back to Thessalonica (2:1–6, 17–18).

The Pastor as Mother

Of course, nothing could have been further from the truth. But notice how Paul defends himself. Significantly, he introduces his point with the powerful image of a mother's heart. In fact, the metaphor could be translated "nursing mother." Paul wanted them to remember his deep affection for them. The picture of mother and child unmistakably suggests tenderness. Few portraits of a mother's heart are more mysteriously powerful than that of a mother nursing her child. Stroking, cuddling, cooing, a mother gently holds her child, giving her very body and soul away in love. It is nurture personified. And that is what Paul modeled in Thessalonica.

The substance of the image defines the pastor's heart. Paul's point is the gentleness that characterizes motherhood and his pastoral ministry. He goes on in verse 8 to say he loved them so much he "[was] delighted to share . . . not only the gospel of God but [my life] as well." A mother's heart is willing to make the ultimate sacrifice—life itself. From conception she willingly gives her body away, exchanging her life for the child's. Paul's audience knew full well that in their world pregnancy and childbirth often took the life of the mother.

The picture of mother and child lies deep in the human soul. Our art, music, literature, and culture are filled with it. It is a picture that captures all that is noble and good in human experience. In seminary I served as youth pastor in a Chicago metropolitan church. Between pastors, we had a kindly old interim pastor. One Sunday an infant started crying in church. The mother tried to hush the child, but nothing worked. The child kept crying as people sitting nearby became more uncomfortable. Finally, the old pastor stopped his sermon and said, "What more beautiful sound in all the earth than mother with child." The tension was broken by the powerful picture of motherhood. (I filed that one away for future use and have used it sparingly and effectively!)

The figure of mother is more than beauty; it is sheer power. In Yad Vashim, the Holocaust museum outside Jerusalem, stands an awful picture that captures the horror of the Holocaust and the power of motherhood. It is the picture of a mother and her children standing in front of a trench, about to be shot by Nazi soldiers. All of them are naked. The mother asks the soldiers to take her life and spare her children. Weeping, she holds out one hand for mercy while covering the eyes of her small son with the other. Paul writes that he gave the Thessalonians his very life. Mothers and pastors do that.

I think I understand that kind of love. I know my mother would lay down her life for me. My wife would give her life for our children, and so would I. But I must confess that I do not understand the depth of Paul's pastoral heart in Romans 9:3 where he says he was willing to be damned if it meant Israel would be saved. Like his Savior, Paul was ready to crawl up on an altar to die for the sake of others. Dare any of us pray that God will give us a heart in the shape of a cross?

I do know the reason Paul could think that way. The framework of such a sacrificial heart is the amazing grace of God. In 1 Thessalonians 2:4 Paul says that he is a man "approved by God to be entrusted with the gospel." Scripture clearly asserts that no human being dares to claim God's approval outside of sheer grace. Approval and acceptance by God comes only through the work of Christ (Eph. 2:8–9). And who dares to suggest that he or she deserves to be entrusted with the gospel? Most of us have enough trouble balancing our checkbooks. Yet God trusts us with his reputation, his church, and his truth. That is sheer grace.

The Necessary Grace of Motherly Ministry

God's grace forms the character of the Christian ministry. We are givers of grace because we have received sheer grace. Yet we often fail to realize the power of the grace we are able to give.

I learned that lesson in the heat of the pastoral battle. Vicki, an unmarried fifteen-year-old foster child of a couple who were members of our church, was pregnant. Her foster mother forced her to talk to me. She came into my office, sullen and unwilling to talk. I tried everything I could think of to get her to tell me what she was feeling or thinking.

Nothing worked. She sat as silent as a stone. Finally, in what I now think was divine insight, I said, "Vicki, on behalf of this church and in the name of Christ, I forgive you." She melted like ice in the July sun. Tears poured from her eyes as God unlocked her heart.

I did not give God's forgiveness. That came later. But I gave her the grace that is enfleshed in a congregation of God's people. That word of forgiving grace opened the door to God's ultimate grace. And, thank God, that congregation gave her loads of grace to accompany God's.

The same grace forms the church. No one deserves to be part of God's family. We are accepted because of Christ's sacrifice in our behalf. The kind of grace must form the character of the church and be given away lavishly by the ministers and people of Christ's church.

Mothers know about the gentle power of grace. Once I discovered Paul's mother metaphor, I began to listen to mothers carefully. I discovered a mysterious and powerful umbilical cord of the spirit that joins mothers and children.

A seventy-five-year-old woman came to see me for pastoral counseling. She sat down and with copious tears told me the sad story of her son. Now fifty years of age, he had fought a losing battle with alcohol all his adult life, and the latest battle had landed him in prison. She stopped in the middle of her story and asked if I thought it odd that an old woman was weeping for her middle-aged son. Then she said words that are imprinted in my mind: "A mother's heart never stops beating and cannot stop caring." This is grace in human form.

A mother's grace keeps the door open at all times. She always has a listening ear, a warm embrace, and an encouraging word. Her acceptance has no limits and her forgiveness no boundaries. She cannot give up on her own. Her heart has no eraser that can eliminate her love, which is like that described in 1 Corinthians 13:4–7: "Love is patient, love is kind. It does not envy, it does not boast, it is not proud. It is not rude, it is not self-seeking, it is not easily angered, it keeps no record of wrongs. . . . It always protects, always trusts, always hopes, always perseveres."

But because a mother's heart is gentle, wrapped in bands of love, it breaks easily. I recall a mother's telling me about her broken heart. Her son was a college student who delighted in belittling her. I suppose it was the first signs of independence, but the price was exceedingly high. He pointed out her intellectual deficiencies and personal faults. He made her feel small, dumb, and unappreciated. Above all, she felt unloved by one to whom she had given life.

Every pastor lives with a broken heart. We give the greatest gift anyone can give—our lives. The years spent in any church are time that can never be recovered. So when that gift is rejected, it is heartbreaking. Paul knew that. The church in Corinth rejected his leadership, despised his looks, and mocked his preaching. Second Corinthians is, in part, the testimony of Paul's broken heart. Yet in the middle of the book stands a remarkable statement: "We have spoken freely to you, Corinthians, and opened wide our hearts to you. We are not withholding our affection from you, but you are withholding yours from us. As a fair exchange—*I speak as to my children*—open wide your hearts also" (6:11–13, emphasis added).

My heart was broken early. The hurt was intense because my love was strong. A little congregation taught me grace and loved me. They surprised me with their affection. More than any other factor, they formed me into a Christian pastor and taught me how to love. I fell in love with them quickly, intensely, and irrevocably. I told them so. They are still my first love with a special place in my heart.

Yet out of the wonderful love story of those early years rises another pervasive theme: They hurt me deeply. That figures. Those we love have the capacity to hurt us most. I guess I thought that loving me meant they wouldn't criticize me. Their criticism cut me to the core. Some thought I spent too much time with a couple in the church. Others thought a powerful man controlled me. Someone thought I didn't like women. Another didn't like my voice. It didn't matter that only a few complained, nor did it ease the pain to know that I am sinfully critical myself and deserved some of the criticism. It seemed more than I could bear, and I marked my journal with bitter tears as I recorded each incident. I cried because I cared, and the real surprise was that I didn't stop loving them. When I left that church, I thought my heart would break in two. I still love them two decades later with the love of a mother's heart.

None of this should surprise us. After all, God is often pictured in the Old Testament as Israel's mother. One of the most touching pictures is the prophet Zephaniah's description of God singing a lullaby to Israel, quieting Israel with love (3:17). The prophet Isaiah portrays God holding Israel's hand and teaching Israel how to walk (Isa. 66: 12–13). In the New Testament, Jesus wept over Jerusalem and said many times that he wished he could be a mother to his people, protecting them like a hen who hides her chicks under her wings (see, e.g., Matt. 23:37).

Some congregations are easier to love than others. I suspect that the longer one remains in ministry, the more difficult it is to fall in love with a people and stay that way. Long memories and accumulated scars create caution, even fear. But love is the vocation of the Christian pastor. God so loved the world that he sent his Son. And God sends us in the name of his Son to bring his infinite love to the world, including the most unlovable of people. If more of us were biological mothers, we would understand that much better. In the meantime I keep asking God for a mother's heart.

A FATHER'S HEART: URGENT MERCY

It is probably no surprise to any of us that a pastor is like a father. It may be quite surprising, however, to note that the work of the pastor-father is "encouraging, comforting and urging." That's not quite the image of father we might expect. It's a far cry from the stereotypical stern, aloof, and distant father.

Our Heavenly Father

But Jesus taught us to call God *abba*, the familiar term for a father, perhaps best translated as "papa." It is a tender, affectionate, and gentle word. Jesus filled in the definition of *abba* in his story about the waiting father and his prodigal son, a story of marvelous and amazing grace. The *abba* in the story patiently waited for his wayward and foolish son to return. When he saw him far in the distance, he ran to him, robe flowing behind him, arms outstretched, and tears coursing down his cheeks. He welcomed the boy home with not a word of recrimination—no "I told you so," "It's about time," or "See what you've done to your mother." His every word and gesture spoke of acceptance, affirmation, forgiveness, and unconditional restoration. To prove his point he threw a party to end all parties. What motivation for the poor lost boy! How encouraging and comforting when the best he expected was slavery. How unlike the motivation in most families and churches where acceptance follows achievement and affirmation must be earned. The waiting father is God's description of himself, fathers, and pastors.

The Heart of a Father

Even if we don't act like the waiting father, deep inside we know about grace. When my oldest son was a high school freshman, he set an ambitious goal. He wanted to earn a varsity letter in track. He went to the coach and asked what he had to do. The coach told him that if he ran the mile under five minutes, he would earn his letter.

Since I was a high school miler, I helped my son set his strategy. I went to all the meets and shouted my encouragement. The season progressed, and he was right on schedule. Soon it was time for the last meet of the season, his final opportunity. He was ready, and I went to help.

During the race, I stood by the finish line with my stopwatch. Each lap I called out his time and told him how close he was to the schedule he had set. He was right on time the first three laps. As he headed into the last lap, I could see he was tired. I knew it would be close. Up the backstretch he began to labor but was still all right. As he headed into the last turn, he began to struggle. As he came out of the turn and into the homestretch, all my world reduced to the figure of my struggling son. Suddenly, to my surprise, I heard myself utter a primal sound from a place so deep in me I didn't know it existed. His agony was mine, and all I could do was groan.

He made his goal and won his letter, and I received another lesson in pastoring that day. Being a father to God's children includes encouraging and urging that comes from so deep in the soul it defies location. That groan for God's children finds its source in a love straight from the heart of God. It is a gift given to pastors who ask for a new heart. I have spent twenty-five years now groaning for my spiritual children in the race of Christian faith. Sometimes the intensity of my groaning surprises me, and it reminds me of that call from God that grips my soul and will not let me go.

But my pastoral education was not complete the day of the track meet. My daughter participated in sports too. Basketball was her great love. Every game day, I took her to breakfast, and we would talk strategy. I quickly learned that she was different from her brother. For every criticism, I needed to give her at least ten encouragements. She responded powerfully to encouraging words, but critical words singed her soul. My groans for her came from the same place, but along the way the technique for delivery had to change. I knew I had succeeded when one Father's Day she told me the one word that characterized me as father was "encourager." I thanked God.

The role of pastoral father includes a large measure of encourager. We assist the Great Encourager, the Holy Spirit, who gives the gift of encouragement to the church. We are, in part, God's cheerleaders for his children. We ache for their success, and when their lives take on the character of the Gospel, we have no greater joy.

My youngest son grew up in the shadow of these two overachievers. He competed by not competing. He wanted to carve out his own space and do his own thing. One night at the dinner table we were having our usual discussion centered in sports activities and accomplishments. Suddenly, he dropped his fork and said, "Do you have to be a jock to be in this family?" I was stunned, and that is when I began another chapter in learning about being a father.

Later that evening, after I had thought a bit, I sat him down and made him look me in the eye. I told him what I should have told him every day of his life. "Son," I said, "your value in this family comes not from anything you do or don't do. Your value lies in the name you bear. You have my name! You cannot make me stop loving you."

The Pastor As Father

That experience with my youngest son helped me realize how much of church life centers in the overachievers who earn our respect and affection by their works. Meanwhile, many of God's children wonder if they have a place in the family. Wise pastors know how to spread encouragement wherever they go.

In fact, one of the lessons I find most difficult to learn is that I need to tell every congregation again and again that I love them. I suspect that most male pastors withhold those words from their congregation for the same reason we seldom express our love to those we love best. Saying "I love you" is about as intimate as we can be. It brings great vulnerability with it and the voluntary surrender of power. We are giving away the deepest part of our being, yet gaining the most valuable experience of life: love.

I suggested to some pastor friends that we should tell our people we love them more than we do. None of them agreed with me. One even admitted that he didn't feel much affection for his congregation, and another said such talk would rob him of power necessary to lead. I am convinced that nothing could be further from the truth. Real leadership power flows from gospel values centered in loving affection. And a pastor with little affection for his congregation needs a ruthless vocational evaluation.

All of us know the power of a loving, encouraging, and comforting word. When I was preparing for the ministry, I was intimidated by the prospect of being a pastor. The requirements seemed impossibly high and the tasks incredibly difficult. Since I grew up in a pastor's home, I knew some of the challenge and the pain. I came home from seminary, and in my despair told my dad that I didn't think I had the stuff to be a pastor. I half expected him to agree. After all, he knew me and my inadequacies perhaps better than I.

He quickly responded, "Oh, yes, you do!" That was God's word to me for that moment. I believed him because he was my father, he was a pastor, he knew me, and more important, he loved me. The power of that encouraging word still sustains me. As pastors we can encourage people in precisely the same way.

Now I often find myself giving encouraging words to individuals and to the church. By God's grace those words carry divine power, and sometimes I don't realize just how much power. But time after time, people tell me that a simple word said in passing made a difference in their lives.

One time I was able to encourage our entire church when it was in need of a new building. The church was not large and did not have great financial resources. They wondered if their meager supply could possibly meet a million-dollar challenge. The church had never had a very high opinion of itself, never hoped for much beyond the ordinary. The most visionary leader in the church thought we could probably raise two hundred thousand dollars.

I believed we could rise beyond all our expectations for the sake of the kingdom of God. I spent lots of pulpit time urging the congregation to believe that God is big enough to do great things. I encouraged the congregation's leadership to think big because the challenge before us was huge. I tried my best to say to doubting people, "Oh, yes, we can do it by the grace of God." I knew them and loved them. I was convinced they could accomplish far more by faith than they imagined.

By grace they believed God would do it. What a celebration we had the day I announced that the congregation had made financial commitments of more than a half million dollars! Encouraging people in the power of God does amazing things.

Wise fathers also know that some children need tough love and hard words. A couple in our church was on the brink of defecting to a cult. They didn't need encouragement or comfort as much as they needed powerful urging. I did something I seldom practice: I sat them down and said, "By my authority as the shepherd of your souls, I demand that you forsake your foolish ways, leave this dangerous group, and return to Christ's church." To my amazement, they repented and returned! Sometimes being a father is difficult and uncomfortable, but God's grace transcends human efforts to accomplish divine things.

More often, though, we need to give comforting words. I recently talked to a young man who was struggling at the beginning of his career. He went to his father to tell him of the struggle. According to the son, his father immediately began to tell him that the son's problems were nothing compared to his—hardly comfort and certainly little encouragement.

Another time the phone rang deep in the night. The voice at the other end told me that a young man named Darrell had been killed in a car wreck, and his mother needed me. Trembling, I dressed and made my way through the dark to the family home. *What could I possibly say at a moment like this?* I wondered. I no sooner got through the back door than she grabbed me and sobbed and sobbed. I thought she would never let go. Finally, in a moment of what I believe was divine insight, I said, "I don't know what to say except this. God understands your pain. He lost a boy too." It was God's word for the moment. Spiritual fathers bring comfort to God's children.

I am continually amazed at the power of pastoral words. The Word of God preached with conviction encourages, comforts, and urges. People actually remember, and those words accomplish eternity in their souls. But words spoken in private also carry divine weight. A young man is in ministry today because I told him that he was gifted and could do it. A woman knows forgiveness because during Communion I looked her in the eye and said, "Neither do I condemn you. Go and sin no more."

Recently I preached in a church where for several decades they have made the love of God the center of their congregation's life. The senior minister and the rest of the staff talked and lived the amazing love of Jesus. One of the assistant pastors was my host for the day. Everywhere we went, she introduced me to people and told me how wonderful they were. She also gave an encouraging word to them as we moved on. It was astonishing how the atmosphere of the congregation overflowed with encouraging love, and this chain reaction of encouragement all started with the love of a pastor for his people. He was bold enough to tell his people that he loved them and powerful enough to give power away in his words of affection.

The grace of the waiting father forms the church and its ministry. We can never fully understand it or manifest it as God does, but hints of it lie deep in the hearts of mothers and fathers. Perhaps that is why Paul says that being a pastor is like being a father and mother. I do know this: Being a Christian pastor is, at a very fundamental level, having a heart shaped by the grace of God.

What a terrifying responsibility. No wonder Paul asks, "Who is equal to such a task?" (2 Cor. 2:16). God trusts us with his children. We are foster parents for God. These children of his carry infinite value and are the objects of the incomprehensible love of God. For God's sake we love them with all our hearts.

9

FARMERS AND BUILDERS: GROWING CHRIST'S CHURCH

What, after all, is Apollos? And what is Paul?
Only servants, through whom you came to believe—
as the Lord has assigned to each his task. I planted the
seed, Apollos watered it, but God made it grow. So
neither he who plants nor he who waters is anything,
but only God, who makes things grow. The man who
plants and the man who waters have one purpose,
and each will be rewarded according to his own labor.
For we are God's fellow workers; you are God's field,
God's building.

—1 Corinthians 3:5–9

I have been intimidated by medicine, disease, and hospitals ever since I can remember. So when the search committee of my first congregation took me to the hospital to visit the man who would be my predecessor, I was less than eager.

When they told me he was on his deathbed, I cringed. I had never talked to a dying person before, and of course, I had never met a predecessor either. He wanted to meet me, and I needed to know him.

I wasn't ready for the sights, sounds, and smells I encountered when we walked into the room. The effects of a massive stroke had paralyzed half the man's body. His breathing was labored and assisted by an oxygen tube in his nose. There was little conversation, since his lopsided mouth could barely form words.

He got right to the point. In fact, his point was one of my concerns. He planned to retire the next month and had fixed up a little house next door to the church for his wife and himself. With great effort he told me that he wanted me to know that he wouldn't do anything to jeopardize my ministry. I'm sure he meant every word.

Nevertheless, I was worried. My dad's horror stories about retired predecessors who stayed in town loomed larger than this predecessor's sincere promise. I knew a person couldn't give twelve years of his life to a congregation like this man had and suddenly forsake that investment without a thought, word, or gesture. Especially when that person lived next door!

As it happened my predecessor's promise to me was among his last words. He died within a week—before I began my ministry. His widow moved into the house next door where she served as a delightful neighbor and wise counselor. Her private and public support of me never wavered, but when the church began to grow and the Spirit moved in power she told me she was troubled.

"Why" she wondered aloud, "didn't these blessings from God come when my husband was pastor?" When that moving of the Spirit reached across the entire community touching most of the churches in town, she asked the same question at a gathering of the clergy and spouses. She was genuinely troubled. In human terms I had succeeded where her beloved husband hadn't. She made her very human question sound spiritual, but even spiritualized, it came out pretty much the same. I had received the blessing of God denied my predecessor, her husband. The church was on fire with the Spirit. The congregation loved me and thought I was pretty wonderful. They told me so. Of course, I loved every minute of it. Needless to say, her late husband suffered by comparison.

Our clergy group listened quietly as she talked. I think all of us felt her pain. Finally, and it seemed reluctantly, she paused and said, "[Paul] planted, Apollos watered; but God gave the increase" (1 Cor. 3:6 KJV). With a bit of reluctance myself, I admitted to myself and to her that she was absolutely right. The moving of the grace of God is always a mystery before which we bow, not a formula we devise.

It also dawned on me that the twelve years her husband had faithfully and lovingly served the church were inherently part of the blessing I received. In fact, I stood on the shoulders of all my predecessors, each of whom formed part of the larger story. And none of the story would have happened without hundreds of faithful laypeople who gave their prayers, energy, love, and dollars to the work of God in that place. And amid everything, "God made it grow."

That widow's struggle and citation of 1 Corinthians 3:6 has stayed with me over the years. My own experience and conversations with pastors indicate that jealousy, rivalry, and gossip plague pastors and churches today as in Corinth nineteen hundred years ago. Predecessors have difficulty giving their blessing to their successors, and successors are jealous of their predecessors. Colleagues in ministry are too often rivals, and shoptalk among us includes the very gossip we resent in our parishioners.

I am still waiting for any of my predecessors to give me their blessing or tell me that I am doing well. Of course I don't want to ask them for it or seek other advice either. I am weary of rumors about me and my congregation that circulate among my colleagues, but I admit that my ears are wide open for bad news about my colleagues or their churches.

It seems that we are a lot like the church in Corinth. As Paul puts it, we evaluate each other and the Christian ministry as "mere men" (1 Cor. 3:3). Too often our pastoral and ecclesial sight falls short of a biblical vision. First Corinthians 3 and 4 give us a glimpse of the church and its ministry that is both apostolic and divine. This word may, in fact, be a necessary and prophetic word for church and pastors today.

A CHURCH IN CONFLICT

From the beginning, conflict between the human and the spiritual has been part of Christian congregations. It is obvious from the most casual observation that Christian conversion is not perfection and that we bring our fallen humanity to church with us. It's the dark side of congregational life.

A Church Captive to Its Culture

The Corinthian church bore all the marks of humanity. Converted from Greco-Roman paganism, the Corinthians brought the deepest and darkest corners of the human heart into the light of their new Christian faith. Most commentaries note that the Greek verb "to Corinthianize" meant to corrupt someone's morals. A "Corinthian girl" described a woman of low moral standards.

Corinth's legendary low sexual standards were encouraged by cultic prostitution associated with the Greek and Roman fertility gods. Sexual promiscuity was not a matter of secular humanism in Corinth; it was part of the divine order of things. In Corinth, sexuality was spirituality.

Though converted, some of the Corinthian Christians didn't leave all of Corinth's immorality behind them. The church overlooked, even encouraged, a strange case of incest forbidden even to pagans (1 Cor. 5:1). Some evidently continued to see temple prostitutes (6:12–20). All of chapter 7 is devoted to marriage, celibacy, and the single life. Yet it is interesting, perhaps even profoundly prophetic, that Paul's primary concern about that messed-up church is not their sexual deviance. Most of our churches today begin church discipline with sexual transgressions. We seem preoccupied with the sexual behavior of our members and leaders.

I recently attended a pastor's conference at which two of the keynote speakers spoke powerfully about the tragic and shameful sexual misbehavior that seems epidemic in our time. As each speaker eloquently noted, sexual transgressions by church leaders are terribly destructive. Men and women of God, along with churches, denominations, and Christian movements are devastated by the fall of pastors and leaders.

It may be, however, that sexual misbehavior is a symptom of a larger and even more destructive evil. At least, Paul seemed to think so. The first issue he deals with in 1 Corinthians and a theme that ties the entire epistle together, is disunity and conflict in the church. Such behavior denies the very nature of the gospel and of the church that that gospel forms.

Conflict: The Church at War with Itself

The Corinthians had gathered themselves around various leaders in the Christian movement. They formed parties and boasted that they belonged to Paul or Peter or Apollos. Whether the parties were formed around theological platforms or human personalities, the result was the same. They so violated the character of the gospel that Paul warned them that God may destroy them (1 Cor. 3:17).

The Destructive Character of Conflict

Note that the terrible threat of divine destruction is directed at conflict in the church. And that threat comes before Paul's directive to deliver the man involved in incest to Satan for his destruction (1 Cor. 5:1). I am not sure anyone knows what either of these destructive acts may be, but one thing is quite clear: God and the apostles take church conflict seriously—at least as seriously as sexual deviance, perhaps even more. Our ranking of sins seldom reflects this biblical approach.

When Paul lists the works of the flesh, the polar opposites of the fruit of the Spirit, he lists "discord," "jealousy," "selfish ambition," "dissensions," and "factions" right along with "sexual immorality," "idolatry," "witchcraft," and "orgies" as some of the dangerous and destructive human tendencies the gospel comes to root out. Paul ends the thought by declaring that people who practice such behavior have no place in God's kingdom (Gal. 5:19–21). Those are frightening and very relevant words in any century. Who of us takes "minor" sins like discord or jealousy that seriously?

Ten years ago when I was called to pastor a very large church, I talked to everyone I could about ministry in unique churches. One pastor put it simply: "Pastoring a large church is managing a variety of competing special-interest groups."

Well, I thought to myself, *that's not too different from what I have been doing for the last fifteen years!* And it wasn't. I was just managing more of them, and more seemed at stake. People were more intense about their "corner" of the church and more likely to fight for their spiritual and ecclesiastical rights. The lines between ministries and causes were clearly drawn.

Some of those groups gathered around the names of former pastors. One of my predecessors stayed in the community and was an active member of the congregation. While he was very ethical and supportive of my ministry, it was quite apparent that his loyal followers would never consider me their pastor. They could not switch their loyalty to a man young enough to be their son.

Both of us were speakers at a weekend retreat where his group made up the majority. The group dynamic was fascinating. I could tell that I was respected and heard, but he was their pastor and leader ten years after he had retired. They called me "David." They called him "Pastor." I didn't mind. He and I had a good working relationship, and in effect, he was an unpaid staff member who provided leadership and pastoral care for part of the congregation. Nevertheless, it is a sad commentary on the human tendency to gather around humans about whom we boast and to whom we belong.

Smaller churches and pastors do the same thing in different form. When I was a graduate student, I pastored a little country church part-time. Our church was three and a half miles from the little town where most of the members lived. Another church in the same denomination, also a part-time pastorate, was about three and a half miles from the other side of town. First Church in town was larger than the two country churches but not large enough to afford a full-time pastor. All three churches were more than a century old and were founded when people rode horses and buggies to church. Three and a half miles was too far to travel to church, and these "country cousin" churches solved that problem.

Early on, I suggested to my board that since distance was no longer an issue and all of us lived in the same small town, we should think about some form of merger. The merged church would be able to afford a full-time pastor and perhaps even a part-time youth pastor. It made little sense to me to continue limping along too small and weak to walk, let alone run.

When I first brought up the idea, one of the deacons quickly poured very cold water on it. He said he would never go to church and share a pew with those people at First Church! "Besides," he went on, "who would take care of the church's graveyard?" That was the end of the discussion.

Our loyalties have very human boundaries that limit the power of the gospel. According to Scripture, that is no small matter. In our dictionary of sins, conflict and party spirit are safe sins, but the gospel declares otherwise.

The Cause of Conflict

The Corinthians held a dangerously defective human viewpoint of the church and the ministry. Twice Paul calls the Corinthians "mere men" when discussing their vision of their church and its leaders (1 Cor. 3:3–4). They had reduced the church to a human institution and had defined and evaluated its work by human standards. Appearances became more important than reality. Human agendas replaced God's agenda for his people, and the gospel was reduced to merely human dimensions.

Paul, Apollos, and Peter were the figures to whom allegiance was given. Leadership style, preaching skills, and theological positions became rallying points. Members of each group thought themselves superior to the others. Hero worship accompanied worship of the Lord Christ, and the church lost its focus. Loyalty to humans divided people from each other and destroyed the unity of spirit created by the power of the gospel.

Gordon Fee notes that the Corinthians' view of the ministry was simultaneously both too low and too high. They valued their leaders too highly and gave them status and authority independent of apostolic teaching about the church. Their view of the ministry was too low, for they judged their preachers and leaders by human standards of excellence and success. In the process they missed the whole point of pastoral ministry and lost the proper mission of their church.[1]

The Contemporary Scene

The Bible is remarkably relevant, and 1 Corinthians sounds as up to date as any text in Scripture. In fact, it reads like an account of the late twentieth century.

Paul, Apollos, and Peter in Modern Dress. Today's Christians gather around radio preachers and Christian TV personalities. I heard a well-meaning Christian declare, "I'm a Swindoll man!" A leader in my church thought he had settled a sensitive issue in a board meeting when he said, "John MacArthur said just yesterday. . . ." Most pastors in our time know the penalty of disagreeing with most anything James Dobson says. I am sure that most Christian celebrities (a Christian oxymoron if ever there was one!) have no intention of creating parties. Nevertheless, with human nature being what it is, division is inevitable. We sound just like Corinth—"I follow Paul," "I follow Apollos"—judging by human standards.

In our day, dividing by evangelical personalities may be more dangerous than ever before. In our era of extreme individualism and electronic communication, a subtly heretical view of the church creeps in unaware. People follow leaders they have never seen and will never know. Their source of nourishment is no longer flesh and blood but a disembodied voice. In fact, many become impatient with the imperfections of pastors and churches and choose to exist in a splendid spiritual isolation without a real church and ministry to upset their vision of the faith.

Special-Interest Christianity. Churches continually find creative ways to divide into informal factions that each claim divine sanction. We have taken some of our cues from modern society, which is increasingly divided into special-interest groups, each lobbying for power and/or money. "Me first" is a way of life in our world and, too often, in the church.

Some people judge my entire ministry according to their political agenda. They want me to sign on to their political views and to make that a centerpiece of the church's ministry. My resistance to their politics can't seem to be merely a difference of opinion. The discussion always escalates into conflict involving accusations, anger, and finally, rejection. I think the real tragedy is how little these political zealots desire the highest values of the gospel such as love, joy, and peace.

To my everlasting sadness, I have seen even the missionary program of a church become a special-interest group that battles the rest of the church for money, loyalty, and energy and judges everyone, including the pastoral staff, according to their loyalty to the mission program. The mission of the church is confused with a particular program for missions, and woe to the pastor who thinks otherwise.

Pastors easily fall into the same trap. Our agenda driven by our vision for the church can become an idolatrous measuring rod by which we judge parishioners' value or orthodoxy. We sometimes confuse loyalty to us with loyalty to the gospel. We also tend to measure our colleagues on grounds that have little, if anything, to do with the values of the gospel.

Personal Loyalty and the Church. Multiple staff churches live with divided loyalty. People generally cannot divide their pastoral loyalty evenly. That is not necessarily bad. We humans, clergy and laity alike, tend toward favoritism. One of my successors in a single-pastor church said that it takes four pastors before a church has experienced one full pastorate. Paul plants, Apollos waters, Peter teaches, and God makes it grow. We each have our gifts and emphases. Multiple-staff churches are able to have several pastors simultaneously. It seems that the churches of the New Testament had multiple leaders, and that was good.

However, all too often the divided loyalty of the congregation turns into civil war in the church or in the staff. Power struggles and turf battles are common. I have seen both open and cold war by staff members protecting their turf. I have had laypeople use unwitting staff members against one another and against me. Fortunately I have only seen it from a distance, but some staff members gather loyal followers and use them against the senior minister or the board of the church, creating a lose-lose situation.

Measurement by Human Standards. Pastors also measure themselves and churches by human standards. Pastoral or ecclesial success in our time is inevitably the size of the congregation. I am weary of the question, "How large is your church?" It seems my value or the worth of my congregation is determined by numbers. I am also sad that I measure myself by that standard. I love numerical growth and tend to think that it is the great blessing of God for a church. I know better, but my humanity leaps over my convictions all too often.

Pastoral shoptalk is increasingly technique oriented. Management specialists have replaced wise pastors at our listening posts. The theology of the church and its ministry is lost in a maze of human effort and techniques. I hasten to add that not all of this is bad. We need to listen to those who know how to lead and manage human institutions, because the church is a sociological reality. But the church marches to another drummer. We obey the norms of the gospel and organize our life and work around apostolic standards.

The clergy do not stand alone. Church boards increasingly think corporately. I find it more and more difficult to get churchs board to think biblically. Discussions inevitably drift toward corporate thinking. In one church we had a long discussion regarding the organization of the church. For hours we talked about contemporary structures and management processes. When I referred to the apostolic or biblical norms for church organization, one man who should have known better said, "I want to know why we're discussing a book that is two thousand years old."

He wouldn't have said that about any of the key doctrines of the faith. I am certain he thinks I should be a defender of biblical orthodoxy. But like so many church leaders, he has removed the church and its ministry from theological or biblical discussion and has placed them under human norms and thinking.

Some time ago ecclesiology and pastoral theology were removed from the canon of theology and came under the order of sociology and psychology. (I have discussed this devolution more fully in chapter 4.) First Corinthians 3–4 is a classic and prophetic discussion of the consequences of such a viewpoint. We may grow gigantic churches, produce evangelical celebrities, catch the eye of the media and the admiration of management leaders, but if all this so-called progress is fueled by human strength, trapped by its own immanence, and measured by human standards, it will come to little or nothing. This is just another phase in the very long story of the Christian church.

TOWARD A PROPER VIEW
OF THE CHRISTIAN MINISTRY

First Corinthians 3:5 begins Paul's rejoinder to the Corinthians' defective view of the ministry. If this human way of viewing Christian leaders is wrong, how should we regard pastors?

God's Servants and Fellow Workers

Paul begins his answer with a simple word. We are God's "servants." The word translated "servant" is *diakonos*. Paul often used the word to describe Christian ministry. Later, it came to be the church office of deacon, but Paul's meaning here is much simpler.

Since servants are ones who serve others, by nature servants occupy a lower place than their masters. As servants, Paul, Apollos, and Peter all stand under God and are, therefore, merely the instruments by which God does eternity's work. We pastors are the ones "through whom" God works (1 Cor. 3:5). The credit and allegiance belong to God. The servants of God, by the nature of their work, deflect praise and loyalty to God. To gather around human leaders and to evaluate them independently of the God who works through them is a fundamental error in judgment.

Paul sums up his thought in verse 9 with another word: "We are God's *fellow workers*." Paul uses the term often, usually to refer to his co-workers in ministry. The emphasis shifts from working *for* God to working *with* each other. Since we all work for God, rivalry and envy are unnecessary. In fact, conflict among the clergy denies the nature of the gospel and inhibits the work of God. Again the force of Paul's thought throws the emphasis from the human workers back to God. God assigns each of us a task (v. 5), and he is responsible for both the role we play and the results of that ministry. What God is doing in the church and for the church is the real issue. What we can do together in labor for God should cancel any conflict our humanity creates.

But what is this work of God done through us, and how can it be measured? Paul elaborates on his thoughts with the use of two metaphors.

God's Farmers

I come from a long line of farmers, and I served in rural churches full of farmers for a decade, yet I have never heard a farmer take credit for growing crops. Farmers are very aware that they plant, fertilize, cultivate, and harvest but that germination and growth to maturity lie completely outside their ability. In farming communities there is talk about and credit given for straight and clean rows. The mark of an amateur is a crooked row, and the sign of a lazy farmer is weeds in his fields. But no farmer, regardless of straight rows and weedless fields, thinks he grows plants.

All Ministry Is a Matter of Grace. Paul considered his apostolic work as farming for God. He planted the seed that became the church in Corinth, but God caused the seed to germinate and sprout from the earth. He also knew that the work of ministry had to continue after his labor was finished. Apollos took up where Paul left off, and watered the growing church. But God made the church grow. And Paul is careful to note that all of the growth was a gift of grace (1 Cor. 3:7). Not only did God make the church come to life, but Paul's calling and talents for ministry were also gifts. As always, Paul deflects the praise to God.

Ministry Points to the Glory of God. Paul asks, why, then, this inordinate attention to the farmers? Shouldn't the praise, credit, and glory go to God who makes the church grow? Paul and Apollos, a skillful apostle and an eloquent pastor, served a larger end than themselves or their gifts. The church should point all its energy and attention to that same goal. The church and the ministry are about growing the church of Jesus Christ. Anything that retards that growth, whether undue attention to God's servants, friction or rivalry among

God's fellow workers, or conflict in the church over trivial or important issues, reveals a defective view of the church and its ministry.

The Unity of the Ministry. Each of God's servants has a unique ministry. One plants, another waters, and extending the metaphor, others cultivate, fertilize, and harvest. God assigns us our ministry (1 Cor. 3:5). Yet these varying ministries are, in fact, one ministry (v. 8). Literally translated, the first part of verse 8 reads, "The one planting and the one watering *are one.* . . ." What a revolutionary way of viewing the pastorate! All rivalry, jealousy, and envy are obliterated by the gospel reality that all of us form a single ministry under God's grace and power.

Our possessiveness disappears too. Paul emphasizes that the church is "God's field, God's building" (v. 9). All our pastoral labor, along with that of every other pastor on earth, leans in a single direction. God is growing his church. God gives us the honor of planting, watering, and harvesting, but those tasks have no inherent value. Growth by God's grace is the sum total of our work. We have no status, significance, or power apart from God, who works in and through us. We should not judge ourselves or anyone else by another standard than God's. Pastors in little places, in small churches with perhaps few gifts, serve precisely the same end as the most famous pastor in the world. The well-known have no more standing before God than the pastor of whom only a few will ever hear. Their ministries are one. We exist to grow Christ's church by the power of God. Any other motive is subbiblical, and any other goal less than fully Christian.

God's Master Builders

Paul abruptly changes the metaphor from God's field to God's building (1 Cor. 5:9). Paul's ministry and ours is to be God's master builders. The word Paul uses is *architecton.* A *tekton* is a carpenter, but an *architecton* is the craftsman who serves as the architect, contractor, and engineer.

The One and Only Foundation for Ministry. Paul's apostolic work was not just formative but normative. His specific role was to lay the foundation on which the church would be built. That foundation was Jesus Christ, and all other pastoral work for all time must make that Christological foundation its reference point. Jesus Christ is the integrating center of all church life and pastoral ministry. He is the focus of attention, the source of our ministry, and the goal of all our labor. Whatever pastoral work might mean, it is summed up by Paul in Colossians 1:28, " ... that we may present everyone mature in Christ" (NRSV).

At the very least and at the highest level possible, the growth of the church, which moves the people of God toward Christ, is a unity that comes from love. That is the point of Paul's letter to the fractured Corinthian church. By the nature of things—God's nature, that is—the church is one (1 Cor. 12:12–31). Jesus taught that such visible unity would be the certification to the world that God sent Jesus to the world (John 17:22–23).

This corporate and visible unity is the natural result of the ultimate work of the gospel, the love of God that is poured out in our hearts (Rom. 5:5). First Corinthians 12–14, in which Paul teaches that all spiritual gifts and divine energy should proceed from and contribute to the unity of the church, has at the center Paul's great hymn of love in chapter 13. Elsewhere Paul declares that all the Law and the Prophets are fulfilled in the love command (Rom. 13:8–10). He was quoting his Lord who said that divine love is the mark of the church (John 13:35).

The Result of Authentic Ministry. The work of the church and its ministry points toward specific Christian behavior—that is, unity born of love. As God's farmers and master builders, loving unity should form the sum and substance of our labors. All else is a means to that great biblical end. Yet that truth is seldom heard in the church these days. The criteria for success and the techniques for achieving great things for God seldom include love or unity. Pastoral conferences and seminars are long on methods but short on the great goal of a truly apostolic ministry.

And, I must admit, farming and building for God easily loses love as the primary motivation. Reality squeezes love from our souls and replaces it with a variety of human motives. Above all, we buy into the performance-based criteria for success that characterizes fallen society. We match the church's special-interest agendas with our own personal interest. Inevitably, this combination shoves the real mission of the ministry, growing Christ's church, to a place behind the struggle to gain supremacy for our personal agendas.

Most dysfunctions in the church and ministry could be corrected at this point. The issue behind much church discussion and conflict is really power: who has it and how it's handled. In fact, we are all God's servants and should be satisfied to give God the credit. What God wants to do through us farmers and builders is to grow/build his church. The foundation of that growth is the same as its end, unity that springs from love—not just any love, but the love God pours into our hearts. And we must always remember that we cannot serve there whom we do not love.

THE CHURCH OF THE HOLY SPIRIT

When I was in seminary, I worked as a custodian for a nearby Lutheran church. The pastor was a mentor and friend. The name of the church was "Church of the Holy Spirit," a name I thought sounded odd at the time. When the secretary answered the phone with, "Lutheran Church of the Holy Spirit," I smiled to myself and sometimes cringed. This "high church" didn't talk much about the Holy Spirit. Moreover, this was not a standard name for a church. It even seemed theologically dangerous.

The Church as the Temple of God

I have learned better. Paul moves his discussion of pastoral ministry as building the church to a powerful conclusion that makes a theological point much needed in our time. The church, Paul argues, is the temple of the Holy Spirit (1 Cor. 3:16). The edifice we pastors labor to build beautifully and skillfully, the church of Christ, is, in fact, the residence of the Spirit.

Paul is often misunderstood here. We usually think that he is referring to our individual bodies as temples of the Spirit. That argument comes later (1 Cor. 6:19). Here the church is the temple of the Spirit. Paul is making an analogy to the Old Testament temple of God. The word he uses for temple (*naos*) has a special reference in the Greek Old Testament, the Septuagint, where it refers not to the entire temple complex, but to the Holy Place where God dwelt. That special reference seems to be Paul's point in this powerful image of the church.

In the new covenant, the church is where God dwells through the presence of the Holy Spirit. The people of God, especially when they are assembled in worship, is the holiest place on earth, the place where God comes to meet his people. That is why Paul was so concerned about decency and order in church worship later in this letter (1 Cor. 12–14). When the church worships as it should, he writes, God's presence is so obvious that even non-Christian visitors will be affected. They will fall to their knees in repentance (14:25). Needless to say, we need to reform our worship in that direction.

Pastors As Priests in God's Temple

Paul is making another equally powerful point. The work of the ministry, whether lay or clergy, is no small matter. Like the priests and Levites in the Hebrew temple, every day we handle holy items and work in the holiest place. The church is not a human organization to be manipulated according to anyone's will or agenda. The church of Jesus Christ is the temple of God; it is where God lives on earth. Thus the presence and power of the Spirit must mark all of the life of the church and each task of pastoral ministry. Because each one of God's people is a temple of the Holy Spirit and collectively they form the temple of God, pastors and leaders must deal gently and carefully with Christ's church. The attitude, character, and techniques of pastoral ministry have a divine reference point and standard. All must be appropriate to the nature and character of the church as the temple of the Holy Spirit.

In fact, the nature of the church as a church of the Holy Spirit, should force us to new focus on the Holy Spirit as the mark of a Christian church. The character of the church as the temple of the Holy Spirit calls into question a technique-driven ministry and eliminates the contemporary vision of the church as little more than a human organization that exists to meet personal needs and agendas.

A Sobering Conclusion

Paul ends his thought with a devastating prophetic word for both Corinth and church leaders in our time: "If anyone destroys God's temple, God will destroy him; for God's temple is sacred, and you are that temple" (1 Cor. 3:17). The great Baptist New Testament interpreter, A. T. Robertson, paraphrases it this way: "The church-wrecker God will wreck."[2] His point is clear: Division into parties formed around personalities, regardless of how wonderful, brilliant, or successful that person may be, is ultimately destructive. It diverts the vision of the church away from its Lord and frustrates the purpose of the church, which is growth toward godliness and God's plan as enabled by the Holy Spirit. Church members need to tremble before this prophetic word.

The reverse is equally true. Pastors must take care not to become the center of special interest and power. Robertson comments on this passage, " There is warning enough here to make every pastor pause before he tears a church apart in order to vindicate himself"[3]

Paul goes out of his way to dethrone himself in Corinth while, at the same time, recovering his real apostolic authority. Biblical authority comes not from personal power or skillful leadership but from the power of the gospel and the presence of Christ in a pastor's life. That is a difficult attitude to maintain, especially when God gives a pastor great gifts. Nevertheless, Scripture is filled with dire warnings about the consequences of pride and power turned in the wrong direction. We need to repeat over and over, "Glory to God alone"—and mean it.

Rather than divide into human categories, the church should live in and grow toward the unity of the Spirit that Christ's love creates. Human agendas and personal preferences fade behind this larger purpose for the church. Pastoral methods and leadership strategies must all point toward building the church into the temple of the Holy Spirit of God. Being the church is much larger than the vision of our time, and pastoral ministry is much holier—and dangerous—than most of us want to admit.

SOME NOTES ON PASTORAL THEOLOGY

Paul's vision of the church and its ministry works against the trends of the past century. Because his ecclesial vision is apostolic, it stands in judgment of our pastoral methods and offers to any generation a foundation for church and ministry appropriate to any person, church, or era.

The Essential Work of the Pastor

While our pastoral work involves an incredibly wide variety of tasks and responsibilities, and while our role in the church and community offers us many opportunities to use our gifts and abilities, all our labors are merely means to a divine end. We ourselves are a means God uses to accomplish a divine purpose. God calls pastors to grow or to build the church.

When I came to my current pastorate, I joined a long line of pastors who serve the same end. We are all different, and we have different emphases, opportunities, gifts, and results; but our goal is singular: We exist to build the temple of the Holy Spirit. We are called to grow Christ's church.

It is easy to confuse means and ends. Every individual and church does it. Yet the result can be tragic. A church I served had a successful and well-known lay evangelism program. As seems to be inevitable, the leaders and participants of that ministry thought it was the most important ministry in the church. People were judged by their allegiance to the program, and other churches were graded by their willingness to learn from our program.

Over time, the end of evangelism was replaced by the means of a particular program. When the program ran out of gas and no longer worked as it once had, the discussion was always limited by commitment to this method. We couldn't talk about evangelism apart from this method. It could not be questioned or even evaluated honestly. Blame and faultfinding became the name of the game. The laypeople were blamed for their lack of zeal. The clergy and lay leadership were cited for their failure to promote and participate in the program. I could not get the program leaders to talk about changing the program or implementing other means of evangelism. Their loyalty to a means blinded them. In the end, the program and evangelism failed.

Pastors, too, are means and not ends. In business and in the church long tenure tends to blind excellent leaders. One of the best leaders I know stayed too long. The church outgrew his ability to lead, and he refused to see the handwriting on the wall. It seemed as though he thought he was the end rather than God's means. He wouldn't listen, change, or grow. The end was very sad. Saddest of all, a church suffered terribly.

The True Nature of a Christian Church

Paul's discussion indicates the Trinitarian nature of the church. He refers to the church as God's field and building, the temple of the Holy Spirit, and Christ's foundation. The significance could not be greater. The very essence of the church is its divine nature.

As a matter of integrity, the life and work of the church must bear witness to the person and character of the triune God. All we do as pastors and leaders in Christ's church must point to the development of the people of God into a people who reflect the God who reveals himself in Jesus Christ. The church always bears in itself a certain transcendence that makes it different from its environment. We bear witness to eternity in a world that stands with its back toward God and is in love with itself.

Apostolic pastoral leadership understands that although the church lives incarnationally and becomes all things to all people in order to win some (1 Cor. 9:22), we must never abandon the one thing that makes us relevant to the world—that we are the dwelling place of Almighty God. Being properly contemporary or relevant does not imply that we must empty our worship, preaching, or corporate lifestyle of the divine. In fact, to be truly sensitive to our unbelieving neighbors, we must have hold of the transcendent. What else can speak to those whose lives have been reduced to godless nothingness by the emptiness of humanism?

My twenty-something son caught me up short the other day. He is a church dropout trying to find his way home. He loves God but has real trouble with churches. In the name of God some people in a church hurt him deeply. Still, he is considering giving church another try.

I was telling him about a church in his neighborhood and mentioned that it had both traditional and contemporary services. He quickly told me that he wasn't interested in contemporary worship. He said it appeared to him an attempt by Christians to be "cool." "Christianity's not cool," he said. "It's supposed to be different."

That's worth thinking about. As a pastor committed to and leading contemporary forms of ministry, I am giving it a lot of thought. Traditional or contemporary, the real issue is the real presence of the very real God.

The Role of the Christian Pastor

At first it may seem that Paul is depreciating apostolic and pastoral ministry when he says that we farmers and builders are nothing while God is everything (1 Cor. 3:7).

Some pastoral traditions have featured self-loathing and an accompanying low view of the ministry. But that is not Paul's point at all. Rather, he is combating a wrong and devastating high view of the ministry. The Corinthians admired and honored the leaders for their human abilities. Apollos was the great orator and Paul the superb theologian. Others admired Peter for an alternative theology that some attributed to him. The nature of the church and the character of the ministry were nowhere in sight. Such a view lowered the ministry to a powerless human level. A correct view of ministry flows from an accurate doctrine of the church and its gospel character.

My brother-in-law is a builder, and he takes me to see his work from time to time. He loves to see the work of his hands and is justly proud of his craftsmanship. He is always talking about how he builds things and how things work. But he doesn't for a moment think he owns the houses he builds. They belong to those who paid for them. His task is building, and his pride is in a job well done. Likewise, the church must be built with great skill and care. Nothing is more satisfying than ministry that is accomplishing something in people's lives and is creating a living church of God.

When I look back over a quarter century of ministry, I am proud of the work I have left behind. But by God's grace I don't think any of it was my doing. I was the faithful farmer who watered what others planted, while God made it grow. I don't own any church, and I will not let my lips form the words "my church." God owns the church; Christ paid for it with his life, and it is the residence of the Holy Spirit. God chose me to work in his field, to build his house. That should be enough.

The danger we all face is improper focus. Honor is due those who labor for God. Paul speaks of his "rights" as an apostle in 1 Corinthians 9; in 1 Thessalonians he demands that parishioners honor their leaders. "Respect those who work hard among you ... and who admonish you. Hold them in the highest regard in love because of their work" (5:12–13). This should go without saying, since the nature of the gospel demands that we love, respect, and honor one another and since the character of the church requires that leaders lead and be respected and honored for it. But, unfortunately, holding our leaders in high esteem is no longer the standard. Perhaps it is because all authority and institutions are suspect these days. In any case, poor treatment has left pastors a discouraged lot.

A wise man once told me that pastoral ministry is a high-demand, low-stroke environment. I sense that more and more as we slip toward the end of this century. Study after study shows that pastors who have served for some time uniformly have less self-esteem than when before they entered ministry.

I was talking to a lay leader in a great church not long ago. He asked how I was doing and then said that he was worried about his pastor. We had a few minutes of truth telling about the difficulties of church leadership, especially the loneliness of it.

Finally, he said, "What can we do for you guys, anyway?" I was taken by surprise—no one had ever asked me that. "Just love us," I said. In all the expectations, demands, and pressures of church life, love is what seems to be lacking. Ironic, isn't it, given the nature of the gospel?

I suppose all of us pastors know we are loved. If nothing else, we find out the depth of love when we resign. Some people do make it a point to tell us they love and support us, but seldom do we sense a wellspring of loving encouragement there to sustain us in the heat of battle. It dawned on me one day that most of the praise and honor I receive from the congregation comes because I am good at what I do. I wondered what would happen if suddenly I developed a stammer or was horribly disfigured. *Would they come and listen? Would they be "proud" of their pastor? Would they hope I might have the good sense to find a less prominent place of service? And could I be happy and comfortable with myself if suddenly I wasn't good at what I do, just faithful?*

The other side of the coin is equally though differently destructive. Because some of us are very good at meeting expectations, performing at a high level, and producing what passes for success, we do receive high marks, loads of honor, even bits of prestige. Because this is a performance-based world, those who are excellent at tasks receive rewards—very human rewards, I might add.

It is probably impossible not to be wrongly proud of the works of our hands or to rely on our abilities to get things done. Frankly, the more successful I become and the longer I do ministry well, the more I tend to depend on my accumulated wisdom and achievements. It came as a huge shock in the spring of 1995, when, for the first time in twenty-five years, I was unable to get done the one thing I thought necessary for the future of the church. I just figured that the church would see the light because I had and that they would follow me because they should.

It is not that what we do and are lacks significance. Ministry in and of itself carries significance because it bears God's name. And all of us carry immense significance because we are sons and daughters of God and are called to ministry. The difficulty is balance. We sometimes forget that everything we are and have is a gift and that, therefore, nothing we accomplish has any real significance independent from the power of God in the gospel. The wonder is that God continues to honor the gospel even when we are blowing our own trumpet. That's grace. From beginning to end, it is God's church, Christ's body, the Spirit's temple. We proclaim the gospel of God not ourselves. G. K. Chesterton once said, "The angels can fly because they take themselves so lightly." That's good wisdom for earthbound pastors.

A BIT OF WISDOM FOR PASTORS

Shortly after I came to Park Street Church, I was at a small gathering of pastors where John Stott was the speaker. He was interested in me because of his long-standing relationship with Park Street Church. As we talked about the burden of historic churches and distinguished predecessors, he put his hand on my shoulder and gently said, "Just be yourself, dear brother." It was the best advice possible for me at the time and, I think, for all pastors everywhere. However, like lots of excellent wisdom, being myself is easier said than done. It requires a good measure of self-knowledge, an understanding of one's gifts, and a profound sense of the uniqueness of God's call.

Understand Your Unique Role and Fill It

As I mentioned earlier, my very first pastoral call was to the bedside of my dying predecessor. He had come to this particular church to retire. He had given the best he had to offer but was sick much of the last few years of his tenure. He died after I was hired as his successor but before I arrived in town.

This man's legacy to me was overwhelmingly positive. He had been a kind and good pastor, and the congregation had loved him and cared for him in his physical decline. Beyond that, my predecessor was not a strong preacher, which made my preaching look better than it perhaps was. His illness made my youth appear more vigorous than it was. And my strong leadership style quickly filled the gap in leadership. It was quite clear that we were two very different pastors with different emphases, strengths, and gifts. I believe we had different callings. Our larger calling to ministry and to that church was the same, but the role our specific callings required during our tenures was very different.

Building on his (and his predecessor's) foundation, I laid some stones of ministry that built that church toward the image of God as revealed in Christ. I realized God brought me there to take a wonderfully good group of God's people who had grown tired and inward in a new direction. All my pastoral leadership was directed at taking that congregation from where it was toward where God wanted it to be. My work and my specific calling was directly related to the work of my predecessor, the character of the church, and my uniqueness as a pastor. Nothing was to be gained and everything lost if I demeaned or discredited my predecessor or his work. I watered what he planted, and God made it grow.

It was apparent to me when that chapter should end. I took the church as far as I could and handed the baton to my successor, whom I helped select. He took the church another gigantic step in its growth, and when that chapter was finished he handed the baton to his successor, who wrote another chapter.

During the tenure of my second successor there, I visited the church. Nearly ten years had passed, and God was writing wonderful lines in the new chapter of the church's life. During a Sunday morning service, the pastor talked a bit about succession and ministry. He is the one who said, "I think it takes three or four pastors before a church has a complete pastorate."

I think he's right. Long-term pastorates certainly have great advantages, but a healthy succession of pastors may, in fact, offer a church better and fuller ministry and leadership. I know that that church was better for it.

Knowing when your work is finished is as important as knowing your role and filling it. Not knowing when to leave can easily destroy the good that has been accomplished. One of my successors in that church agrees with the church that he stayed a couple of years too long and damaged the good work all of us did for god.

Build God's Church Very Carefully

I thank God for the church-growth movement. It has taught important principles of human and institutional behavior but, more important, it has caused pastors, laypeople, and theologians to take another look at the doctrine of the church. Even if the rhetoric gets a bit too heated, the present spotlight on what it means to be and grow the church is illuminating.

In any discussion, definitions are crucial. Growth, as Paul defines it, goes far beyond the popular usages in the contemporary church. Numerical growth has ascended to near-divine status in our time. People and pastors are preoccupied with how large churches are or how fast they are growing.

I will never forget my first exposure to church-growth thinking. I was with two pastor friends who exchanged their growth charts. They did it off to the side since my church wasn't growing like theirs. It seemed that success or failure and certainly significance hung on rapid growth. Somehow that above all else indicated God's blessing.

It may. But rapid growth may just as easily indicate skillful programming, attractive personalities, and sociological momentum, even pandering to human desires. "Easy come, easy go" is often the rule for large churches. If people are attracted because of human factors, they will leave for the same reason. I once heard Chuck Swindoll say that he could lose three hundred people by wearing a bad tie. He wasn't altogether serious, but he made a point.

The New Testament in general and 1 Corinthians in particular define proper church growth. Growth always involves moving people toward Christlikeness (e.g., 1 Cor. 2:16; Col. 1:28–29). Paul gives no praise for size; rather, he commends churches large and small for their Christlike character, for matters of the soul such as love, hope, and faith. God alone gives the increase, and we should be satisfied with that.

The bottom line for pastors, as we know and teach, is the object of our trust. Do we rely on our gifts, skills, and experience, or on the Lord of the church? Is our trust in techniques and methods, or in the living God? Most of the time I want it both ways. I do trust in God, but I rely on my power at the same time. Paul renounced his own stuff, powerful as it was, preferring instead the genuine power of God. Human objects of faith inevitably falter and finally fail.

Realize the Power of Pastoral Succession

As I said earlier, my first predecessor was a faithful, loving pastor. I entered a world of trust and affection that was the legacy of his ministry. My congregation expected me to be a good man and to do good ministry. Their expectation created a climate for powerful ministry. Even my predecessor's final illness was a part of that legacy, for the church learned to care for a pastor. My youthful energy was such a jarring contrast to his last years that it created momentum by itself.

My second pastoral charge could not have differed more dramatically. I followed a pastor who for a variety of reasons created a legacy of suspicion. His final pastoral act was to lead a small group of church members in a church split. They set up a new church down the road. This was a small town, and the consequences of that church fight were devastating.

Needless to say, the chapter I wrote in that congregation's life was quite different from my first pastorate. Now I was in a "binding up" ministry. I came to a small group of wounded, disillusioned, and often angry Christians. I had to listen very carefully, watch my words, and guard my spirit. I had to win support, and in some cases I failed. Mistrust had penetrated too deeply to move aside. Five years of ministry did not erase the damage of my predecessor's two-year pastorate.

Sometime in that second pastorate I learned that a predecessor largely determines early perceptions of the new pastor—especially when there has been conflict. It is equally true following a long-term pastorate, for the predecessor becomes the frame of reference in which the new pastor is perceived.

What has happened in the past determines how and where we lead and the texture of our ministry. In that second church, I had to go slowly, be careful, and continually reassure the congregation that they were worthwhile and that I was trustworthy. It was exhausting but worth it. My successor is a long-term and successful pastor. The church regained some of its former health and once again is reaching out to the community.

I also must add that a predecessor can hinder or even destroy one's ministry. I know of a church where the retired former pastor is trying to get rid of his young successor. He lives in the same community, which is not a wise thing to do. He disagrees with the new directions the church has taken under his successor and has been meddling in the internal affairs of the church for more than two years. The church board has told him to keep his hands off, but he continues to spread poison and undermine his successor. The young successor is deeply wounded and may not survive.

Be Ethical and Careful With Succession

A pastor is, after all, only one minister in the one church of God. We pastors don't own God's church. When our chapter is finished, we should honor our successor and trust the congregation to handle its own affairs. Few things so debilitate ministry as outside influence, especially a former pastor to whom loyalties die hard.

I learned early on that it is wise to honor my predecessors and successors by carefully monitoring my attitude toward them. I try to avoid conversations that are negative and, when possible, I give my blessing. My father taught me that when I leave a church, I'm gone. Common pastoral ethics require us to stay out of God's field when it has a new farmer unless invited back in. I will not perform acts of ministry at a former church unless invited by the present pastor. Church boards should know and enforce this basic ethical standard. I tell my friends from former congregations that negative discussions about the church and the pastor are out of bounds. If I really love Christ's church and rely on the Lord of the church, I should be content to support its ministry and pray for its pastor—regardless!

A Final Word About Rivalry

One of the least attractive features of pastoral life is competition among pastors. Since pastoral ministry is overwhelmingly male, I suppose it follows that we carry our competitive spirits into our work.

A neighboring pastor took me to lunch one day and forthrightly told me that he wanted to meet me so he could size up the competition. From that moment, try as I may, he seemed more a rival than a brother in ministry.

Gatherings of pastors often resemble the gorilla cage at the zoo. The male gorillas continually jockey to become the dominant male of the group. They beat their chests and otherwise attempt to demonstrate their prowess. In the end, one always prevails. We pastors gather, and out of our insecurity and with our competitive drive, we jockey for position, show our strength, brag about our accomplishments, and size up one another. We love to hear stories about one another and about our churches. We especially lean toward bad news about our brothers and their congregations.

A friend of mine was with a pastor in our denomination who was unaware of our friendship. This pastor told my friend that he had "heard" that I was a "New-Ager." On hearing this, my own competitive drive kicked into gear, and I was ready for a fight. But on reflection, and because of the Holy Spirit's restraint, I became saddened that a brother I didn't even know listened to and then spread the gossip. I was sadder still that he didn't check to see if the rumor was true. How different from Paul's image of a single ministry with numerous builders working together to build a great house for God. It is time for us to act as one ministry in loving support of each other and with a steadfast refusal to participate in the bad news tendencies of our own hearts.

We need to hear Paul's prophetic warning loud and clear and tremble before the Word of God. The church belongs to God not us. We are called to a single ministry, and together we are building the temple of the Holy Spirit. If anyone destroys God's temple, God will destroy him. That is the Word of the Lord.

10

SERVANTS AND STEWARDS: THE POWER OF PASTORAL INTEGRITY

Pastoral life is disillusioning, often crushingly so. I certainly had my pastoral ideals emptied in a hurry. I should have known better—I grew up in a parsonage. But with the arrogance of the young and strong, I created the church in the image of my seminary course in ecclesiology. I loved the "idea" of the church. Then reality hit.

CHECKING UP ON OURSELVES

Reality Check

The pulpit committee of my first congregation, like all search committees, didn't tell me about the realities; instead, they sold me the positives. I bought the store! I wanted the church to be like my seminary dreams. And, of course, I didn't tell them about my weaknesses either.

The weekend that I candidated to be their pastor was a wonderful whirlwind of goodwill, meetings, smiles, and good cheer. I loved it. I loved them. They loved me. It was delightful if not altogether realistic.

On Sunday morning I preached to a packed house. They were glued to my every word, and I preached with gusto and great hope. On Sunday evening the members met and voted unanimously to call me to be their pastor. I was stunned. Dad told me that nobody receives a unanimous vote. I flew back to Chicago on an airplane, but my soul seemed to fly by itself, borne by wings of optimism.

Three months later I arrived. The first service I conducted was a traditional midweek prayer meeting. I anticipated a crowd of eager members who would come to learn and pray. I worked up a humdinger of a lesson on prayer. I waited in my office, nearly breathless with anticipation. *Who knows,* I thought, *maybe revival would break out on the spot!*

I walked out into the Fireside Room to meet my waiting and expectant congregation. Thirteen people sat scattered among the folding chairs. Twelve were elderly women. I felt betrayed. Where was the search committee? Where was the packed-out church I remembered so vividly? Most of all, I lamented, where was the prayer? These people said words, but they sounded routine, trite, and mechanical. And the prayers did not reflect any of the wonderful lesson I had just finished. I walked home silent and wounded.

My first board meeting came the following week. I had never been to a board meeting in my life, so I really didn't know what to expect. In fact, I don't recall a single discussion of board meetings or board members in my three years of seminary. I didn't even know enough to form an agenda, and I couldn't find anything in the church files to help me.

I arrived first and sat alone in the room nervously awaiting my board, several of whom I hadn't met yet. Only three board members showed up, and they arrived together. The youngest, a sixty-five-year-old man, helped the other two men into the room. Neither was steady afoot nor able to attend church any longer. I smiled and greeted them. Then I died inside. There wasn't much to talk about. They told me that one of the deacons had joined a cult group and was no longer around. We chatted a while and went home. I walked home that night wondering what I had gotten myself into.

The next week was the monthly trustees' meeting. Unfortunately, all of them showed up, including three who no longer attended church. The chairman had an agenda, utterly without religious content. The discussion seemed to have a hard edge. That night I walked home scared.

Then came the Christian education committee meeting. The longest discussion was whether or not to let a Mormon continue to help her husband teach the third-grade Sunday school class. They hoped that participation in church activities would bring her to Christian faith. But there was more—much more. Two church officers were having an affair. A couple of choir members told me they often held their feet off the floor during the sermon in order to fight their hangovers and stay awake. Plus there were the inevitable long-term grudges and hurts common to small-town life—or to any church community.

I was fortunate. The church officers were not typical of the heart of the church. No church boss manipulated me, the congregation loved me, and the Holy Spirit came in power. People were converted and lives were changed, including the couple having the affair; and the townspeople took notice.

But in the midst of God's blessing, human nature raised its ugly head. Several people came to share their "concerns." I have learned that that word usually means criticism is coming! Some weren't sure that I was filled with the Holy Spirit. A group claiming wide support demanded that we change the style of music. Another group said that if we did change the music they would leave. Some thought one man controlled me; others said a group of people dominated me. One said I preached too loudly; another complained she couldn't hear me. An early supporter decided I hated women and withdrew her blessing from me.

I couldn't believe it. The church was being transformed. We were packed out every Sunday. The old prayer meeting was full and alive. People in the community were coming to faith. Yet some of those who claimed the deepest spirituality couldn't seem to see anything except negatives. My humanity kicked in full force. I complained in my journal:

> So this is the pastorate. For three years I lived in a dream world. Now I see. I hear some resent the L's because they idolize me. Others don't want us to spend time with the P's. Some are praying for me because my sermons are too boring. C told me I'm a "hard" person without compassion. K said he would never set foot in church again because of me. L said I quench the Spirit. Is this the ministry? To be misunderstood, unappreciated, alone, and misquoted with no hope of correction? This is a painful, lonely business. What can I do?

Sometimes I preferred the bad old days when the church was dead and everything was sheer religious routine.

It's a Matter of Integrity

Regardless of the self-pity in my journal, I did have a point. Pastoral ministry is the strange combination of being loved and despised, affirmed and criticized, followed and rejected. It's part exhilaration, part depression. Peaceful contentment mixed with destructive discontent. Lots of affection and sometimes even more anger. It's the power of the gospel and the weakness of humanity all wrapped up in one experience.

Pastoral disillusionment is the child of betrayal. We live and work in the living body of Christ, a community born of the gospel, which, by its nature, is called to demonstrate the love, grace, and holiness that mark the gospel of God. The church is the objective means through which God shows his character to the world. Therefore, the character of God is integral to the character of Christ's church. And therein lies the problem.

Because it bears the unmistakable character of humanity, the church falls far short of its Lord. People who should know better substitute small human forms of religion for the righteousness demanded by the gospel. Pastors are fully human and bear the weight of fallenness too. This universal humanness is part of the burden and joy of the ministry. What is integral to the church, the character of God and Christ's gospel, is not natural to fallen humans. The gap between our profession and reality challenges the integrity of the church and the ministry.

Galatians 5 describes the character of humanity in contrast to the work of the Spirit. It is remarkable and too often ignored that sin and righteousness in that text are largely relational. When the church fails in relationships, which is the location of original sin in the church, it hurts deeply. Some Christians and churches vigorously enforce correct doctrine but allow bitterness, hostility, and gossip to go unchallenged. That is failure at the most basic level: the great command (John 13:34–35). Lovelessness destroys pastors and their families, but it destroys the church too. People for whom Christ died seem less important than petty self-interest. Institutional values seem to conquer gospel values regularly. This betrayal not only disfigures Christ's church, it frustrates the progress of the gospel. It is no small matter. It is, in fact, a matter of integrity.

The reverse is equally and profoundly true: Pastors regularly disillusion congregations. Our betrayal of the Word we preach by attitude and action destroys people for whom Christ died. That betrayal is, too often, a tragedy of what we call moral failure. My father pastored a church where one of his predecessors ran off with a woman in the church. Twenty-five years later the consequences remained.

Or, our betrayal may be far more subtle but equally destructive. Arrogance and other forms of pride undermine the work of God. My father-in-law, a long-time lay leader and church officer, helps me see things from the other side of church life. He once remarked that it seemed to him that pastors acted as if they were infallible. Perhaps he overstated the case, but if we are not careful, we give the impression that we alone know God's will for the congregation.

Pastoral Integrity

Power provides a great capacity for corruption. Pastoral life is about power. Pastors have organizational power, personal power, spiritual power, pulpit power, and financial power—the power of trust and office and souls.

Abuse of power is as basic an evil as there is, and it lies at the heart of pastoral and ecclesial failure. The antidote is the foundational Christian value of submission. Every pastor needs to be in submission not only to God but also to Christ's church. A body from within the congregation needs to look out for our souls. Denominations should spend far less time tinkering with organizational matters and more time pastoring pastors. And most of us need relationships with others outside the congregation who make us answer the hard questions about our lives and our faith. As a matter of integrity, our lives must match the gospel we proclaim just as the inner life of the congregation must reflect the character of Christ.

Back when I first hit the wall of disillusionment, I recall looking in Paul's writings to find a word for my roller-coaster life of altitudinous highs and even deeper lows. I certainly didn't want to resign my spirit to cynicism and develop a bitter core in my soul. I had seen that happen to others in the clergy, and it frightened me. I turned to the Corinthian letters because I knew that Paul's experience with them was far worse than anything I had run into. Sure enough, Paul felt all the highs and lows I knew. In chapter 4, after a long passage about what apostolic ministry means, he says that he was cursed, slandered, and persecuted. He was regarded as "the scum of the earth, the refuse of the world" (v. 13). My journal never reflected that sort of intensity.

Paul handled his own disillusion well. He said, "When we are cursed, we bless; when we are persecuted, we endure it; when we are slandered, we answer kindly" (vv. 12–13). Apparently Paul was able to turn the other cheek when under the lordship of Christ. His submission to Christ created triumph in his heart. His remedy for disillusionment in pastors and in our churches is a helpful word for our time. Pastors often feel betrayed by their seminary education, by denominational officials, and by their congregations. Laypeople, young and old, sense betrayal everywhere, even in the church.

Disillusionment is an opportunity for integrity. Another Pauline double metaphor will help modern-day pastors in the struggle for integrity. Paul told the Corinthian church to regard him and his fellow ministers as "servants of Christ and stewards of the mysteries of God" (1 Cor. 4:1, my paraphrase).

SERVANTS OF CHRIST

A local pastor was under severe attack. Although he had been quite successful elsewhere, things were not working out in his new church. In fact, rumor had it he was about to be fired. A pastor friend and I took him out for lunch and encouragement. We both were stunned by his remarkable calmness and apparent self-assurance. The all-out assault on his gifts and style didn't seem to phase him at all. The reason, he said, was an unswerving sense that God had called him to that church.

My friend and I talked afterward. We agreed that we were different. Under attack we questioned everything, including our call to pastoral ministry. Since then I have often wondered where that man's calm sense of call came from, especially since the church did fire him!

Paul was remarkably calm under fire too. The Corinthian church didn't like his looks, his preaching, or his style (2 Cor. 10:10; 11:5, 12). Under all the criticism was a mistrust of Paul's motives. They doubted his integrity (1:15–2:4), and he questioned theirs (11:1–15). Yet in 1 Corinthians 3–4 he is quite sure of himself. His pastoral identity is certain despite the attacks. In 4:1–5 he uses the dual image of servant and steward to reveal the character of his ministry and himself.

The Word *Servant*

Paul often refers to himself as a "servant" (*diakonos*) or "slave" (*doulos*) of Christ. Both of those words are general terms for a servant. The two words used in 1 Corinthians 4:1, *huperetes* ("servant") and *oikonomos* ("steward," or as the NIV translates it, "those entrusted") give specific content to the idea of pastoral servanthood.

Huperetes is relatively rare in the New Testament but common in ordinary Greek. More often than not, it is misunderstood in popular preaching and teaching. Based on etymology, the word is often linked to the Greco-Roman galley slave who rowed his master's ship. Literally the word means "under rower." The image portrayed is lowliness and servitude.

In common usage, however, the word meant something rather different.[1] Ordinarily the word described someone who was commissioned to speak and carry out orders in behalf of another. In Greek literature Hermes and the prophets of Delphi in their role as spokesmen of Zeus and Apollo are called *huperetai*. Cynic and Pythagorean philosophers were also *huperetoi* who served as spokesmen for the higher authority of their philosophy. A physician's assistant was a *huperetes* who treated patients on behalf of and at the order of the physician. Hellenistic Jewish literature provides an even sharper example of the word. The historian Josephus describes Moses as God's *huperetes* who led Israel to the Promised Land.

The New Testament use of the word is similar. In the Gospels *huperetes* is used to describe one who carries out the edicts of a court of law (Matt. 5:25). In Acts, John Mark is Paul and Barnabas's *huperetes*, or assistant. In each case the *huperetes* renders a service by executing the will of another. In

1 Corinthians 4:1, Paul explains the pastoral role played by himself and Apollos with this word. Paul, an apostle, and Apollos, a pastor, are both *huperetai* of Christ. They represent and speak for the Lord. They are Christ's assistants in the church. They do not speak or act on their own behalf but on Christ's.

The Pastoral Leader As Servant

Paul uses the servant image to defend himself against attack. In view of the Corinthians' rejection of him, they needed to know some basic pastoral facts of life. First and foremost, Paul answered to Christ not them. Note how strongly he fills out the picture in 1 Corinthians 4:3–5. (my paraphrase):

> I will not be judged by you. I don't work for you. I'm Christ's assistant. If your don't like my leadership or my message, *you* have the problem! I'm Christ's agent and spokesman, not yours. Moreover, what the watching world thinks of my person and office is also a matter of indifference to me. I don't answer to public opinion. In fact, I don't even judge myself! The only accurate measure of anything is Christ and his Word. I cannot trust your opinion, public opinion, or my own opinion.

This is not professional anarchy. Paul did not arrogantly flaunt his apostolic independence from outside authority; he was deeply submissive to Christ. All human opinion, including his own, he writes, stands before that solemn court. Paul was also submissive to the apostolic tradition he taught the churches. First Corinthians, in particular, is a call for the church to pay attention to that authoritative tradition (cf., e.g., 11:16, 23; 15:3).

Nor should this image and its context encourage pastors to defy local or denominational church authority. Mutual submission and accountability under the lordship of Christ are necessary checks on the human tendency to serve our own personal ends.

This picture does, however, offer a profound sense of pastoral identity and integrity. Paul knew who he was, and he knew his conscience was clear. More important, the whole matter was under Christ's authority. The Corinthian church had apparently escaped that authority in order to serve its own ends. Paul is bringing the church back to its first principles.

The corrective to a defective pastoral self-image is focus on the One whom we serve. Focus on the Christ who calls us to ministry would also quiet much of the discontent in the church at large.

"Remember Who You Are"

A number of years ago, a small but vocal group in the church decided they wanted me to go. I was never sure how many were in the group, since secrecy shrouded their maneuvering. And I never really understood what the issues were, although I did know that they disliked my style and direction of leadership and that some even doubted my Christian faith. They refused to communicate openly or to identify themselves. I only knew that several spokesmen told me they represented "many" concerned members. (I learned later always to ask for names and numbers, since the critics are seldom more than a handful and should not be taken seriously if they won't talk publicly.)

It made me sick. Literally. I recall sitting on a deacon's porch talking it over with a group of deacons. My whole body shook and my voice trembled as I tried to talk. The board supported me unanimously, the larger congregation affirmed me openly, and these deacons had gathered together to encourage me, yet in the heat of battle their support meant little to me. Because the rejection had caught me by surprise in the midst of otherwise good pastoral times, it devastated me.

I felt horrible. The pastoral instinct to care deeply came home to haunt me. It usually does. The more we care, the more rejection hurts. That's the way it is with love. Pastors have big hearts, and that heartfelt affection seems to create

213

thin skin. I was ready to pack it in. I knew I had reached an all-time low when one afternoon I found myself reading the want ads looking for another way to make a living.

My road back to health included a phone conversation with my dad, who had walked the path of rejection more than once. His counsel was wise and rooted in Paul's pastoral self-understanding.

"Remember who you are," he said. "You are the pastor there until God moves you on. Act like it!" He didn't mean that I should be stubborn, arrogant, or unsubmissive to authority. He did mean that I should remember for whom I was working. The Christological reality was stunning. I could not wither in self-pity or retreat inside myself, for the nature of the pastoral call demanded self-assurance born of my identity as Christ's assistant.

My father's exhortation was simple yet difficult to put into action. Instead of following the natural human tendency to gain confidence from our own accomplishments, we must realize that all our gifts and skills rest on the foundation of Christ's person, words, and work. If I take my orders from him and speak his truth, no human court of opinion is ultimately relevant. Pastoral integrity rests in our relationship to the One who calls us.

Unless controlled by the lordship of Christ, this can be a dangerous image. We must not use it to justify stupidity, mistakes, saying the wrong things, or leading in harmful ways. We may be dead wrong and the congregation right. That afternoon on the porch, I listened to two men I trusted. Their wisdom supported Christ's lordship. As fellow-elders of the church, we were mutually accountable. They affirmed what I knew was true: God had called me to be Christ's spokesman in that place. I had to act like it. My call from Christ compelled me to stand before the church in the name and power of the Lord Christ.

Years ago I found a quote from C. H. Spurgeon, which I framed and hung on the wall by my desk. Listen to his firm sense that he is Christ's man:

> I have striven, with all my might, to attain the position of complete independence of all men. I have found, at times, if I have been much praised, and if my heart has given way a little, and I have taken notice of it, and felt pleased, that the next time I was censured and abused I felt the censure and abuse very keenly, for the very fact that I accepted the commendation, rendered me more sensitive to the censure. So that I have tried, especially of late, to take no more notice of man's praise than of his blame, but to rest simply upon this truth—I know that I have a pure motive in what I attempt to do, I am conscious that I endeavor to serve God with a single eye to His glory, and therefore, it is not for me to take either praise or censure from man, but to stand independently upon the rock of right doing.

Remember Who Is Lord

Any pastoral theology or practice with biblical integrity will be Christologically centered. That is no mere theological proposition. The presence and power of Christ form the heart and soul of the church. The very life-force of Christianity in its individual and corporate forms is the real presence of Christ. Leadership in the church, lay or clergy, takes its identity and its cues from its Lord.

Gordon Fee reminds us that 1 Corinthians 3–4 is not only deeply Christological but equally eschatological.[2] Apostolic eschatology meant far more than a focus on the end times. Paul and the early church lived in the powerful awareness that for Christians the future is guaranteed because of the past. Christ's death and resurrection ushered in the new age of the Spirit. The future is anchored in the work of God accomplished in the past. Therefore, the present, regardless of its difficulty, is guaranteed by that future. Or, as Paul put it elsewhere, "He who began a good work in you will carry it on to completion until the day of Christ Jesus" (Phil.1:6).

Trust in Christ is, by its nature, hope. Reliance on the work of Christ is, at the same time, the firm belief that Christ's death and resurrection determine all human history. In a world without hope beyond its own fading dreams, the message we preach is powerful indeed. And if we proclaim it, we must be formed by it. We who stand in the name of the Lord of the universe know who is Lord of the church. Regardless of appearances, God is not finished with any church. God will make everything work for good and his glory. We dare not live by any other vision than the lordship of Christ. Nor must the church serve any other vision. Hope is who we are and how we live.

That same lordship determines our work and forms our integrity—at least it should. We are not left to our own devices. Against principalities and powers coupled with enough human realities to make us weep, we speak for a Lord who will triumph in us, in the church, and in history.

I talked to a layman who simply could not get his act together. His circumstances at home and on the job kept him off-balance spiritually, and he couldn't seem to grow in faith. He wanted to know what he could do.

Puzzled myself, I desperately searched through my mental file to find some word of hope. Finally, I said, "Harold, you are a man whom Christ raised from the dead. Now act like it!"

I was amazed when he said, "Okay!" I was more amazed when his life began to change. What I had really said was, "Live in faith in the One who claims you."

Christian pastors are servants of the Most High God. We bear and proclaim the name of the Lord Christ. Now act like it! More simply, believe what you say you believe.

STEWARDS OF GOD

Again Paul shifts his metaphors to enrich his description of the ministry. He wanted the Corinthian Christians to see their pastors in a new way. He calls Apollos and himself "stewards" (Gr. *oikonomos*).

Stewards in the Bible

In both Testaments a steward is one entrusted with the management of another's wealth. Ordinarily, in the ancient world, stewards were household slaves who managed the entire estate. Joseph, for example, was Potiphar's steward. He was responsible for the management of everything Potiphar owned. Joseph's responsibility was so complete that Potiphar concerned himself with nothing except the food on his table (Gen. 39:4, 6). The only part of the household not under Joseph's authority was Potiphar's wife (v. 9). Joseph was in charge of the other slaves, the finances of the estate, Potiphar's business affairs, and the administration of the entire household. As a result of Joseph's wise stewardship and of God's blessing on Potiphar's household for Joseph's sake (v. 5), Potiphar's wealth increased and his household was well managed—except for his wife! Needless to say, few citizens were more important to ancient culture than stewards, for they formed the administrative structure of society. They managed the wealth of the nations and oversaw the affluent households that supported civilization.

In the New Testament, the role of stewards was the same. The parable of the so-called unjust steward is a case in point (Luke 16:1–18). In fact, he was not unjust at all (note that the NIV calls this the parable of the "shrewd manager"). The parable seems strange to our ears. A steward was accused of mismanagement, and his master called him to account for his actions. The steward quickly sized up the situation and made plans for survival should he lose his position. His actions seem to indicate that he was a poor steward paving the way for new employment. He called in his master's debtors and offered them deals they couldn't refuse. He cut one debtor's bill in half and offered another debtor a 20 percent reduction. All his master's debtors received deals they couldn't refuse. The master got wind of the steward's arrangements and, surprisingly, we think, commended his dishonest steward for his shrewd deals.

Interpreters are puzzled by what appears to be Jesus' justification of dishonesty. However, the steward's dishonesty is more likely his actions previous to these phenomenal deals. As J. Duncan Derrett points out, the laws of agency that regulated the behavior of stewards gave them nearly absolute privilege and power. The steward, as an agent, could make and cancel debts independently of the householder. He set interest rates and arranged repayment. The steward's authority was so complete that his decisions were legally binding on the master.[3] Thus the steward in Jesus' parable was entirely within his rights to change interest rates and cancel debts. He was using his agency to better his own position. He was not unjust and did nothing illegal at this point of his stewardship. His master's commendation of his shrewdness was probably also a rebuke for not advancing the household's fortunes in a similar fashion.

The One Necessary Quality of Stewards

The point of Jesus' parable is that a steward's primary quality is trustworthiness. Those who can be trusted with little, who are shrewd like the steward in the parable, will be trusted with much (Luke 16:10). An earthly steward ran the entire household, managed slaves, saw to the care and education of the children of the manor, and controlled the cash flow and investments of the family. He was in charge of capital and people. He was top man in the household apart from the master. Therefore, he must be trustworthy. Too much hangs in the balance for the steward to be anything less than a man of integrity.

Paul's point bears both emphases of the metaphor. Stewards have enormous privilege and therefore must be trustworthy. Eternity hangs in the balance.

THE PASTOR AS STEWARD

The steward metaphor was perhaps more powerful for Paul's first readers than for us. *Oikonomos*, or steward, is part of a word group that the authors of the New Testament often use to describe the church and the economy of God. The root word of the group is *oikos*. Usually translated "house," the word means much more than that English word. A better translation is "household." It means the entire extended family, even a clan, including slaves and servants.

Paul called the church the "household of God" (*oikeioi tou theou*), a people being built together into the temple of the Holy Spirit (Eph. 2:19–22). The whole church of Christ is God's extended family. Moreover, all of human history is under God's stewardship (*oikonomian*) and is moving toward its consummation in Christ (Eph. 1:9–10).

No wonder Paul says the stewardship of apostles and pastors is managing a mystery (1 Cor. 4:1). As God's under-stewards we are part of the drama of the ages as we lead God's people toward their certain future in Jesus Christ. It's the mystery of pastoral seeds we plant and God causes to grow (3:6). We work, and God builds his house (3:10–14). We preach the message deemed foolish by modernity, and it is the wisdom of God to women, men, and children who have been given ears to hear by the Spirit (2:6–10). We speak in weakness that becomes God's power (1:18). Meanwhile God takes ordinary people like ourselves and our congregations and builds a house for his Spirit (1:25–30). It is a mystery indeed!

In Ephesians 3 Paul broadens the concept of the mysteries of God to include the entire enterprise of the ministry of the gospel. Hidden for centuries, this mystery is now being revealed in the church, which includes people of every tongue, tribe, and nation. Paul was a steward of this mystery who led the progress of the gospel westward through the Mediterranean world. Apollos was a steward of that mystery in Corinth.

The work of the Christian ministry is managing a mystery. God puts his pastors in charge of his estates here on earth. The wealth of eternity, the power of the kingdom, the precious cargo of human lives, and the very oracles of God found in holy Scripture are entrusted to us to invest wisely. No wonder stewards must be trustworthy (1 Cor. 4:2).

The Shape of Pastoral Stewardship

Paul's steward metaphor speaks powerfully to the disillusionment of the church and its ministry. The church must readjust its perspective, for too often it tries to pour pastors into a mold of expectations alien to the spirit of Scripture, the history of the church, and the calling of Christ.

Competing Expectations. After I had been with my first congregation for a year or so, the mother of a teenage girl told me that she had readjusted her expectations of me. She was on the search committee that called me and confessed that she wanted a young pastor like me because the teenagers in the church needed someone with whom they could identify.

While there was nothing wrong with wanting a pastor to minister to the youth of the church, the woman's expectations were a serious distortion of pastoral realities. Interestingly, the search committee had never brought up the subject in our discussions. Therefore, as so often is the case, the expectations by which I would be judged were unspoken. I learned about them when I broke the mold.

More important, my call to pastoral ministry and my call to that church were far larger than ministry to a specific group in the church. I came to care for the souls of everyone, without distinction. By God's grace that mother learned the larger truth and thanked me for it.

Years later I was in a group of pastors who were talking about the traditional evening service. The consensus was that the traditional Sunday night service had not served its purpose well and needed either substantial reformation or a decent funeral. We talked about some options and about the experiences of those who had changed or done away with the old evening service. After a while one of the pastors made a comment that changed the discussion. He said, "I'm bothered by this discussion. God called me to be a teacher in the church. The kind of reforms we're talking about take away a significant part of what God called me to do."

I think my friend was wrong in his analysis but correct in his sense of identity. There may, in fact, be better ways to teach the church than the traditional Sunday evening service. Nevertheless, he was right about one thing: He evaluated ministry discussions against his sense of calling. As a steward of the Word of God, he refused to be forced into a ministry mold alien to his calling.

Proper Shape for Ministry. Paul wanted the Corinthian church to know it had a distorted vision of the ministry (1 Cor. 4:1). They wanted eloquence, style, and high-fashion leadership. They were forming a human mold into which Paul refused to be poured. He did not meet their expectations. In response, he defended his style along with Apollos' very different style by defining pastoral ministry in terms of the gospel of God.

Proper expectations may be substantially different than what some people in the congregation desire. For instance, Paul reminds the Corinthian church that high-powered spirituality along with charismatic leadership do not necessarily equal valid ministry. If eloquence and spiritual fireworks are not accompanied by love, he writes, the result is nothing more than noise. Financial success and leadership prowess without love equal zero (1 Cor. 13:1–3).

Paul puts it even more bluntly in 1 Timothy 1:5, where he sums up the ministry of teaching: "The goal of this command is love, which comes from a pure heart and a good conscience and a sincere faith." The bottom line of pastoral ministry is simply the behavioral fruit that only the gospel can produce. Genuine gospel ministry produces gospel fruit. That should be the expectation congregations have of us and our ministry. My friend, who measures his ministry by his calling to teach the church, needs to add an important point: Teaching ministry, like any other form of ministry, is a means to a gospel end.

While much disillusionment with pastors would disappear if the church (and perhaps not a few pastors) changed the mold of their pastoral expectations, pastors need an integrity check too. We must admit that the behavior of some pastors and church leaders has brought shame on the church and suspicion on all of us. And we must confess that all of us fall short of God's glory and the integrity required of stewards of the mysteries of God. Let those of us who are still standing take heed and humbly repent before God and our people before we fall.

The Integrity of God's Stewards

God trusts us with the management of his property. Every day we shape people's lives and mold the church's character as we direct God's work on earth. We leave our indelible mark all over the church (see chapter 7, "God's Penmen"). Careless, casual, or half-hearted ministry betrays the character of our work and lacks integrity.

I repeatedly tell our seminary interns to take great care when they lead worship. When people assemble in Christ's presence and open their souls to the living God, they are at their most vulnerable. Therefore it is necessary to think before one speaks, to weigh one's words, and to offer them in the spirit of the Lord Christ. The nature of the church demands it.

Most important, those called to manage the mysteries of God must themselves be under the authority of God's truth. We cannot make the goal of our ministry "love from a pure heart and a good conscience and a sincere faith" if those gospel values are not at work in us.

The easiest mistake to make in ministry is to examine God and Scripture as objects and then teach about them rather than making them subjects we know and love. The most dangerous part of seminary education is spending three or more years objectifying God and his Word as things to be inspected, understood, and appreciated rather than taking time to know and love God and his Word personally. We tend to love the objective truth and revel in teaching it at the expense of our love for God himself. It takes most of us years to recover from theological education. In some ways we never do, because another sermon or lesson is always out there waiting for us. We study and talk and talk, sometimes never stopping to deal with God or with what the text means to us.

I heard Howard Hendricks tell about a time early in his teaching ministry when he worked up a humdinger of a series on prayer. At the end of his study he knew more about prayer than he had ever imagined he could know. He had worked it into a grand presentation and couldn't wait to preach it. As he walked toward the podium to give the first lesson, it dawned on him that he hadn't prayed about the lesson or the series. That has happened to all of us too many times. We know the truth and teach the truth but are not ourselves transformed by that truth. We are not as good as our word.

The one requirement of a steward is faithfulness. In Greek, "faith" and "faithfulness" are the same word (*pistis*). English faintly maintains the connection. Originally, faithful meant "full of faith"—that is, what comes out in life corresponds to the thing believed. A faithful steward is one whose life inside and out matches what he or she proclaims as true.

At its most basic, the meaning is devastatingly simple: The sum and substance of Christian proclamation and, therefore, Christian ministry, is Jesus Christ. Because he is the object of our faith and the subject of our message, he is also the criterion for our behavior. The love we proclaim is the love of Christ, so we need to ask ourselves, "Is that love, making headway in me?"

Former Mayor Koch of New York City used to ask everyone he saw, "How am I doing?" That is a very gutsy question for anyone in public life. Pastors should have the courage to ask their people constantly, "How am I doing?" We should be interested in whether our sermons connect with people. We had better know if people are following our leadership. In a world where perception determines so much, wise leaders want to know how they are perceived.

Most of all, we should put our soul on record. The bottom line of the question "How am I doing?" is the question of integrity. At the least, our key leaders should monitor our spiritual progress. It is frightening to be spiritually submissive to people we are called to lead, but the alternative is more frightening. When we are not accountable we easily betray the truth we proclaim by our actions and our attitudes. Most of the time we are not aware of what is obvious to others. Greediness, pugnacity, quarrelsomeness, and pride invade our souls and change our character very quietly. They show, but we seldom see them. We need someone who loves us enough to tell us the truth.

Some Good News for God's Stewards

Paul's metaphor implies that stewards should be successful. After all, the wealth of the master is given to the steward to be managed well, which includes the growth and profit of the estate. Pastors are called to grow or build the church (1 Cor. 3:5–16; see chapter 9, "Farmers and Builders"). God does not entrust us with his truth and his church so that we can maintain the status quo. The very nature of the gospel demands growth and expansion. The apostles speak of growth, however, not in material terms but in spiritual terms.

The steward metaphor clearly agrees with Jesus' teaching that faithfulness is the one great requirement. In Jesus' parable of the talents, in which good stewardship demands results, note the master's commendation, "Well done, *good and faithful* servant!" (Matt. 25:21, 23, emphasis added).

The requirements for a pastor listed in 1 Timothy 3 feature qualities of faithfulness. Human standards of success are not listed. Most are inner character qualities that match the nature of the gospel: "temperate, self-controlled, respectable, hospitable, . . . not violent but gentle, not quarrelsome, not a lover of money. . ." (vv. 2–3). The only skills listed are the abilities to teach and manage well. And again the objective signs of success are surrounded by a context of integrity. A pastor's character must correspond to the message he or she proclaims.

Nevertheless, God requires results from his stewards. The gospel is inherently ambitious, and so are its stewards. How can we live well in the tension of that demand on the one hand and the great requirement of faithfulness on the other? What does God really want?

I think the answer lies in the proper relationship between our ambition for results and our passion for integrity. The New Testament witness clearly makes integrity our priority and leaves the results to God. Human nature tends to reverse the order of priority. I naturally think more about my resume than the state of my soul. I like results because they make me feel good about myself and create the credentials that increase my ranking in the pecking order of the church.

Another way of putting it is to say that we need to reform our understanding of success. Perhaps the most successful pastor I have known was a member of my staff. He had come to work for our church after a lifetime of faithful pastoral service. He was semiretired and worked for us part-time. We said his job description was to walk around and love people. He fulfilled his job description wonderfully. He was one of those remarkable men in whom grace worked so powerfully you just had to love him. The entire congregation looked to him as a model of what God wanted of us.

This man had never pastored a large church, and he wasn't a distinguished preacher or a master teacher. He wasn't particularly handsome. In fact, he was short and rather ordinary looking. He wasn't stylish, nor did he have the "class" that was so important in our neighborhood. He was, however, conformed to the image of Christ. He was wonderfully successful in the one thing that counts in life. And he was a splendid success in pastoral ministry. Everyone in the congregation looked to him as a model of faith—and faithfulness. In fact, I determined that when I am an old man that is the kind of man I want to be by God's grace.

He had remarkable ambition for the kingdom of God and was part of the staff of a large and growing church. His ambition, however, rested comfortably in the grace of God that was making him Christ's man and therefore a man of Christian impact. He knew his gifts and calling, and while he worked hard, he left the results with God. At the end of such a pastoral career, what better epitaph could be given a person than this: "Good and faithful servant"?

What the World Needs Now

In a world with little integrity and a church that struggles to be faithful to its Lord, integrity is the pastoral pearl of great price. Government, business, education, and, too often, families fail to live by their original principles. As a result, not many dreams are left uncrushed, and cynicism pervades.

A well-known public political figure moved into my Boston neighborhood. It is one of the most densely populated neighborhoods in the country and is also a historic neighborhood where ancient buildings are often more important than people. Most of the buildings on the block are not wired for cable TV because the cable company can't get by the politics of the local historical society. Not long ago a utility company tore up the entire street to bring fiber optics to our prominent new neighbor's house. No one in the neighborhood seemed surprised—power serves power, and politics has little to do with those served.

In Boston I ministered in a congregation filled with young adults who have had enough of that kind of world. They don't trust institutions because they have seen too much. They are wary of the church, too, because they have been let down by God's people. I worry about whether a man of fifty-something can communicate with a congregation of twenty-somethings. But they see me as a model of integrity because I have lasted twenty-five years in ministry and have been married for thirty years. They don't see much of that. When I teach them, many of them see the father they never had.

It is a frightening responsibility, but stewards must be found faithful. Will the next generation find a church that is as good as its gospel and pastors that are as good as their word? Pastoral ministry in the future will increasingly demand integrity from its practitioners and from its congregations.

A Word of Grace

This is the age of self-help books and do-it-yourself spirituality. We want formulas for success in life and faith. Pastors want formulas for pastoral success. We prefer that someone else do the hard work instead of having to take responsibility ourselves.

I have no helpful hints for faithfulness, no lists to guarantee integrity. I've heard enough of them to know that while they are true, no list or human aid can deal with the human heart.

Recently I attended a pastors' conference where speaker after speaker aimed at the moral breakdowns among the clergy and offered ways to avoid temptation. I believe every one of their cautions and words of wisdom are true. But when a Delilah confronts us, human wisdom flies out the first open window. We are left alone with our soul and temptation. And when a long string of success inflates our ego and blinds us, all the advice on humility in the world fails, good as it may be. Or, when the sting of criticism wounds us so deeply that we cannot find words to frame the hurt, what will keep our heart from bitterness or anger? Human advice and, indeed, human effort, fail.

The final word must be the word of grace. Sanctification is no more accomplished by human works than justification is gained by human righteousness. My poor soul needs the powerful grace of God that is capable of making me able to look Delilah, pride, and anger straight in the eye and say, "No thanks!"

In the face of an increasingly secular and hostile world, pastors must develop a breadth and depth of spirit unknown to most of us. We must turn from forms of spirituality that feature mechanical activities and find wells of the Spirit that nourish and enrich the soul. Our hearts must become so much like the character and spirit of Christ that we cannot find it in ourselves to betray the gospel.

John Stott once said that every morning of his life since his days as a university student, he has meditated on the fruit of the Spirit in Galatians 5:22–23. If the fruit of the Spirit is the bottom line of the grace of God, it makes sense to meditate on, pray about, and devote one's attention to it. Don't you suppose that much of the power and integrity of John Stott's character and ministry flow directly from that soul-expanding exercise? It is not the method of meditation that made the man. Rather, it is the Spirit and Word of God that transforms any of us into the image of Christ.

In pastoral ministry as nowhere else, integrity is essential. Men and women who bear God's name and proclaim God's Word must, by the very nature of things, model the values and character of God.

As I talk to young adults these days, I'm impressed by the number of times they mention integrity or authenticity. The rising generation want the church and its ministry to walk what it talks and mean what it says. They want us to be as good as our word—and God's Word. And they're right.

11

Ambassador and Preacher: The Pastor's Authority

We are therefore Christ's ambassadors, as though God were making his appeal through us. We implore you on Christ's behalf: Be reconciled to God.
—2 Corinthians 5:20

"Frank" was a grizzly bear of a man. Years of farm labor had hardened his body while a hard country religion had petrified his soul. He was a deacon in a church I served. Never short for words, Frank always told it like it was. He could be brutal. His wife and children cowered before his harshness, and they loathed him for it.

After church one Sunday, the deacons and I went out for lunch to discuss the state of the church. Things didn't seem to be going well. Frank wasted neither time nor words. He raced through his meal, put down his fork, and blurted out,

"The problem with the church is that the preacher ain't preaching evangelistic sermons."

Frank spoke volumes more than he thought. I was sitting next to him, yet he referred to "the preacher" as if I were absent. He had distanced himself from my ministry, and his words showed it. By evangelistic preaching, Harold meant that I should aim my sermons at non-Christians and at those Christians who needed to get right with God. He assumed that he was in neither camp, and therefore he wanted my preaching to leave him alone. He regularly got angry when I touched issues in his life like anger, racism, or compassion.

One Sunday I preached from the text, "Blessed are the peacemakers . . ." (Matt. 5:9). I thought the passage was relevant since court-ordered busing to force school integration had created near-riot conditions in nearby Louisville, Kentucky. I asked the congregation to consider what the Christian response to that kind of anger and hate should be. The church was small enough to allow conversation, and I used the last part of the sermon time for discussion of the question.

Frank spoke first. His face was red with anger, and he more or less yelled a question at me. "Why'd you bring that up here today?" he asked. He obviously didn't want to think about it.

Frank granted me very little authority as his pastor. His framework of faith and life excluded any human from having spiritual oversight of his soul.

A CRISIS OF AUTHORITY

Frank is a rough-hewn symbol of our time. We live in a culture in which submission to authority, especially moral or spiritual authority, is anathema.

An Authority-Resistant Culture

The Western world is at the end of a long battle against authority. Long ago, individual rights and personal sovereignty overthrew the centuries-long moral authority that resided in the state and the church. Now about the best our culture can do for moral authority is offer some vague notion of shared community standards determined by the larger culture. The moral voice of the church is mocked as hopelessly irrelevant for a world like ours.

Other authorities are under attack as well. It seems that nobody trusts the government anymore. Public figures, governmental or otherwise, have a brief day in the sun before they are discarded for new and more congenial figures. Public figures who speak with moral authority are viewed as hopelessly out of touch, even dangerous. Somehow Billy Graham escapes the cynicism of our time, but few Americans view him as a moral authority for their lives. The pope, a towering figure of moral strength for many people of Christian faith, is a figure of ridicule in the media and in some quarters of his own church. We are living through a tremendous cultural evasion of authority.

Leaders in business, education, and government agree that it is more difficult to lead in our day than in any time in recent memory. Leaders who live in the public eye suffer from overexposure and from the reactions of a fickle public, and they seldom survive more than a decade. Add to this mix cultural unrest fueled by ethnic and racial conflict, economic uncertainty, and moral and family breakdown—it is no wonder some think we are at the brink of a "culture war." Such an environment naturally creates a resistance to all claims of moral authority.

An Authority-Resistant Church

Naturally, deep cultural trends spill over into the church. The cultural conflict and resistance to authority of our time make pastoral ministry increasingly difficult.

All throughout Christian history a certain authority has been granted to the clergy. Power and authority are inherent to the office of pastor. And although pastoral authority has been abused in every generation, it has nevertheless been granted as necessary—until our time. Now the office of pastor is shrinking to the size of congregational expectations shaped by a culture that is deeply committed to the values of consumers and their inalienable natural rights.

The results are deeply disturbing. Surveys of pastors indicate the trauma of leadership in our time. Self-esteem is plummeting while conflict and self-doubt soar. Pastors are being fired and are leaving the ministry in alarming numbers. All of this is, in part, the result of a devaluing of the office and authority of the Christian pastor.

Pastoral counselor Lloyd Rediger has coined the phrase "clergy abuse," which he says is the natural result of a social movement in America that is characterized by escalation of violence and incivility. His definition of clergy abuse is simply "intentional damage" that is physical, sexual, verbal, or emotional. He points out that when traditional paragons of virtue in a society are intentionally targeted, that culture is in deep trouble.[1] The church in that culture is in deeper trouble. We are living in an ecclesiastical crisis of authority.

Even at its best, the church in this culture devalues the work and authority of pastors. The rise and dominance of technology creates norms and expectations that traditionally trained clergy cannot meet. Some technically trained parishioners have difficulty respecting and listening to ministers trained in language and ideas. The escalating trust in management models along with our native American pragmatism erode the theological and biblical base on which pastors have always done their work. The triumph of individualism in America has created a church filled with people who refuse to let anyone tell them what to believe or do. The consent of the governed, a sign of democracy, has become the lord of many a church and its pastor.

I was recently in a conversation with several church members from another congregation. I asked them about their hopes and dreams for their church. Most of their responses indicated a deep longing for spiritual renewal. One young man, however, made an interesting and telling remark. He said he hoped for a church where the teachers would only *suggest* what he should believe and do. He was tired of preachers and teachers *telling* him how to behave and what to believe. It's a sign of the times. Modernity wants the Ten Commandments to become the Ten Suggestions.

One member of a pastoral search committee told me early in the selection process that, in his opinion, preaching was not very important. He said all his Christian growth came from one-on-one relationships with Christian friends. He was signaling me in no uncertain terms that he would not submit to my teaching authority, nor would he let me pastor him except on his terms. That he was a leader in the church indicated to me an institutional resistance to pastoral authority.

More recently a university professor gave a failing grade to a report prepared by a committee of our church board. The committee didn't give proper attention to process in its attempt to encourage biblical goals for the board. He said that at his institution such a report would be laughed out of school. He was telling the board and his pastoral staff that he was sovereign over them and that in order for him to respect the work of the church, it had to proceed under a management model of his choosing. I don't suppose I will ever have much influence on his soul.

Long ago I learned an important lesson about the church, pastoral ministry, and spiritual growth. Only those who open their hearts and souls to me and my ministry will grow from my ministry. Those who resist me or my pastoral authority not only tend to be unhappy, but they cut themselves off from the spiritual nourishment at the center of the church. One cannot be served well by someone to whom one will not open one's soul.

Wise leaders distinguish carefully between the authority conferred by an office and the authority earned over time. An insightful man once told me that in the church only a fool uses official authority without sufficient earned authority to back it up. Sadly, in our time the length of time needed to win the consent of the governed is growing longer and in some cases will never happen.

As we come to the end of the twentieth century, pastoral ministry is more and more difficult. In large measure that is due to the reduction of the authority of the pastoral office to a mere shadow of what it was only a generation or two ago.

A CRISIS FOR PREACHING

In no area is authority more significant for pastoral ministry than in preaching, for it is in the pulpit that we speak the Word of Christ. The tone of our leadership is set in the moral and spiritual authority we model in our preaching. Preaching is the public demonstration that the Word of God is at work in us, and it is the tool that God uses to speak to the church and the world. Preaching without authority robs the Word of God of its essence; it is like an army without weapons. The gospel of Christ demands the authority inherent in it.

A Culture Without Ears

Preaching in our time is increasingly difficult. The technological age, in particular television, works powerfully against reasoned oral discourse. Images and sound bytes characterize the electronic communication that bombards us day in and day out. And the younger the audience the more difficult oral communication becomes. Those raised on MTV think in vivid and repeated images that burst on the imagination.

We preach to people young and old whose attention span is shortening. Our audience sits before us with a remote channel-changer in their minds. Increasingly passive recipients of powerful electronic stimulation, American audiences seldom listen with a will to become actively engaged in our sermons. Attention is more difficult to gain and even more difficult to keep.

Beyond the electronic challenge of our age, our larger culture conspires against preaching. The idea of a single person's standing with moral authority and speaking a truth that demands obedience is ridiculed. The verb *preach* in ordinary conversation is a negative term, and among the worst things to be said about a public figure is that he or she is "preachy." That mentality cannot escape those who fill our pews on Sundays. They bring either a conscious or unconscious bias against the authority of preaching. Thus, we seldom dare to tell people what to do and are instead consigned to gentle persuasion.

Moreover, our congregations are more and more consumers of religion with less and less taste for hard thinking, challenges to their presumptions, and theological reasoning. Sermons in our time reflect that distaste for thinking, challenges, and theology.

A friend of mine is a Catholic priest in a large and thriving parish. He told me that a young couple in his church recently informed him that they had decided to attend a large and growing Baptist church because it had a better children's ministry. But, they assured him, they would be back when their children were out of elementary school. What a challenge for that Baptist pastor!

When I was in suburban ministry, nearly every week some young couple came by the church to interview our children's pastor and inspect our facility. They weren't very interested in what we believed or in much else besides the best religious package they could find for their children. I was glad that we attracted these undiscriminating seekers of God—what an opportunity! But at the same time, preaching became more of a challenge as the congregation grew wildly diverse. Preaching and teaching was forced toward the lowest common denominator. I could no longer presume anything as I prepared. That's the religious world in which we live.

A Church with Itching Ears

Christians have always wanted to bend their preachers into their own image. Paul warned Timothy of that pastoral fact of life (2 Tim. 4:3–4). None of us likes to hear disturbing truths or to have our assumptions challenged. Meanwhile, we all want to hear our favorite themes and have our presumptions affirmed. Inevitably, the church wants its ministers to become chaplains of their religious expectations and guardians of their cherished traditions. Most of us learn from hard experience that when we violate institutional values, we will be hurt. It is a sad fact of church life that these institutional values are usually guarded more carefully than the gospel.

I was once in a committee meeting in which a staff member suggested we change the location of the church library. He listed a number of good reasons for the change, each of which would have enhanced the purpose for which the library existed. Suddenly a member who had been quiet during the long preceding discussion about the future of our church's mission nearly came out of his chair. With uncharacteristic passion he argued against moving the library since that would upset some long-time members.

I have sat through hundreds of board and committee meetings in my ministry and have heard long and passionate discussions about the church name, the gender of church ushers, and the color of the carpet. Yet I have never heard a discussion with the same kind of emotion about our lost neighbors or the poor at our doorstep. No wonder my impassioned sermons on the mission of the church receive such a cool reception. That is not what turns most Christians on these days. Preaching God's Word into the contemporary church's preoccupation with itself and its values is difficult indeed.

Add special agenda groups dedicated to that very human tendency to serve our own interests, and preaching and leading become even more difficult. People listen for their special agenda to be addressed and then judge the pastor and the church on that basis. I hear from people regularly who have but one theme: I haven't addressed their special interest sufficiently.

The first Sunday I was pastor of a congregation, one of the choir members caught me before the service and told me that he hoped I would preach strongly on sin. He added that they hadn't heard that theme much from my predecessor. I knew he would be judging me on how often I preached on sin.

In that same church a certain woman held a high position in party politics. During an election year she called to tell me she could arrange for one of the presidential candidates to speak on a Sunday morning at our church. When I gave her a variety of reasons why I thought that was a bad idea and that I wasn't interested, she was quite upset and told me I was out of date. Her idea of a modern church featured partisan politics. I don't think my sermons or my ministry got past the front door of her heart after that.

This woman was part of a special interest group that continually put pressure on the church leadership and staff and judged everything according to their vision of a political church. That was but one of many agenda-driven groups to whom I spoke each Sunday. Preaching with pastoral authority in the contemporary church is very difficult. Fewer and fewer Christians, it seems, want a spiritual authority independent of their control.

All of us, pastors and people, bring to every Sunday worship service our own personal agendas that drive us and form the shape of our hearing and speaking. As a pastor I must make sure my preaching and my life stand under the Word of God I preach so that my agendas don't shape what I preach. My wife and my board help keep me honest. I cannot create that kind of integrity on my own.

I have learned that my ministry in any Christian's life is dependent on that person's willingness to submit to my pastoral and teaching authority. Resistance to me or my ministry creates a fortress around the soul. Consequently, I have also come to understand that the level of satisfaction in my congregation is directly related to their willingness to open their lives and souls to my care.

Paul understood the difficulty of communicating to a resistant culture and church. Corinth, of course, is the biblical laboratory for learning how to minister in a dysfunctional church. Once again Paul drops a couple of metaphors into his letters to Corinth that help us stand before our world and the contemporary church in proper pastoral authority. One of the metaphors, Christ's ambassador (2 Cor. 5:20), is rare, used only here and in Ephesians 6:20. The other metaphor, a preacher or herald, is quite common in the New Testament. Paul emphasizes his authority as a preacher in 1 Corinthians 1–2.

Both metaphors taken together are a healthy antidote for the flagging sense of pastoral authority in most of us preachers.

CHRIST'S AMBASSADOR

I served on the board of a Christian college for several years. During that time, the government of Swaziland wanted to recruit Christian school teachers to come to their country and help them set up a Christian school system. Swaziland is a monarchy, and this was the desire of the king.

Swaziland's ambassador to the United Nations, Nelson Malinga, came to the college to interview students. I was privileged, along with another board member, to serve as his host for two days. It was an eye-opening experience. My lifetime in a democracy had not prepared me for the power of a monarchy. I had never before met a government official, and I discovered that ambassadors are a very special type of governmental official. Ambassadors of a king are even more unusual.

The first thing I noticed was Mr. Malinga's sense of dignity. It was quickly apparent that he was the personal representative of a king. His office bore an inherent power that gave the ambassador great confidence. From his behavior it was clear that he was well aware that he spoke for a king. He was quick to say, "Well, the king says, . . ." If anyone had questioned his authority or his word, he could have simply replied, "Call the king!" Mr. Malinga's dignified confidence rested in his assurance that he spoke for a monarch who had nearly absolute power.

Because the ambassador spoke for the king, a certain authority accompanied everything he did or said. At the same time, however, the ambassador was quite reserved. At all times he deferred to the king, from whom his confidence and power came, for neither the message he spoke nor the mission he was on were his own.

At night when the meetings were over and we went back to the hotel, Mr. Malinga had one last task. He called home to talk to the king. He had known the king all his life and represented a king he loved and respected. I think that much of the ambassador's dignity and quiet sense of authority came not just from his high office but also from his relationship with the king. He knew what the king thought and desired. He lived to make the king's wishes come into being.

Paul, Christ's Ambassador

Paul lived in the powerful awareness that he was an ambassador of Christ the King. He stood before his critics and enemies in Corinth with the power and dignity of the one who sent him. Despite the opposition to his ministry in the church and to the gospel in the larger culture, Paul spoke and acted with authority because he was a man under the authority of the King.

Paul needed the power and authority of Christ in Corinth. The church was enamored with appearances. They had poured their ministers into the mold of their expectations, and the results looked good and acted powerfully. Paul came out on the short end (2 Cor. 5:12). So Paul reminded the Corinthians that the gospel comes with its own persuasive power through the appeals of ordinary men like himself (v. 11).

Though some might think Paul a madman (2 Cor. 5:13), he wanted them to know that his sole motivation for ministry was the love of Christ that "compelled" him to preach the gospel (v. 14). Love compelled his ministry, because love is the nature of the gospel, which is a message of reconciliation (v. 19). Hence, Paul no longer viewed himself or his ministry from a human point of view (v. 16). He was driven by a divine energy, the love of Christ, and an eternal mission, the reconciliation of humankind to God and each other.

Paul closes this section on reconciliation by saying, "We are *therefore* Christ's ambassadors, as though God were making his appeal through us. We implore you on Christ's behalf: Be reconciled to God" (2 Cor. 5:20, emphasis added). Paul's use of "therefore" indicates that he is drawing a conclusion. He stood before the world and the church as the ambassador of Christ as though God were making his appeal through him. Hence, Paul "implored" the Corinthians to be reconciled to God, to each other, and to himself. Loving reconciliation is inherent to the gospel, is in the nature of the church, and is the goal of the ministry.

The Pastor As Ambassador

The pastoral role of ambassador lies in great tension. On the one hand, we speak for the King of kings and Lord of lords. When his Word and will are clear, we cannot help but speak boldly come what may. Our own ideas or interpretations cannot be spoken with the same boldness. Paul himself distinguished between the word of the Lord and his own opinions (1 Cor. 7:25). Nevertheless, he spoke with pastoral confidence as one with experience in the church and with the Lord. Pastors need to know the difference between the sure word of Christ and our own counsel, and we need to show our congregations the difference.

On the other hand, we ambassadors of heaven live on earth and bear witness to a Lord of the Incarnation. Christ spoke his divine Word in a manner congenial to his culture. He was sensitive to his environment, and even when he spoke harsh words of judgment he spoke the truth in love.

A few years ago I visited the country of Burkina Faso in West Africa. Our little delegation traveled to see the American ambassador to Burkina Faso in the capital city of Ouagadougou. He was most gracious and arranged for us to eat breakfast with him the next day. The topic of discussion at breakfast was how American Christians could assist that poor sub-Sahara African nation with its economic and social needs.

The ambassador was a veteran in the diplomatic corps and had spent most of his career in poor African nations. West Africa is a backwater of American diplomacy. The State Department operates on the assumption that few matters of American national interest are at stake in the region. Hence, the ambassador said, little American aid or attention is given to countries like Burkina Faso.

As he talked, I was struck by his deep understanding of and compassion for Africa. He seemed genuinely to care about the people and their future. He refused to give up against enormous, even impossible odds. He welcomed the support of churches and aided us in getting in touch with the proper sources so that we could assist the country.

As I watched and listened, I couldn't help but think of Christ's ambassadors. We represent Almighty God on this fallen planet. Many pastors may even think they serve in forgotten outposts of Christ's kingdom where very little strategic activity ever occurs. Nevertheless, we are called to minister for Christ in a manner that bears the dignity of our King, with confidence appropriate to envoys of God, and with the loving concern of our King who died for the world.

Our work demands that we appreciate and understand the citizens of this far-off country. We speak Christ's Word into a very specific set of circumstances to people bound by time and space. Our message must also bear deep sensitivity and love for the poor lost citizens of earth to whom we are sent to help.

I know that I fall short in both of these areas. Too often I am afraid of offending someone. Last winter I pulled out sermons from early in my ministry and was surprised at my youthful boldness. Over the years I have grown shier and have even blunted the sharp sword of the Spirit. I have learned that it is safer to go after some issues indirectly, and perhaps I have acted less like Christ's ambassador and more like a skillful politician.

We need to remember for whom we speak and to do so with the dignity, authority, and deference appropriate to ambassadors. We need not shrink from this anti-Christian culture nor from power brokers in the church. Our conduct should command the respect that Paul says is appropriate for ambassadors of the great King (1 Thess. 5:12–13). I have to remind myself from time to time that Christ did give the power of the keys of the kingdom to his church and its ministry. Sometimes I forget and think that the keys of the kingdom rest in congregational opinions or in powerful people. It is time for Christian pastors to act like ambassadors of God.

However, Christ's ambassadors must maintain balance in their position of authority. Paul says that the Lord's servant "must not quarrel; instead he must be kind to everyone, able to teach, not resentful. Those who oppose him he must gently instruct, in the hope that God will grant them repentance" (2 Tim. 2:24–25). That's a tough balance to keep. In fact, only under the power of the Spirit can we act like the king's ambassadors and gentle shepherds at the same time (1 Peter 5:1–3).

When I go to the hospital, when I am counseling or at a board meeting, preaching or in casual conversation I remind myself of who I am and whom I represent. I am the handpicked ambassador of Christ the King sent to represent him among the almighty God's children.

GOD'S PREACHERS/HERALDS

The work of the pastor is summed up in the pulpit. When we take up the Word of God in the temple of the Holy Spirit, God creates a moment that is uniquely divine and unrepeatable.

The ministry of the apostles is likewise summed up in the word *preachers*. Preaching was their top priority, and in so doing they were simply continuing the work of their Lord (Mark 1:14).

I once heard Dick Lucas, rector of St. Helen's Church in London, say, "God had only one Son, and he made him a preacher." It's true, and it is a source of great encouragement in these days of hostility to preaching and preachers.

The Importance of Preaching in the New Testament

The Greek word group from which come the English words *preach, preacher,* and *preaching* are among the most theologically significant in the New Testament.[2] Suffice it to say here, the concept of preaching lies at the heart of the apostolic faith. John the Baptist and Jesus came "preaching," and Peter stood and "preached" on the Day of Pentecost. Preaching is the characteristic work of the apostles and prophets in the book of Acts. Paul declared that God chose to save the lost through the "foolishness of what was preached" (1 Cor. 1:21). He commissioned pastor Timothy with these words: "In the presence of God and of Christ Jesus . . . I give you this charge: Preach the Word; be prepared in season and out of season; correct, rebuke and encourage—with great patience and careful instruction" (2 Tim. 4:1–2).

Throughout Christian history, preaching has consistently played a foundational role in the work of the church. While the term *preacher* may be a term of derision in our time, Paul was pleased to refer to himself as one appointed "a preacher and an apostle" (1 Tim. 2:7 KJV; NIV "a herald and an apostle").

While New Testament interpreters have discussed at length the distinction between the words *preach* and *teach* in the apostolic tradition, it is clear in the New Testament and in the life of the ordinary parish pastor that preaching and teaching are deeply intertwined. If, as contemporary scholarship suggests, preaching in the New Testament is primarily the proclamation of the Good News to unbelievers and teaching is ordinarily instruction in the church, it is also true that both are held together by their subject, Jesus Christ. We do proclaim Christ to the lost, but at the same time preaching is also a proclamation of the claims of Christ to believers. Teaching the church is instruction, but it is also proclamation, for what is it we teach except the truth found in Jesus? All our work as pastors is proclaiming and teaching Christ.

The Authority of Preaching

The preacher or herald in the New Testament world was a member of the royal court and a spokesman of a prince or king (later for the state). These heralds carried a scepter to signify their royal dignity and majesty and typically spoke with a loud voice to declare the word or orders of the king. They came to have religious standing as spokesmen for the gods and were called on to perform religious functions for the state. In short, heralds, like ambassadors, were envoys for the king and therefore acted and spoke for the king. Inherent in the concept is that the heralds carried in themselves the power and authority of the king.

The apostles described their work and the work of the church as preaching. They were certain that the King of kings commissioned them to declare to the world and to the church the good news contained in God's final revelation, Jesus Christ. Furthermore, they were equally and mysteriously convinced that when they spoke on behalf of King Jesus, he himself spoke, "as though God were making his appeal through us" (2 Cor. 5:20).

Such proclamation or teaching must be made with authority or it subtracts from the dignity and sovereignty of God. Preachers in our day need to recover that confidence. We dare not waver before the hostility of the watching world nor the self-centered agendas of contemporary churches. We come in the name and authority of Christ the Lord. Meanwhile, we preachers need to brush up on what Jesus said and how the apostles interpreted his words so that our message will be an authentically Christian word.

Much is said about the deplorable state of preaching in our time. I am convinced that the root of the problem is theological. Pastors find it increasingly difficult to stand and speak as heralds of the Lord. We suffer from a failure of confidence because we depend on our own ability and take far too many cues from our audience. Too often we preach as if asking permission for a hearing. Shy preaching denies the nature of the One for whom we speak and the character of his Word.

The Power of Preaching

To a world and church that questions appropriateness or efficacy of a person standing before a group with moral authority, the apostolic tradition offers the miracle of the Word. Somehow, mysteriously and under the hand of God, preachers stand each Lord's Day and with faltering human speech incarnate the living Word again. That Word goes out in power and strikes human hearts in ways we preachers cannot begin to imagine. The Word of God is sharp and powerful, and it never comes back empty (Heb. 4:12–13).

I am awestruck at the power of the preached Word to touch a world that has been programmed to reject it. I regularly preach to a congregation of which the majority are younger than I. They are a high-tech congregation, and the younger members reflect the values and lost dreams of this generation. Yet they listen to me, a man old enough to be their father. And time after time, when I communicate God's Word in my own human manner, it transforms lives in small and large ways. Once a couple on the verge of divorce were struck by the power of the Word in a sermon and decided to give their marriage another chance. Often people report that my preaching or a particular sermon turned their life around. It is a wonder and a privilege.

I recently traveled to the countryside. Life is simple there, and so is church. On Sunday the preacher stood with Bible in hand and a congregation of country folk before him. His sermon was homey—properly so—and made a profound gospel point in simple terms. God reached out of eternity, penetrated my proud, educated heart, and made his point. I was changed. It was the miracle of preaching, the foolishness that is the power of God.

It is time for preachers to remember who they are and stand in the name and authority of Christ before congregations who are skeptical of their preaching. Without apology or wavering we must stand as Christ's envoys and heralds to do God's work. And by God's grace we will.

In his wonderful book *How Shall They Preach?* Gardner Taylor sums up preaching in a wonderful application of the story of the valley of dry bones in Ezekiel 37.

> Scattered grimly throughout the silent desert were the bleaching bones of what once had been a proud and gallant army. Rusting spears and rotting regimental standards and wheelless chariots told their story of martial splendor and of some great battle once fought on this scene now so stark. . . . Now there is nothing but stillness, ominous, deathly stillness and a man and some bones and, yes, off on the other end a God who initiates conversation.
>
> Is this what life is all about, green valleys that turn to dust and silence? Are our marching hopes and vibrant dreams fated for nothing more than to lie at last wasted and still? Is this what the preacher confronts in the brokenness of human life, the high resolves and royal vows which come to nothing? Is all that doomed to perish in a people become pygmied and uglied by their own cravenness and selfishness and bigotry?
>
> The man is addressed by God. . . . It is that voice which sounds in varying tones of joy and sorrow in every preacher's inmost self, challenging, summoning, examining, accusing, encouraging. . . . "Son of man, can these bones live?"
>
> Can life come where death has breathed its chill? Can springtime come when winter has frozen the earth in its icy grip? Can old men dream the dreams of young men? . . . "Son of man, can these bones live?" There will be those facing every pulpit who know they have failed their Lord in word and work. . . . In their own way they ask the question which God asked of Ezekiel, "Son of man, can these bones live?" It is God's question. . . .
>
> A quick and easy answer "Yes" is more than half a lie, for the preacher cannot help having doubts. On the other hand, if he or she surrenders to that doubt and

says, "No . . ." the preacher impeaches the power of the Eternal God. Thus there ought to be some central hush in the preacher's utterance, for he or she stands in the midst of life and death matters, with God very much in the midst of it all. . . .

Withal, it is a glorious task to be called to preach the gospel. This no man's land just described above merely accentuates and sweetens the task of the preacher. Wherever one's preaching lot is cast, there will be men and women long in captivity, their eyes unaccustomed to the light which belongs to those who know the glorious liberty of the Sons of God. In darkened cells of the spirit, half dead, they sit. And, then, please God, on the edge of the mountain they see the running feet of the courier and know by his garments that he is the King's messenger. They know also, that he bears welcome and long longed-for word of the mighty battle and a great victory, and that because of that victory soon their cell doors will swing wide and thy will stand free in the sunlight once again. That the courier's feet are not well formed, that the bone structure is not symmetrical, that there are ugly deformities showing through the leather of his footwear all count for nothing. He bears good news and glad tidings. Is there any wonder that a cry rings through the prison? Now and then, couriers of the great King, you will hear it or some variation of it, "How beautiful upon the mountains are the feet of him that bringeth good tiding . . . that saith unto Zion, 'Thy God reigneth!'"[3]

BENEDICTION

There you have it, a summary of the Christian ministry. We are sacramental persons who bear in our being and words the very power of God. We are benedictions of God to the King's people. In the biblical world, benedictions were far more than pretty words. They carried the weight of eternity because they were spoken in the name of the Most High God.

That is what we pastors are and do. We are sent by the King to bless his people with our words and deeds. Lately I have begun to take benedictions—and myself as a benedictor—more seriously. I deliberately lay hands on people and give them God's blessing and mine. I have changed the way I see God's people and my work as God's herald.

To the church of Jesus Christ and all the pastors who stand among God's people I say:

> *The LORD bless you*
> *and keep you;*
> *the LORD make his face shine upon you*
> *and be gracious to you;*
> *the LORD turn his face toward you*
> *and give you peace.*
>
> (Num. 6:24–26)

NOTES

Introduction: Welcome to the Ministry

[1]Walt Russell, "What It Means to Me," *Christianity Today,* October 26, 1992, 30.

[2]Russell Chandler, *Racing Toward 2001* (Grand Rapids: Zondervan, 1992); Leith Anderson, *A Church for the 21st Century* (Minneapolis: Bethany House, 1992); Leonard Sweet, *FaithQuakes* (Nashville: Abingdon, 1994).

[3]George Hunter, "Communication to Secular People," The Church in the 21st Century Conference, Dallas, Texas, June 15, 1993.

[4]Loren Mead, *The Once and Future Church: Reinventing the Congregation for a New Mission Frontier* (Washington, D.C.: Alban Institute, 1991).

[5]Greg Asimakoupoulos, "The New Endangered Species," *Leadership* (Winter 1994), 123.

[6]Ibid.

[7]Louis McBurney, "A Psychiatrist Looks at Troubled Pastors," *Leadership* (Spring 1980), 109, 114.

[8]H. R. Niebuhr, *The Purpose of the Church and Its Ministry* (New York: Harper & Row, 1956), 48.

[9]James Smart, *Rebirth of Ministry* (Philadelphia: Westminster, 1960).

[10]Seward Hiltner, *Preface to Pastoral Theology* (1956; reprint, Nashville: Abingdon, 1979).

2 What's My Address? The Significance of Geography

[1]Roy Oswald, *Crossing the Boundary Between Seminary and Parish* (Washington, D.C.: Alban Institute, 1980).

3 What Time Is It? The Question of Date

[1]Tom Peters, *Thriving on Chaos: Handbook for a Management Revolution* (New York: HarperCollins, 1991), xiii.

[2]Loren Mead, *The Once and Future Church: Reinventing the Congregation for a New Mission Frontier* (Bethesda, Md.: Alban Institute, 1991).

[3]John R. Stott, *The Contemporary Christian* (Downers Grove, Ill.: InterVarsity Press, 1992).

[4]Robert Bellah, *Habits of the Heart: Individualism and Commitment in American* Life (New York: Harper & Row, 1986).

[5]Martin Seligman, "Boomer Blues," *Psychology Today,* October 1989.

[6]Ibid.

[7]Vance Packard, *A Nation of Strangers* (New York: McKay, 1972).

[8]James D. Hunter, *Culture Wars: The Struggle to Define America: Making Sense of the Battles over the Family, Art, Education, Law, and* Politics (New York: Basic Books, 1991).

[9]Daniel Patrick Moynihan and Nathan Glazer, *The Melting Pot* (Cambridge: MIT Press/Harvard University Press, 1963).

[10]Daniel Patrick Moynihan, "Pandemonium," *Newsweek,* January 4, 1993.

[11] *Fortune,* December 12, 1993.

[12]*Forbes,* September 14, 1992

4 Whose Church Is This? The Question of Ecclesiology

[1]Cited in John Jefferson Davis, *Foundations for Evangelical Theology* (Grand Rapids: Baker, 1984), 6.

[2]Os Guiness, speech entitled "The Challenge to Faith of Modernity," Dallas, Texas, August 21, 1991.

[3]Robert Patterson, "In Search of the Visible Church," *Christianity Today,* March 11, 1991, 36–40.

[4]Ibid., 38.

[5]Millard Erickson, *Christian Theology* (Grand Rapids: Baker, 1985), 3:1025.

[6]Ibid.

[7]Helmut Thielicke, *The Evangelical Faith* (Grand Rapids: Eerdmens, 1982), 3:203.

[8]Hans Küng, *The Church,* trans. Ray and Rosaleen Ockenden (New York: Sheed & Ward, 1968), 25.

[9]P. T. Forsyth, *The Church and the Sacraments* (1917; reprint, Naperville, Ill.: Allenson, 1955), 93.

[10]Karl Barth, *Church Dogmatics*, ed. G. W. Bromiley and T. F. Torrance (Edinburgh: T. & T. Clark, 1936–), 4:66.

[11]Ibid., 4:679.

[12]Jürgen Moltmann, *The Church in the Power of the Spirit: A Contribution to Messianic Ecclesiology*, trans. M. Kohl (New York: Harper & Row, 1977), 6.

[13]Thielicke, *Evangelical Theology*, 3:244.

[14]Küng, *The Church*, 23.

[15]Stanley J. Grenz and Roger E. Olson, *20th Century Theology: God and the World in a Transitional Age* (Downers Grove, Ill.: InterVarsity Press, 1992).

5 Christ's Prisoners: The Pastor's Call

[1]*Charles Grandison Finney: An Autobiography* (1876; reprint, Westwood, N.J.: Revell, n.d.), 27.

[2]Timothy George, "From the Senior Editor," *Christianity Today,* Dec. 13, 1993, 15.

[3]Alfred Plummer, *A Critical and Exegetical Commentary on the Second Epistle of St. Paul to the Corinthians.* International Critical Commentary (Edinburgh: T. & T. Clark, 1956), in loc.

[4]A. T. Robertson, *The Glory of the Ministry: Paul's Exaltation in Preaching* (1911; reprint, Grand Rapids, Baker, 1967), 40.

[5]Scott Hafemann, *Suffering and Ministry in the Spirit* (Grand Rapids: Eerdmans, 1990), 21.

[6]Hafemann, *Suffering and Ministry*, 19-34.

[7]Plutarch, *Aemilius Paulus*, 33.3–34.2: quoted in Hafemann, *Suffering and Ministry*, 24.

[8]Victor Paul Furnish, *Second Corinthians*, Anchor Bible Series 32A (New York: Doubleday, 1984), 173.

6 Jars of Clay: The Pastor's Burden

[1]Richard Baxter, *The Reformed Pastor*, rev. and ed. Hugh Martin (1656; reprint, Richmond: John Knox, 1956). See also John T. McNeill's *History of the Cure of Souls* (New York: Harper & Row, 1951) for an instructive history of pastoral ministry.

[2]W. G. T. Shedd, *Homiletics and Pastoral Theology* (1873; reprint, London: Banner of Truth Trust, 1965), 323–24.

[3]*Lectures to My Students* (reprint, Grand Rapids: Zondervan, 1954).

[4]Leonard Sweet, *Faithquakes* (Nashville: Abingdon, 1994), 9.

[5]Richard Jackson, *Leadership*.

[6]*Leadership,* Summer 1995.

[7]Peter Drucker, as quoted in Russell Chandler, *Racing Toward 2001* (Grand Rapids: Zondervan, 1992), 216.

[8]Lloyd Rediger, "The State of the Clergy," *Clergy Journal,* March 1995, 20, 48.

[9]Peter Drucker, as quoted in Sweet, *Faithquakes,* 18.

7 God's Penmen: The Pastor's Impact

[1]Frederick Beuchner, *A Room Called Remember: Uncollected Pieces* (San Francisco: HarperCollins, 1984).

9 Farmers and Builders: Growing Christ's Church

[1]Gordon Fee, *1 Corinthians,* New International Bible Commentary (Grand Rapids: Eerdmans, 1987), 4.

[2]A. T. Robertson, *Word Pictures in the New Testament* (Nashville: Broadman, 1930–33), 4:99.

[3]Ibid.

10 Servants and Stewards: The Power of Pastoral Integrity

[1]Cf. K. H. Rengstorf, "ὑπηρέτης, ὑπηρετέω," in *Theological Dictionary of the New Testament,* ed. Gerhard Kittel, trans. Geoffrey W. Bromiley (Grand Rapids: Eerdmans, 1964–76), 8:533–34.

[2]Gordon Fee, *1 Corinthians,* New International Bible Commentary (Grand Rapids: Eerdmans, 1987), 157.

[3]J. Duncan Derrett, *Law in the New Testament* (N.p.: n.d.), 48–77.

11 Ambassador and Preacher: The Pastor's Authority

[1]Lloyd Rediger, "Beyond the Clergy Killer Phenomenon," *Clergy Journal,* August 1995, 19–24.

[2]Cf. Gerhard Friedrich, "κηρυξ," in *Theological Dictionary of the New Testament,* ed. Gerhard Kittel, trans. Geoffrey W. Bromiley (Grand Rapids: Eerdmans, 1964–76), 3:683–718.

[3]Gardner Taylor, *How Shall They Preach?* (Elgin, Ill.: Progressive Baptist Publishing House, 1977), 52–56. Used by permission.